Prove it

by

Paul McCauley

Prove it

How you can know and show
that the Bible is God's word

by

Paul McCauley

Decapolis Press

Printed in the UK

Contents

Acknowledgements

Very few meals stand out in my memory, yet if I had only eaten the ones I remember I would be in a bad way! The daily and unremarkable intake of good food is a lot more important to our physical well-being than the Christmas dinners and birthday celebrations. In a (kind of) similar way, there has been a steady diet of wholesome spiritual food that has been fed to me all my life. I could never thank all the people who have catered to my soul and consequently made this book possible. Family members, Sunday School teachers, Bible class leaders, overseers, Bible teachers, and friends have all furnished me with the resources I have drawn on in this project. I pay tribute to them, Heb. 13. 7, and I am grateful that the Lord has recorded all their labour and will reward it in a coming day.

Getting thoughts from my mind on to the page is one thing; doing it in a way that means those thoughts get into the mind of the reader is another. I am indebted to the help of Jonathan Caldwell and David Williamson in this regard. These two friends have been kind enough to hack away at what I presented to them so that your pathway through this book will be a lot smoother than it otherwise would have been. I thank them on your behalf, and also thank David for his willingness to provide the foreword. Working with him in the spread of the gospel has sharpened my thinking and deepened my appreciation of God and His word immeasurably.

My thanks to the editorial team and publisher for their helpful input. It has been a pleasure to work with them.

I especially want to pay tribute to my wife, Karen – truly, 'you excel them all', Prov. 31. 29, NKJV.

And to my wonderful boys, Luke, Zach, Jacob and Levi – may you grow to be God's men, 2 Tim. 3. 15-17.

Foreword

'Thy word is truth', John 17. 17.

Almost two thousand years ago Pilate asked 'What is truth?' John 18. 38, and never waited for an answer to his question. Many today raise questions concerning truth, but few distinguish themselves as honest seekers willing to examine the evidence to discover what truth is and where it can be found. Historically, the Christian has believed that all truth is God's truth and that He has communicated it to us primarily and perfectly in His word, the Bible.

But is this confidence in scripture justified? By placing trust in the Bible, is the Christian building upon a solid or shaky foundation? Are we believing facts or fiction? This is the subject of this book, and within its pages you will find a clear and coherent defence of God's word.

Many are the accusations levelled against the Bible. Some attack its morality, others sneer at its miracles. Some believe it is full of discrepancies and contradictions, others view it merely as a book of mythology. Most feel it should be offered for sale only in the fiction section of the bookseller. These attitudes have been encouraged by a growing willingness on the part of mainstream media to ridicule the biblical record. From many sources, and on many fronts, the truth of scripture is being attacked and its claims undermined. The person with an interest in knowing God is confronted by a cacophony of voices, among which the only harmonious note is a warning against placing any confidence in the Bible.

What is the Christian to do? Just as any loving husband would (and should) rush to the defence of his wife if her character was being unjustly vilified, so the Christian who loves God and His word should feel compelled to stand up and speak out when these objects of his love are maligned or misrepresented.

However, many believers, while fully convinced that the Bible is God's inerrant word, and feeling a duty to answer the ridicule and scorn heaped upon it, are unsure how to present a convincing case for its defence. In this book, Paul McCauley has done us a great service. He has condensed many evidences for the inspiration of scripture into five chapters under headings which can be easily remembered using the acronym PROVE.

Taken in isolation, any chapter of this book should provide sufficient evidence to the open mind for the reliability of scripture. Taken collectively, there can be no doubt that the Bible is the God-breathed word, and is perfect. The sheer volume of evidence presented in favour of divine inspiration caused me to rejoice and wonder again at the miracle which is the Bible.

As the reader will discover, many of the arguments and evidences here presented have been hammered out on the anvil of personal evangelism. Some are the result of personal challenges to faith which, while unpleasant at the time, have resulted in deeper study of God's word, and firmer conviction of its truth. Others are the fruit of Paul's own meditation on the riches of divine revelation. Others still have been gleaned from wide reading in the area of Christian apologetics. All are profitable for strengthening faith in God's word, and assisting us to better communicate this confidence to others.

I have been privileged to work with Paul regularly in evangelism, and hold him in the highest regard as a lover of scripture and a lover of souls. I know of no-one more suited to write this book. May the Lord be pleased to bless it to the edification of believers and the salvation of the lost.

David Williamson
October 2016

Introduction

'I don't believe the Bible. But if it is true, then I'll be in big trouble'.

This was the candid admission of a Navy colleague of Frank Turek.[1] He saw that there is a lot riding on the question of the authority of scripture.

The Bible doesn't present itself merely as a code of conduct or a source of comfort; it presents itself as the self-revelation of the true and living God, containing the one way of being reconciled to that God and saved from the eternal punishment our sins against Him deserve. So if the Bible is the word of God it has a message we can't afford to ignore; its warnings aren't idle and its promises aren't empty. However, if it's not the word of God then those who base their beliefs and build their lives on it are on a faulty foundation, and those who chart their course by it are lost. It's vital that we know, because if the Bible isn't right then who or what is? Atheism? Some other religion?

The question, then, is, can we know? If we could prove the Bible to be the word of God then every competing worldview automatically loses, but many people think that is too high a standard to reach and we can never be sure.

I remember asking a man (Stuart) if he ever thought about what happened after death. He told me he didn't. 'You really ought to', I said, 'because if the Bible is the word of God then . . .'.

At that point he cut me off with the words, 'Well, no one has ever been able to prove that'.

My reply was, 'I think I can, and I think I can do it in less than two minutes'.

---

[1] NORMAN L. GEISLER & FRANK TUREK, *I Don't Have Enough Faith to Be an Atheist*, Crossway, 2004, p. 67.

He raised his eyebrows sceptically and said, 'Come on in'.

I took no more than two minutes to share with him one of the arguments of this book. Stuart's response was that I had given him something to think about. I told him I really did hope he would think about it, because if the Bible is the word of God then we don't have to speculate about what happens after death – it tells us there is a God to meet, an eternity to face and a judgement to come, and Jesus Christ is our only hope of salvation.

Stuart had been generous enough to invite me into his home to give me an opportunity to prove the Bible is God's word, and I am glad that you have given me that opportunity as well.[2]

We will look at five proofs of inspiration and we are going to use the letters of the word PROVE to hang our headings on.

Prophecy
Reality
Oneness
Verification
Experience

As we look at these five subjects we will see that they all point in the one direction and they all proclaim the same message – the Bible is God's word. If you are a Christian, my prayer is that this study will give you confidence and courage to take your stand on the truth of scripture. You have no need to blush when you say you are a Bible-believing Christian. I also pray it will lead you to an increased appreciation of the word of God and the God of the word – to see His greatness and glory in Holy Scripture and be more committed to Him than ever before.

---

[2] It is true that on one definition of the word 'proof', it is really something that belongs to the fields of mathematics and logic alone, but we are using the word here in a wider and less formal sense, i.e. 'evidence sufficient to establish a thing as true'.

If you are not a Bible-believer, please read this book with an open mind and don't back away from the challenge it presents. If the Bible is God's word then it is your duty to bow to its message and receive the Saviour it presents. This will mean big changes in your life. Many people are not prepared to go where the evidence leads because they are not willing to do what the Bible says and they do not want the change that salvation brings. I want to encourage you to count the cost, but to make sure you factor eternity into the equation. You may be thinking of the cost of accepting the Bible's authority and receiving the Saviour, but nothing compares to the cost of rejecting the Bible's authority and refusing the Saviour. There is a lot at stake.

Chapter 1: Prophecy

'Show the things that are to come hereafter, that we may know that ye are gods', Isa. 41. 23.

'knowing this first, that no prophecy of Scripture is of any private interpretation, for prophecy never came by the will of man, but holy men of God spoke as they were moved by the Holy Spirit', 2 Pet. 1. 20-21, NKJV.

Introduction – Guess work or God's word?

I had just finished preaching, and I called into the nearby petrol station. The lady (Clare) who worked there asked me what I had been preaching about. I gave a summary of my message. She was utterly unimpressed.

I asked Clare what she thought about God and she told me she was an atheist. When I enquired why, her reply was, 'Because of science'. After some discussion it emerged that science had nothing to do with why she was an atheist, and she had no real reason at all.

The shop was empty, so I asked her if I could read something to her and she agreed. I read from a couple of passages we are going to look at in this chapter, Isaiah chapter 53 and Psalm 22.

'Do you know what these verses are talking about?' I asked.

'The death of Jesus', she answered, in a tone that implied it was the most obvious question ever. I agreed with her that it was obvious, 'It couldn't be anything else'.

She nodded as if to say, When are you going to get to the point?

'The point is these passages were written centuries before Jesus, yet we have no difficulty identifying what this is describing'.

I asked her how such accurate, graphic descriptions could be given hundreds of years before Jesus was born.

She was at a loss for words, so I thought I would adapt an illustration I had heard to try to show what is going on. I said, 'Suppose I told you that a red Ford Focus was going to come into the forecourt at 09:02hrs. Suppose I gave you the registration of the car, the names, addresses, ages and occupations of the people in the car. Now imagine you're standing here tomorrow morning and at 09:02hrs in drives the red Focus with everything exactly as I described, what would you think?'

She replied, 'I'd think you'd arranged it'.

Of course she would! There's no way she would have concluded that it was just a lucky guess. When such details are given, there *must* be some arrangement going on behind the scenes.

So the question I had for her, as I pointed to the open Bible, was this, 'Who arranged that? Who gave David and Isaiah the telescope that allowed them to look down the centuries? Who put their hand into the affairs of men to bring about the fulfilment of these scriptures?'

She confessed she had no answer.

The Bible provides us with one – God.

The uniqueness of the Biblical prophecy
There are many ways in which the Bible is unique amongst all the so-called holy books of world religions, and one of those ways is that the Bible is a book of prophecy. This is surely not without significance. If someone claims to be speaking from God and for God then they should be able to tell something about future events which would be beyond the ability of the speaker to guess or influence. No other religion engages in this explicit kind of predictive prophecy, but the Bible abounds in it. Some cults, most notably the 'Jehovah's Witnesses', have taken upon themselves the title of prophet and have

16

set dates for cataclysmic events, only to be left with egg on their face, their claims discredited and their credibility in tatters.[3]

About 30% of the Bible is prophetic literature and many of these prophecies have been fulfilled as a matter of historical record. If it is indeed the case that these prophecies were recorded before the events, that the writer could not have naturally anticipated the details, or effected their fulfilment, and the prophecy did come to pass, then we have proof that God has spoken. It was the proof of prophecy that God Himself pointed to when challenging the gods of the nations to prove themselves:

> 'Produce your cause, saith the Lord; bring forth your strong reasons, saith the King of Jacob. Let them bring them forth, and show us what shall happen: let them show the former things, what they be, that we may consider them, and know the latter end of them; or declare us things for to come. Show the things that are to come hereafter, that we may know that ye are gods: yea, do good, or do evil, that we may be dismayed, and behold it together', Isa. 41. 21-23.

The criteria for authentic prophecy
For a prophecy to provide proof of God's existence there are four things that need to be true:

1. It needs to be a prophecy that is not *deceptively altered*. Obviously the prophecy has to precede the fulfilment. We have to rule out any fiddling or tampering with the text.
2. It needs to be a prophecy that is not *easily anticipated*. Saying the sun will rise tomorrow, or there will be rain somewhere in the next few days, wouldn't count as a divine revelation. Nor would picking a team to win a competition or a candidate to win an election – we know that some team will win the competition, and one candidate will win the election, we are

---

[3] Eventually the Watchtower Society learnt that it wasn't terribly good at prophecy and so it doesn't claim to be God's prophet anymore.

looking for something that can't be put down to luck or good guesswork.

3. It needs to be a prophecy that is not *overly ambiguous*. The horoscopes in the tabloids and the predictions of Nostradamus are so vague that they could have any amount of 'fulfilments' in any amount of ways. There must be clarity in what is being prophesied.

4. It needs to be a prophecy that can't be *deliberately achieved*. Zechariah prophesied the King coming on a donkey (9. 9); there is no question that the Lord deliberately fulfilled that prophecy, and by doing so He was presenting Himself as the King prophesied by Zechariah, but this is not an example of a prophecy that proves the Bible to be God's word. What is required is the action of people who are not setting out to fulfil a prophecy they are aware of.

We will look at three areas of Biblical prophecy:

a) Prophecies relating to the nations;
b) Prophecies relating to the nation of Israel;
c) Prophecies relating to the Messiah.

I would not (and could not) deal with every prophecy in the Bible,[4] but I will confine myself to three from each category and focus on those I find most impressive and demonstrable.

Prophecies relating to the nations

In the Old Testament we find that different nations had their own local deity. This deity served as the nation's lucky mascot, but Israel was altogether different. The God of Israel was not a tribal god with no jurisdiction over other nations. The God of Israel asserted His rights over all nations, and demonstrated His sovereign control over

---

[4] See JOHN F. WALVOORD, *Every Prophecy of the Bible*, David C Cook.

them by the prophecies He communicated. There are lots of examples of these prophecies but we will make do with three.[5]

Four centuries of advanced history, Daniel 11

A casual reading of the book of Daniel will show that it is divided into two parts. The first six chapters make up the first part (the well known part). These are chapters of narrative – exciting stories that have kept Sunday School children enthralled for generations. The last six chapters make up the second part. These chapters are full of visions and prophecy, and make much harder reading (not so easy for Sunday School!)[6]

It has been pointed out that the first six chapters are 'prophetic history' while the last six chapters are 'historic prophecy'. What people mean by that is that in the first six chapters there are, in the narrative, pictures of future events, such as the faithful Jewish remnant being preserved in tribulation days, but in the last six chapters we have prophecies that were future to Daniel but are historic to us – much of what was revealed to Daniel in chapters 7-12 has already been fulfilled.

Is there any real importance to this? Yes, huge importance actually. We can look at the last six chapters and see how the prophecies relating to world empires, the rise and fall of leaders, the coming of the Messiah and the timing of His death, the destruction of the Temple, etc. have been literally and accurately fulfilled, and that should give confidence that the prophecies that relate to our future

---

[5] For more examples, see R. C. NEWMAN (ed.), *The Evidence of Prophecy*, Interdisciplinary Biblical Research Institute, or J. BARTON PAYNE, *The Encyclopaedia of Biblical Prophecy*, Harper & Row, 1973.

[6] That is the division according to a casual reading. A more in-depth reading will show that the division is actually after the fifth chapter, with chapters 6-12 corresponding to chapters 1-5. For more on this see D. W. GOODING's paper, *The literary structure of the book of Daniel and its implications*, http://www.tyndalehouse.com/tynbul/library/tynbull_1981_32_02_gooding_literarydaniel.pdf.

will be fulfilled just as literally and accurately. Daniel is a wonderful book to prove that the God of scripture lives.

This is illustrated in chapter 2. Nebuchadnezzar had a dream and he wanted to know the meaning of it, so he gathered his wise men together and told them to give him the meaning of the dream, but he also wanted them to tell him what the dream was. Could Nebuchadnezzar really not remember his dream? I think he had no difficulty at all recalling it, but I think his real difficulty was in trusting his magicians and enchanters. Like the fortune teller at the fair, it would be pretty easy for the King's advisors to invent some kind of bland interpretation and conjure up a future prediction, but what confidence could Nebuchadnezzar have in its trustworthiness? For this reason, Nebuchadnezzar wanted to know if his advisors really did have any special revelation or supernatural insight, so he asked them to give evidence that he could actually verify. If they were able to tell him what happened last night in his dream, it would be good evidence they were able to tell him what that dream meant. That is the evidential value of the book of Daniel – it can be trusted in relation to the future because it can be tested in relation to the past.

There are so many passages in Daniel we could dip into to see its prophetic accuracy, but we will have to satisfy ourselves with chapter 11.

The passage is so detailed and accurate that it has led many to conclude that it must have been written after the fact. After all, if it was written before the events then that would prove that God was involved, and, for lots of people, that conclusion just isn't allowed! We will deal with the dating of Daniel later, but suffice it to say for now that there are weighty arguments that crush any possibility of a late dating of Daniel.

Let's take a quick walk through this chapter picking out some of the major points along the way.[7]

> 'And now I will tell you the truth: Behold, three more kings will arise in Persia, and the fourth shall be far richer than them all; by his strength, through his riches, he shall stir up all against the realm of Greece', 11. 2, NKJV.

We are told that there would be four more kings in the Medo-Persian empire after Cyrus (Darius was reigning under him) until there would be a stirring up against Greece. The fourth of these kings would be the richest. History records the fulfilment of this prophecy. These four kings following the death of Cyrus were Cambyses, Pseudo-Smerdis, Darius I Hystaspes and Xerxes I Ahasuerus. The fourth was certainly remarkable for his wealth, as it was he who held a feast for six months to show off the 'riches of his glorious kingdom and the honour of his excellent majesty', Est. 1. 4. This wealth allowed him to invade Greece in 480 BC, and resulted, ultimately, in disaster for the Medo-Persian Empire.

For this reason we are introduced at this point to one of history's most remarkable individuals:

> 'Then a mighty king shall arise, who shall rule with great dominion, and do according to his will. And when he has arisen, his kingdom shall be broken up and divided toward the four winds of heaven, but not among his posterity nor according to his dominion with which he ruled; for his kingdom shall be uprooted, even for others besides these', 11. 3-4, NKJV.

This figure can be none other than Alexander the Great. To say he was a mighty king with a great dominion is no exaggeration. He was a

---

[7] The majority of the information in this section has been taken from J. ALLEN, *Daniel Reconsidered*, Scripture Teaching Library, 2013; R. E. SHOWERS, *The Most High God*, FOI, 1994; and WALVOORD, *Every Prophecy of the Bible*.

military genius who never lost a battle, with a larger territory than either of the two empires before him. Daniel prophesied that the kingdom would not pass to any of his posterity, but would, instead, be divided in four, which was literally fulfilled – his kingdom was not passed to either of his sons, but was eventually carved up among four of his generals. The chapter focuses on two of the four divisions, the kingdom of the Ptolemies (based in Egypt – the king of the South) and the kingdom of the Seleucids (based in Syria and Babylonia – the king of the North).

> 'Also the king of the South shall become strong, as well as one of his princes; and he shall gain power over him and have dominion. His dominion shall be a great dominion. And at the end of some years they shall join forces, for the daughter of the king of the South shall go to the king of the North to make an agreement; but she shall not retain the power of her authority, and neither he nor his authority shall stand; but she shall be given up, with those who brought her, and with him who begot her, and with him who strengthened her in those times. But from a branch of her roots one shall arise in his place, who shall come with an army, enter the fortress of the king of the North, and deal with them and prevail. And he shall also carry their gods captive to Egypt, with their princes and their precious articles of silver and gold; and he shall continue more years than the king of the North', 11. 5-8, NKJV.

There was constant conflict between these two kingdoms but around 250 BC Ptolemy II Philadelphus (the king of the South) attempted to make peace with Antiochus II Theos (the king of the North) by sending his daughter, Berenice, to marry him. They married and had a son, but the plan ultimately failed, because Ptolemy II died soon afterwards, Antiochus divorced Berenice and took back his previous wife, Laodice. Laodice wasn't pacified by this, and had her husband poisoned and Berenice and her son killed too. Laodice then had her son installed as king, and he was known as Seleucus II Callinicus.

Ptolemy II in Egypt was succeeded by Berenice's brother ('a branch from her roots'), Ptolemy III Euergetes, and, in retaliation for the murder of his sister, he came against the northern kingdom and plundered it.

> 'Also the king of the North shall come to the kingdom of the king of the South, but shall return to his own land. However his sons shall stir up strife, and assemble a multitude of great forces; and one shall certainly come and overwhelm and pass through; then he shall return to his fortress and stir up strife', 11. 9-10, NKJV.

After some years Seleucus II Callinicus launched a foolish and futile attack against Egypt and was sent home with his tail between his legs. His sons were furious and sought to avenge this humiliation and restore some honour. One son (Seleucus III Ceraunus) was killed in battle. The other son ('one shall certainly come') Antiochus III earned the name 'the Great' because of his success.

> 'And the king of the South shall be moved with rage, and go out and fight with him, with the king of the North, who shall muster a great multitude; but the multitude shall be given into the hand of his enemy. When he has taken away the multitude, his heart will be lifted up; and he will cast down tens of thousands, but he will not prevail. For the king of the North will return and muster a multitude greater than the former, and shall certainly come at the end of some years with a great army and much equipment', 11. 11-13, NKJV.

This riled the king of the South (Ptolemy IV) who scored a victory against Antiochus III. Rather than take advantage of the situation, Ptolemy IV made some real blunders and allowed Antiochus III to regroup. Ptolemy IV and his wife both died, and their five year old son was crowned Ptolemy V Epiphanes.

> 'Now in those times many shall rise up against the king of the South. Also, violent men of your people shall exalt themselves

in fulfillment of the vision, but they shall fall. So the king of the North shall come and build a siege mound, and take a fortified city; and the forces of the South shall not withstand him. Even his choice troops shall have no strength to resist. But he who comes against him shall do according to his own will, and no one shall stand against him. He shall stand in the Glorious Land with destruction in his power', 11. 14-16, NKJV.

Antiochus III was not alone in wanting to fight against Egypt. Philip V of Macedonia was in league with him, there were Egyptians prepared to rebel, and there were Jews who wanted to join the fight ('violent men of your people'). These Jews thought that by joining forces with Syria it would result in their freedom. They couldn't have been more wrong.

The Egyptians were devastated by the forces against them, and took refuge in Sidon, 'a fortified city'. The city yielded, and Antiochus III gained control of 'the Glorious Land', Israel. The Jews were expecting freedom, favour, or, at the very least, fairness, but he stood in the land 'with destruction in his power'.

> 'He shall also set his face to enter with the strength of his whole kingdom, and upright ones with him; thus shall he do. And he shall give him the daughter of women to destroy it; but she shall not stand with him, or be for him. After this he shall turn his face to the coastlands, and shall take many. But a ruler shall bring the reproach against them to an end; and with the reproach removed, he shall turn back on him. Then he shall turn his face toward the fortress of his own land; but he shall stumble and fall, and not be found', 11. 17-19, NKJV.

Antiochus III had determined to further expand his kingdom, so he didn't want Egypt bothering him again. History records that he gave his daughter, Cleopatra, to Ptolemy V Epiphanes to marry. His aim in this was to undermine Ptolemy V and Egypt, allowing him to take control at a later stage, but it didn't go according to plan because

Cleopatra was loyal to her husband, and this resulted in a stable Egypt.

Antiochus III set off to conquer Greece, and it went well until the Romans sent their general Lucius Cornelius Scipio to halt Antiochus III. The Syrians were soundly beaten and utterly humiliated. Antiochus III returned to Syria and sought to strengthen the fortifications for fear of Roman attack. He was killed while attempting to rob a temple in Elymais.

> 'There shall arise in his place one who imposes taxes on the glorious kingdom; but within a few days he shall be destroyed, but not in anger or in battle. And in his place shall arise a vile person, to whom they will not give the honor of royalty; but he shall come in peaceably, and seize the kingdom by intrigue. With the force of a flood they shall be swept away from before him and be broken, and also the prince of the covenant. And after the league is made with him he shall act deceitfully, for he shall come up and become strong with a small number of people. He shall enter peaceably, even into the richest places of the province; and he shall do what his fathers have not done, nor his forefathers: he shall disperse among them the plunder, spoil, and riches; and he shall devise his plans against the strongholds, but only for a time', 11. 20-24, NKJV.

Antiochus' son, Seleucus IV Philopator, didn't have the ambition or aggression of his father. A hefty tribute of one thousand talents a year had been laid on him by the Romans and he was finding finances a bit tight, so he had Heliodorus, his prime minister, collect taxes. Seleucus IV commanded Heliodorus to raid the Temple, but some kind of a supernatural apparition stopped him in his tracks. Seleucus IV's short reign of 11 years ended with a mysterious death, perhaps poisoning, but in any event, it was 'not in anger or in battle'.

In place of Seleucus IV there arose 'a vile person' indeed. Antiochus IV, who gave himself the name Epiphanes. Antiochus was the younger brother of Seleucus IV, and, although none in Syria wanted him, he took the throne by intrigue and with the support of Rome.

The king of the South, Ptolemy VI Philometor, attacked Syria, but they were 'swept away from before him', and Antiochus Epiphanes, with the help of his allies, scored a decisive victory. He took the 'prince of the covenant', probably a reference to Ptolemy VI,[8] and tricked him. Using their treaty as cover, he was able to bring a small army to Egypt without opposition, and he seized the treasures of Memphis, thus becoming 'strong with a small number of people'.

He set his sights on taking the strongholds that could have potentially become sources of trouble and centres of rebellion, but the stronghold of Alexandria escaped his grasp, and he had to leave that task unfinished.

> 'He shall stir up his power and his courage against the king of the South with a great army. And the king of the South shall be stirred up to battle with a very great and mighty army; but he shall not stand, for they shall devise plans against him. Yes, those who eat of the portion of his delicacies shall destroy him; his army shall be swept away, and many shall fall down slain. Both these kings' hearts shall be bent on evil, and they shall speak lies at the same table; but it shall not prosper, for the end will still be at the appointed time. While returning to his land with great riches, his heart shall be moved against the holy covenant; so he shall do damage and return to his own land', 11. 25-28, NKJV.

The king of the South was now Ptolemy VII Euergetes, the younger brother of the previous king. He launched a rebellion against Antiochus, perceiving that his failure to take Alexandria was an indication of weakness. However, Ptolemy VII was not leading a united force, and those who were his advisors, ('who eat of the

---

[8] Some see it as a reference to Onias III, the High Priest of Israel. For the problems with this view see ALLEN, *Daniel Reconsidered*, pp. 531-532.

portion of his delicacies') could not be trusted. This resulted in his defeat. Antiochus Epiphanes returned to his land, laden with the spoil of battle, and he returned via Israel. He took time to deal severely with the God-fearing Jews and to loot the Temple.

> 'At the appointed time he shall return and go toward the south; but it shall not be like the former or the latter. For ships from Cyprus shall come against him; therefore he shall be grieved, and return in rage against the holy covenant, and do damage. So he shall return and show regard for those who forsake the holy covenant. And forces shall be mustered by him, and they shall defile the sanctuary fortress; then they shall take away the daily sacrifices, and place there the abomination of desolation. Those who do wickedly against the covenant he shall corrupt with flattery; but the people who know their God shall be strong, and carry out great exploits. And those of the people who understand shall instruct many; yet for many days they shall fall by sword and flame, by captivity and plundering. Now when they fall, they shall be aided with a little help; but many shall join with them by intrigue. And some of those of understanding shall fall, to refine them, purify them, and make them white, until the time of the end; because it is still for the appointed time', 11. 29-35, NKJV.

Antiochus Epiphanes headed to Egypt again, but his plans were all coming undone, and the Romans told him to withdraw his troops from Egypt and get himself home. This put him in very bad form and so when he heard that the Jews were giving his man, Menelaus (the apostate High Priest), in Jerusalem trouble again, he was filled with rage. He was determined that only those who were prepared to 'forsake the holy covenant' would remain. He desecrated and defiled all that was holy and sacred. He met resistance from 'the people who know their God', and the Maccabean revolt began. This ends the historic prophecy in the chapter. The remainder of the chapter deals with events yet future.

Dating Daniel

From our brief look at this chapter, the accuracy is undeniable. The question is: is this a legitimate prophecy, or was this written after the events? We will look in chapter 4 at an archaeological proof for an early date of Daniel, but, for now, let's go down a different track.

Daniel 9, as we will see later, offers a remarkable prophetic timetable for the death of the Messiah and the destruction of the city of Jerusalem and the Temple. Even taking the latest and most liberal dating for the book of Daniel, we are still in the second century BC,[9] so there is immoveable, unshakeable evidence of genuine prophecy there. Since moving Daniel to the second century BC on the basis of the remarkable accuracy of chapter 11 doesn't eliminate prophecy from the book, maybe the naturalistic presuppositions of the critic need to be challenged and changed, rather than the date of Daniel.

Internal evidence

According to the sceptic, Daniel must have been written after the events of Daniel chapter 11 verse 35, which means it can be no earlier than 164 BC, however, there are internal and external reasons showing that this cannot be so.

DR GLEASON ARCHER, summarizing the work he and others have done on the vocabulary of Daniel, writes:

> '[A] second-century date for the Hebrew chapters of Daniel is *no longer tenable* on linguistic grounds . . . *there is absolutely no possibility* of regarding Daniel as contemporary [with the sectarian documents]. On the contrary the indications are that *centuries must have intervened* between them . . . But any fair-minded investigator when faced with such an overwhelming body of objective data pointing to the temporal interval of

---

[9] It can be no later than the second century because of the presence of the book of Daniel among the Dead Sea Scrolls which dates to the late second century BC. See, for instance, F. M. CROSS Jr, *The Ancient Library of Qumran and Modern Biblical Studies*, Gerald Duckworth & Co., 1958, p. 33.

centuries between the two bodies of literature must conclude that *a second-century date for the book of Daniel is completely out of the question'*.[10]

External Evidence
As regards the external evidence, no fewer than eight scrolls representing the book of Daniel (containing many verses from chapter 11) were found among the Dead Sea Scrolls, dating to the late second century BC. ARCHER is equally clear on the implications of this:

> 'But now that the considerable body of new documentation exhumed from the First Qumran Cave has been published and subjected to thorough analysis, it becomes patently evident that the Maccabean-date theory, despite all of its persuasive appeal to the rationalist, is altogether wrong. Only a dogma-ridden obscurantist can adhere to it any longer, and he must henceforth surrender all claim to intellectual respectability'.[11]

ARCHER is correct. Just consider what the sceptic wants you to believe: sometime after 164 BC some expert historian went through all the tricky history of the previous 400 years, got it all set out with stunning accuracy, and managed, somehow, to get this book out amongst the Jews as a book written by Daniel in 530. The Jews strangely enough swallowed this without choking. It was accepted without qualm or question as the word of God and they put it amongst their sacred scriptures, and it was copied over and over again by the community at Qumran within a few decades. One expert on the Dead Sea Scrolls who adheres to a Maccabean date said:

---

[10] GLEASON L. ARCHER, *New International Encyclopedia of Bible Difficulties*, Zondervan, loc 7159-7165, emphasis mine. He had already stated regarding the Aramaic chapters (2-7), 'based on purely philological grounds – they have to be dated in the fifth or late sixth century; and they must have been composed in the eastern sector of the Aramaic-speaking world (such as Babylon), rather than in Palestine (as the late date theory requires)'. Loc 7145.
[11] *Ibid.*, loc 7171.

29

'One copy of Daniel is inscribed in the script of the late second century BC; in some ways its antiquity is more striking than that of the oldest manuscripts from Qumran, since it is no more than about half a century younger than the autograph of Daniel. It is thus closer to the original edition of a biblical work than any biblical manuscript in existence, unless it be the Rylands Fragment of John from the first half of the second century AD'.[12]

Yes, striking indeed! The striking thing is not that a book is accepted as scripture fifty years after its writing; the striking thing is that a book that claims to have been written about 400 years prior to its actual writing would be accepted as scripture in so short a space of time when it allegedly hadn't been seen before. It's like someone in AD 450 writing a letter in the name of a first century Christian that maps out Christian history from the time of the apostles to the fifth century, and getting Christians to accept that it was actually scripture from the first century! Would such a thing be possible? Would Christians not wonder why such a document had never been heard of or quoted from in the first 400 years of Christian history? Whoever believes that this is possible is far more gullible than they obviously believe the Jews were. There's no way they would have accepted this Johnny-come-lately document as ancient and authoritative scripture, especially when one of the criticisms of the passage is that it goes historically askew after the section about Antiochus.[13]

As DR HASEL pointed out:

---

[12] CROSS Jr, *The Ancient Library of Qumran and Modern Biblical Studies*, p. 33.

[13] It doesn't go historically askew at all; it goes into the end times at that point – it is still future to us. This is made clear by the fact that the figure of verses 36-45 is not the king of the North (see v. 40), but he is obviously one who is in character very similar to him. When we see that Antiochus Epiphanes is described as the little horn in chapter 8 verse 9, and this is the same expression used in relation to a figure from the fourth kingdom in chapter 7 verse 8, it shows that there will be a future ruler who will be like Antiochus Epiphanes.

✝ 'According to current historical-critical opinion, the book of Daniel originated in its present form in the Antiochus Epiphanes crisis, that is, between 168 / 167- 165 / 164 BC. It seems very difficult to perceive that one single desert community should have preserved such a significant number of Daniel manuscripts if this book had really been produced at so late a date. The large number of manuscripts in this community can be much better explained if one accepts an earlier origin of Daniel than the one proposed by the Maccabean hypothesis of historical-critical scholarship, which dates it to the second century BC . . . Inasmuch as Daniel was already canonical at Qumran at about 100 BC, how could it have become so quickly canonical if it had just been produced a mere half century before?'[14]

DR HASEL's conclusion that 'an earlier date for Daniel than the second century is unavoidable'[15] is in line with all the evidence, and is only called into question by the anti-supernatural bias of 'a dogma-ridden obscurantist'. This means that we are dealing with genuine prophecy, far beyond the ability of Daniel to have anticipated, and this proves the truth of what Daniel said in chapter 2 verse 28, *'there is a God in heaven that revealeth secrets'.*

The overthrow of Tyre, Ezekiel 26
This chapter gives a detailed and definite prophecy of the destruction of the ancient Phoenician seaport of Tyre.

'And it came to pass in the eleventh year, on the first day of the month, that the word of the Lord came to me, saying, "Son of man, because Tyre has said against Jerusalem, 'Aha! She is broken who was the gateway of the peoples; now she is turned over to me; I shall be filled; she is laid waste'.

---

[14] DR GERHARD HASEL, *New Light on the Book of Daniel from the Dead Sea Scrolls,* http://www.biblearchaeology.org/post/2012/07/31/New-Light-on-the-Book-of-Daniel-from-the-Dead-Sea-Scrolls.aspx#Article.
[15] *Ibid.*

'Therefore thus says the Lord God: "Behold, I am against you, O Tyre, and will cause many nations to come up against you, as the sea causes its waves to come up. And they shall destroy the walls of Tyre and break down her towers; I will also scrape her dust from her, and make her like the top of a rock. It shall be a place for spreading nets in the midst of the sea, for I have spoken", says the Lord God; "it shall become plunder for the nations. Also her daughter villages which are in the fields shall be slain by the sword. Then they shall know that I am the Lord". For thus says the Lord God: "Behold, I will bring against Tyre from the north Nebuchadnezzar king of Babylon, king of kings, with horses, with chariots, and with horsemen, and an army with many people. He will slay with the sword your daughter villages in the fields; he will heap up a siege mound against you, build a wall against you, and raise a defense against you. He will direct his battering rams against your walls, and with his axes he will break down your towers. Because of the abundance of his horses, their dust will cover you; your walls will shake at the noise of the horsemen, the wagons, and the chariots, when he enters your gates, as men enter a city that has been breached. With the hooves of his horses he will trample all your streets; he will slay your people by the sword, and your strong pillars will fall to the ground. They will plunder your riches and pillage your merchandise; they will break down your walls and destroy your pleasant houses; they will lay your stones, your timber, and your soil in the midst of the water. I will put an end to the sound of your songs, and the sound of your harps shall be heard no more. I will make you like the top of a rock; you shall be a place for spreading nets, and you shall never be rebuilt, for I the Lord have spoken", says the Lord God. Thus says the Lord God to Tyre: "Will the coastlands not shake at the sound of your fall, when the wounded cry, when slaughter is made in the midst of you? Then all the princes of the sea will come down from their thrones, lay aside their robes, and take off their embroidered garments; they will clothe themselves with trembling; they will sit on the ground, tremble every moment, and be astonished at you. And they will take up a lamentation for you, and say to you: "How you have perished, O one inhabited by seafaring men, O renowned city, Who was strong at sea, She and her inhabitants, Who caused their terror to be on all her inhabitants! Now the coastlands tremble on the day of your fall; Yes, the coastlands by the sea are troubled at your departure". For thus says the Lord God: "When I make you a desolate city, like cities that are not inhabited, when I bring the deep upon you, and great waters cover you, then I will bring you down with those who descend into the Pit, to the people of old, and I will make you dwell in the lowest part of the earth, in places desolate from antiquity, with those who go down to the Pit, so that you may never be inhabited; and I shall establish glory in the land of the living. I will make you a terror, and you shall be no more; though you are sought for, you will never be found again", says the Lord God', Ezek. 26. 1-21, NKJV.

No wrangling about dating is going to get this prophecy off the table.

'Ezekiel is probably the most carefully dated of all Old Testament books . . . [W]e here note that the majority of biblical scholars, even of those who reject the inspiration and unity of the Bible, believe most of the book was written in the sixth century BC by the prophet Ezekiel. The prophecy against Tyre in chapter 26 can be dated with great probability at least two centuries before its fulfilment'.[16]

The unity of the book linguistically, and the fact that it is not ordered chronologically, are compelling indicators that the book has not been edited or tampered with after the time of Ezekiel.

'Thus centuries of scholarship have found no good reason to date the book later than the time of Ezekiel. Instead it has been regarded as a remarkably historical book. And chapter

---

[16] Robert W. Manweiler in NEWMAN (ed.), *The Evidence of Prophecy*, loc 356.

26 is in a privileged category in this privileged book. We can say with confidence that the prophecy of chapter 26 was written long before Alexander began his career'.[17]

The details are straightforward and won't require the same amount of information and background as our consideration of Daniel chapter 11. The city of Tyre had an inland part, called Old Tyre, and an island part, called Insular Tyre. The prophecy of Ezekiel chapter 26 deals with both Old Tyre and Insular Tyre. The chapter speaks about many nations coming against Tyre, vv. 3-6, then it speaks about Nebuchadnezzar coming against Tyre, vv. 7-11. The vital thing to notice is that in this section, vv. 7-11, it consistently makes use of the pronoun 'he', referring to Nebuchadnezzar. In verse 12 there is a change to 'they', and the reason for this is that it is reverting to the prophecy of verses 3 to 6 relating to the many nations. Thus, there is a prophecy in verses 7 to 11 of Nebuchadnezzar launching a campaign against Tyre. This is clearly Old Tyre because it refers to his horses and chariots, etc. But verse 12 picks up the thought from verses 3 to 6, a campaign of many nations. What is this referring to? Alexander the Great came on the scene more than two centuries after Ezekiel. His conquests and activities are well documented. He sought access to Insular Tyre to offer a sacrifice to their god, Hercules. He was refused entry, and he was highly offended and deeply vexed. This led to him resolving to take Insular Tyre – no mean feat, but he was no mean general! How was he going to get to this city half a mile off shore?

DIODORUS reports the situation vividly:

> 'The king [Alexander] saw that the city could hardly be taken by sea because of the engines mounted along its walls and the fleet that it possessed, while from the land it was almost unassailable . . . Immediately, he demolished what was called Old Tyre and set many tens of thousands of men to work carrying stones to construct a mole [causeway] two plethora [200 ft] in width. He drafted into service the entire population

---

17 *Ibid.*, loc 495.

of the neighbouring cities and the project advanced rapidly because the workers were so numerous'.

So Alexander used the ruins of *Old Tyre* to build a causeway connecting the coast to the island, and he employed many other nations to do it! Curtius states that "a great amount of rocks was available, supplied by Old Tyre". The ruins of Old Tyre were literally dumped into the sea. Ezekiel could hardly have said it more precisely (vv. 4 and 12)'.[18]

Using this causeway, Alexander led an army made up of 'many nations' and launched a brutal assault. 'The bare ground where Tyre once stood is testimony today of the literal fulfilment of this prophecy. Tyre never regained power after this attack'.[19] This led to the nations around yielding to Alexander, just as Ezekiel said: 'Then all the princes of the sea will come down from their thrones, lay aside their robes, and take off their embroidered garments', v. 16.

The prophecy is clear; it could not have been anticipated by even the most astute political commentator at the time of Ezekiel. This was not a lucky guess, it points to the reality of the God whom Ezekiel claimed to represent. MANWEILER's summary statement is hard to improve on:

'What conclusions should we draw? The Bible claims Ezekiel is God's spokesman, that God Himself has communicated with us through this prophet. In the fulfilment of prophecies such as these, God reveals His own existence and authenticates His prophets along with their messages. The Bible believer, then, is not blindly trusting anyone who claims to have had a revelation. He or she is accepting Scripture on the basis of strong verification that it comes from One who knows, the God who controls history'.[20]

---

[18] *Ibid.*, loc 416, emphasis his.
[19] WALVOORD, *Every Prophecy of the Bible*, loc 2905.
[20] NEWMAN (ed.), *The Evidence of Prophecy*, loc 522.

The overthrow of Nineveh, Nahum

The prophecy of Nahum outlines the destruction of Nineveh, and, unlike the book of Jonah, there is no repentance and rescue for the Ninevites here, Nineveh fell in 612 BC.

The dating of the prophecy

The dating of the book is the key question, and those with an anti-supernatural bias who dismiss the possibility of divine intervention in history have to try to date the book after, at, or just before the events to remove any evidence that God was involved. However, their efforts fail to deal with the facts, and a late date for the book cannot stand. Let's just look briefly at some of the evidence for an early date.

The view that the book was written after the fact takes the drastic step of accusing the writer of dishonesty for the book is written as if the destruction of the city were still future (e.g. 2. 13; 3. 5). Furthermore, it makes no sense to make such an accusation. Why would a writer backdate his work? What would he gain from it? It would be of no interest to anyone to produce a work that people after his death would suppose was a real prophecy. And if that was his aim, why not put a date on his work, and include the names and more details about the peoples who destroyed Nineveh?

The *International Critical Commentary* says:

> 'That we are not dealing with a *vaticinium post eventum* [prophecy after the fact] is clear: the hope of the prophet is too genuine and fresh; the details of the siege and conquest are too minute and would be somewhat superfluous, to say the least; and the total lack of any shadow cast by the knowledge, or even suspicion, that Babylon was a far more severe taskmaster than Nineveh had ever been would be inexplicable'.[21]

---

[21] SMITH, WARD AND BEWER, *International Critical Commentary*, p. 275, cited by Elaine A. Phillips in NEWMAN (ed.), *The Evidence of Prophecy*, loc. 837.

The next suggestion is that the book was written just before the events when the intelligent observer could foresee what was going to happen. This, however, doesn't account for the details given of the siege, the fact that there would be flooding[22] and fire,[23] the implication that the siege would last over the summer meaning that those in the city would need to 'Draw your water for the siege, 3. 14, and the statements that the destruction would be permanent.[24] These are facts of history that could not have been naturally known before they took place.

Another problem with this view is that Nahum refers to the sacking of Thebes (3. 8 – 'No Amon' NKJV) which took place in 663 BC (so that fixes our earliest limit for the date of the book).

> 'Are you better than Thebes that sat by the Nile, with water around her, her rampart a sea, and water her wall? Cush was her strength; Egypt too, and that without limit; Put and the Libyans were her helpers. Yet she became an exile; she went into captivity; her infants were dashed in pieces at the head of every street; for her honored men lots were cast, and all her great men were bound in chains', Nah. 3. 8-10, ESV.

This incident is referenced as a notorious event that would be well known and remembered, but if Nahum was written nearly fifty years after this event why would he not have referenced more recent examples of devastation, especially given the fact that Thebes was rebuilt and remained a city of some (religious) importance (though not politically as it was before).

There is an even more telling blow to be levelled at the late date theory, and that is that Assyria is described as a major power and Israel as being under her heel. Look at the following:

---

[22] Nahum 1. 8; 2. 6, 8.
[23] 2. 13; 3. 13, 15.
[24] 1. 14-15; 2. 11-13; 3. 18-19.

'Thus says the LORD:
Though they are safe, and likewise many,
Yet in this manner they will be cut down
When he passes through.
Though I have afflicted you,
I will afflict you no more;
For now I will break off his yoke from you,
And burst your bonds apart', Nah. 1. 12-13, NKJV.

We can see that at the time of writing Israel was still labouring under this yoke of affliction, and Nineveh was still throwing her weight around and making the lives of many others miserable too:

'Woe to the bloody city!
It is all full of lies and robbery.
Its victim never departs.
The noise of a whip
And the noise of rattling wheels,
Of galloping horses,
Of clattering chariots!
Horsemen charge with bright sword and glittering spear.
There is a multitude of slain,
A great number of bodies,
Countless corpses —
They stumble over the corpses —
Because of the multitude of harlotries of the seductive harlot,
The mistress of sorceries,
Who sells nations through her harlotries,
And families through her sorceries', Nah. 3. 1-4, NKJV.

But just prior to Nineveh's overthrow it was struggling to maintain control over its territories:

'Ashurbanipal died in 627 BCE and his sons fought for control of the throne. The Assyrian Empire was so large by this time that maintaining it was almost impossible. The regions which were subject to Assyrian rule had been trying to break free for

38

years and, finally, they saw their chance. The historian Simon Anglim writes that, "though the Assyrians and their army were respected and feared, they were most of all hated . . . by the last quarter of the seventh century BCE nearly every part of the empire was in a state of rebellion; these were not just struggles of freedom but wars of revenge" (186). Military incursions by the Persians, Babylonians, Medes, and Scythians began in earnest in 625 BCE and the already weakened Neo-Assyrian Empire could not hold off a full-scale invasion for very long. In 612 BCE the city of Nineveh was sacked and burned by the allied forces of the Persians, Medes, Babylonians, and others who then divided the region between them. The area was sparsely populated thereafter and, slowly, the ancient ruins became buried in earth'.[25]

The picture Nahum gives of Nineveh certainly does not fit the description of it from 625 BC onwards.

'W. A. MAIER suggests that Nahum gave his prophecy soon after Thebes fell, between 663 and 654 BC (*The Book of Nahum*, pp.30, 34-37). His arguments include these:
1. The description of Nineveh (1.12; 3:1, 4, 16) does not match the decline of the Assyrian nation under Ashurbanipal's sons, Ashur-etil-ilani (626-623 BC) and Sin-shar-ishkun (623-612 BC).
2. When Nahum prophesied, Judah was under the Assyrian yoke (1:13, 15; 2:1, 3). This fits with the reign of Manasseh over Judah (697-642) more than with the reign of Josiah (640-609).
3. The Medes rose in power around 645 BC as an independent nation, and the Neo-Babylonian Empire began in 626. If Nahum had written shortly before Nineveh's fall to those nations in 612, mention of them would be expected. But since Nahum does not mention the Medes or the Babylonians, he probably wrote his prophecy before 645.

---

[25] http://www.ancient.eu/nineveh/.

4. Most important, however, is the fact that nine years after Thebes was destroyed, it was restored (in 654). Nahum's rhetorical question in 3:8 would have had little or no force if it had been written after 654'.[26]

There seems to be no reason other than an anti-supernatural bias that would lead anyone to deny the evidence that the book of Nahum was written early, at a time when Assyria was a major power, and her destruction was not on the horizon.

The details of the prophecy
Having established that Nahum was written well before the overthrow of Nineveh, let's look at some of the prophecies Nahum made. ELLIOT E. JOHNSON summarises a dozen of them:[27]

Fulfilments of Nahum's Prophecies	
Nahum's Prophecies	Historical Fulfilments
The Assyrian fortresses surrounding the city would be easily captured, 3. 12.	According to the Babylonian Chronicle the fortified towns in Nineveh's environs began to fall in 614 BC including Tabris, present-day Sharif-Khan, a few miles northwest of Nineveh.
The besieged Ninevites would prepare bricks and mortar for emergency defence walls, 3. 14.	A. T. Olmstead reported: "To the south of the gate, the moat is still filled with fragments of stone and of mud bricks from the walls, heaped up when they were breached" (*History of Assyria*, Chicago: University of Chicago Press, 1951, p.637).
The gates would be destroyed, 3. 13.	Olmstead noted: "The main attack was directed from the northwest and the brunt fell upon the Hatamti gate at this corner . . . Within the gate are traces of the

---

[26] Elliot E. Johnson in JOHN F. WALVOORD & ROY B. ZUCK (ed.), *The Bible Knowledge Commentary*, Old Testament, SP Publications, 1985, pp. 1494-1496.
[27] *Ibid.*, p. 1495.

	counterwall raised by the inhabitants in their last extremity" (*History of Assyria*, p.637).
In the final hours of the attack the Ninevites would be drunk, 1. 10; 3. 11.	Diodorus Siculus (c. 20 BC) wrote, "The Assyrian king . . . distributed to his soldiers meats and liberal supplies of wine and provisions . . . While the whole army was thus carousing, the friends of Arbakes learned from some deserters of the slackness and drunkenness which prevailed in the enemy's camp and made an unexpected attack by nights" (*Bibliotheca Historica* 2. 26. 4).
Nineveh would be destroyed by a flood, 1. 8; 2. 6, 8.	Diodorus wrote that in the third year of the siege heavy rains caused a nearby river to flood part of the city and break part of the walls (Bibliotheca Historica 2. 26. 9; 2. 27. 13). Xenophon referred to terrifying thunder (presumably with a storm) associated with the city's capture (Anabasis, 3. 4. 12). Also the Khosr River, entering the city from the northwest at the Ninlil Gate and running through the city in a southwesterly direction, may have flooded because of heavy rains, or the enemy may have destroyed its sluice gate.
Nineveh would be destroyed by fire, 1. 10; 2. 13; 3. 15.	Archaeological excavations at Nineveh have revealed charred wood, charcoal, and ashes. "There was no question about the clear traces of the burning of the temple (as also in the palace of Sennacherib), for a layer of ash about two inches thick lay clearly defined in places on the southeast side about the level of the Sargon pavement" (R. Campbell Thompson and R. W. Hutchinson, *A Century of Exploration at Nineveh*, London: Luzac, 1929, pp.45, 77).

The city's capture would be attended by a great massacre of people, 3. 3.	"In two battles fought on the plain before the city the rebels defeated the Assyrians . . . So great was the multitude of the slain that the flowing stream, mingled with their blood, changed its colour for a considerable distance" (Diodorus, *Bibliotheca Historica* 2. 26. 6-7).
Plundering and pillaging would accompany the overthrow of the city, 2. 9-10.	According to the Babylonian Chronicle, "Great quantities of spoil from the city, beyond counting, they carried off. The city [they turned] into a mound and ruin heap" (Luckenbill, *Ancient Records of Assyria and Babylonia*, 2:420).
When Nineveh would be captured its people would try to escape, 2. 8.	"Sardanapalus [another name for King Sin-shar-ishkun] sent away his three sons and two daughters with much treasure into Paphlagonia, to the governor of Kattos, the most loyal of his subjects" (Diodorus, *Bibliotheca Historica*, 2. 26. 8).
The Ninevite officers would weaken and flee, 3. 17.	The Babylonian Chronicle states that "[The army] of Assyria deserted [lit., ran away before] the king" (Luckenbill, *Ancient Records of Assyria and Babylonia*, 2:420).
Nineveh's images and idols would be destroyed, 1. 14.	R. Campbell Thompson and R. W. Hutchinson reported that the statue of the goddess Ishtar lay headless in the debris of Nineveh's ruins ("The British Museum Excavations on the Temple of Ishtar at Nineveh, 1930-1," *Annals of Archaeology and Anthropology*, 19, pp.55-6).
Nineveh's destruction would be final, 1. 9, 14.	Many cities of the ancient Near East were rebuilt after being destroyed (e.g., Samaria, Jerusalem, Babylon) but not Nineveh.

Regarding this twelfth point, ELAINE PHILIPS says:

✝ 'But there is one point from which we *cannot* escape, the thorough and lasting destruction of the city . . . As the *Cambridge Ancient History* remarks: "The disappearance of the Assyrian people will always remain a unique and striking phenomenon in ancient history"'.[28]

The dating of the book means that Nahum was not prognosticating based on then-current indicators. The details of the prophecies are at such a degree of specificity that we cannot dismiss them as mere lucky guesses, and Nahum wouldn't have risked going on record with such guesses anyway. Why give specifics when generalities would do? The only reason he gave such a detailed account is because he sincerely believed that the burden he had and the vision he saw, Nah. 1. 1, came from God. The remarkable fulfilment of his prophecies bears that out and proves that God is real and has revealed Himself in scripture.

Prophecies relating to the nation of Israel

Israel is the key nation in God's prophetic programme.

'Among all the nations of the earth, the Jews alone have had their history written in advance. There is hardly a notable feature in their entire history, however improbable, that is not predicted with such detail in the Bible that it needs no correction, in spite of the large fraction of Israel's history which has occurred since the Bible was written'.[29]

There are loads of prophecies relating to this unique nation, but we will content ourselves with three.

---

[28] NEWMAN (ed.), *The Evidence of Prophecy*, loc 931. See also Zephaniah's prophecy of Nineveh's complete destruction, Zeph. 2. 13-15, written prior to Josiah's reforms which commenced in 622 BC.
[29] SAMUEL H. KELLOGG, *ibid.*, loc 982.

Blessing for the world, Gen. 12. 1-3

'Now the Lord had said unto Abram, Get thee out of thy country, and from thy kindred, and from thy father's house, unto a land that I will shew thee: and I will make of thee a great nation, and I will bless thee, and make thy name great; and thou shalt be a blessing: and I will bless them that bless thee, and curse him that curseth thee: and in thee shall all families of the earth be blessed'.

It is trendy amongst the sceptical and liberal to deny Moses wrote the Pentateuch, and this is, in part, due to the fact that if he was the author it would mean we have evidence of the genuinely prophetic. However, without getting waylaid, let's set out a few reasons why we can be sure of Mosaic authorship.[30]

- If Moses was not the writer, it would mean the writer(s) of the Pentateuch was/were deliberately deceptive because the Pentateuch claims to have come from the pen of Moses.[31]
- It would mean that the book of Joshua was doctored to fit in with this later story about Moses writing the Law.[32]
- It would also mean that the many references in the Old Testament to the Pentateuch coming from Moses are erroneous.[33] It is the universal testimony of the Old Testament that Moses was responsible for the books of the Law. Surely the ancient Jews were in a better position to know than the liberal professor in his study.
- Christ affirmed that the Pentateuch came from Moses.[34] If He is the Son of God then we have Mosaic authorship confirmed by the highest authority.[35]

---

[30] These are points made by ARCHER, *New International Encyclopedia of Bible Difficulties*, loc 974-1119.

[31] See e.g., Exod. 24. 4; 34. 17; Num. 33. 1-2; Deut. 31. 9-11.

[32] See e.g., Josh. 1. 7-8; 8. 30-35.

[33] See e.g., 1 Kgs. 2. 3; 2 Kgs. 14. 6; 1 Chr. 15. 15; 2 Chr. 23. 18; Ezra 6. 18; Neh. 8. 1; Dan. 9. 11-13; Mal. 4. 4.

[34] See e.g., John 5. 46-47; 7. 19.

- There are internal evidences that the writer was writing from firsthand knowledge and giving eyewitness accounts. The climate, trees and animals are what would be found in Egypt and the Sinai Peninsula, but not in Canaan. A later author writing from Israel would hardly have been able to get all this correct. The geographical references show familiarity with Egypt but not with Canaan, note especially, 'In Genesis 13:10, where the author wishes to convey to his readers how verdant the vegetation of the Jordan Valley was, he compares it to a well-known locality in the eastern part of the Egyptian Delta region'.[36] There are Egyptian names and loan words in the Pentateuch that are not found anywhere else in scripture, just what one would expect if the author had been brought up in Egypt. The name Yahweh of Hosts is never used in the Pentateuch despite the fact that it was used hundreds of times by writers of the period when liberals say the Pentateuch was being written.

There are many other reasons for rejecting a late composition of the Pentateuch, but these are sufficient to allow us to go on.

So in Genesis 12 we have a passage that was written by Moses in the fifteenth century BC, and it contains details that never could have been expected and yet have certainly come to pass.

Moses is recording that Abraham and his descendants would have a worldwide influence. Who could have anticipated it then? But who would argue with it now? Here we are, 4,000 years after Abraham, 3,500 years after Moses, and the influence of Abraham is felt right across the world. The Jews, while not a missionary people, have brought tremendous tangible blessing to the world through their scientific, economic and agricultural achievements. Christianity, which has its roots in the Hebrew scriptures and claims to represent the God of Abraham, has spread around the globe, bringing

---

[35] See chapter 4, *Verification*, for evidence of the deity of Christ.

[36] ARCHER, *New International Encyclopedia of Bible Difficulties*, loc 1024.

tremendous spiritual (as well as physical and emotional) blessing to many. While many people do not concur that the knowledge of the God of Abraham is a good thing, the point is that the one who gave the prophecy (God), the one who received it (Abraham) and the one who wrote it down (Moses) would have believed it to be a good thing, so the fact that the gospel has spread throughout the whole earth bringing millions to worship the God of Abraham means that the prophecy has been fulfilled.[37]

> '[T]he easy-to-understand point is this: Genesis 12 predicted that through Abraham the people of Israel would influence the faith and life of people all over the earth. At the end of the entire Old Testament period, that prediction was not even remotely coming true. However, two millennia later, the worldwide influence of the Abrahamic heritage is an indisputable fact'.[38]

This shows that *even if* the passage had been written when the most liberal scholars suggest, it is still a remarkable prophecy! Thus, late-dating the Pentateuch just cannot get rid of the evidence for the prophetic, and the liberal scholars should just leave the passage where the Bible places it and the evidence puts it.

The statement also contains an indication that the fate of people (and nations) will depend on their attitude to Abraham (and his descendants). History would bear this out as one might pick his steps through the wreckage of empires that opposed the Jews.

Was it a wild gamble from Moses, or a lucky guess that Abraham's name and nation would be so great? Well, we don't have this said of

---

[37] This is not the full and final fulfilment of this prophecy, which awaits the millennial reign of Christ.
[38] KENNETH BOA & ROBERT M. BOWMAN, *20 Compelling Evidences that God Exists*, David C Cook, loc. 1722.

any other individuals.[39] This shows it wasn't a shot in the dark from Moses, it was a revelation of divine light – a genuine prophecy.

Consequences for national disobedience, Deuteronomy 28-31

One section of the Bible that contains many striking prophecies regarding the nation of Israel is Moses' final address to the nation found in the last chapters of Deuteronomy.

Moses warns the Israelites about the consequences of breaking the covenant they had with the Lord. There are several features of this that certainly would not have been expected, and are unique in the history of nations.

A disobedient people

Moses doesn't just warn the people about what would happen if they were unfaithful to God, he told them that they actually would be unfaithful:

> 'For when I shall have brought them into the land which I sware unto their fathers, that floweth with milk and honey; and they shall have eaten and filled themselves, and waxen fat; then will they turn unto other gods, and serve them, and provoke me, and break my covenant. And it shall come to pass, when many evils and troubles are befallen them, that this song shall testify against them as a witness; for it shall not be forgotten out of the mouths of their seed: for I know their imagination which they go about, even now, before I have brought them into the land which I sware', Deut. 31. 20-21.

This is a nation that had experienced the miraculous power of the living God, and yet they would turn their back on this God and turn to the idols of the nations round about. This is something that the nations around wouldn't do, and it's something that no Israelite at the time would have forecast. Yet it is exactly what happened.

---

[39] It was said that Ishmael would become a great nation, Gen. 17. 20; 21. 18, which is true, but it doesn't say his name would be great.

A dispersed people

'The Lord shall cause thee to be smitten before thine enemies: thou shalt go out one way against them, and flee seven ways before them: and shalt be removed into all the kingdoms of the earth . . . And the Lord shall scatter thee among all people, from the one end of the earth even unto the other; and there thou shalt serve other gods, which neither thou nor thy fathers have known, even wood and stone. And among these nations shalt thou find no ease, neither shall the sole of thy foot have rest: but the Lord shall give thee there a trembling heart, and failing of eyes, and sorrow of mind: and thy life shall hang in doubt before thee; and thou shalt fear day and night, and shalt have none assurance of thy life', Deut. 28. 25, 64-66.

Repeatedly Moses tells the people that their disobedience will result in their scattering from the land.

'And such a scattering, please note, is hardly a necessary result of foreign domination. The Romans, for instance, to whom the last and most extensive scattering of the Jews is due, conquered many nations; generally they allowed these nations to remain in their own land if they would submit to Rome. But the biblical predictions of foreign conquest regularly indicate that Israel will not be allowed even this poor consolation. Instead they would be scattered among the nations and many would be sold into slavery'.[40]

So such a pronouncement from Moses was pretty audacious – it is very rare for an entire people to be removed from their land – and yet it was totally accurate, as the nation of Israel has discovered, having been exiled from their land not just once, but twice.

---

[40] Kellogg in NEWMAN (ed.), *The Evidence of Prophecy*, loc 1026.

A despised people

Generally when people are sent into exile they are the objects of pity, but for the Jews they have, by and large, been an object of scorn and contempt. This too was prophesied:

> 'You will become an object of horror, scorn, and ridicule among all the peoples where the Lord will drive you', Deut. 28. 37, HCSB.

No people have been the butt of more jokes and the object of more hatred than the Jewish people. We have a specific word for hostility towards the Jews – anti-Semitism. There is no other nation or ethnicity for which there is a specific word to describe hatred towards them, why? Because anti-Semitism has been so widespread and accepted that it deserves its own word, there's no other antagonism quite like it.

A disobedient people, a dispersed people, a despised people – these features are completely accurate and yet could not have been cleverly anticipated. It is a clear example of divine inspiration.

The second demolition of the city and sanctuary, Dan. 9. 26

This verse comes in a context that we are going to look at again in relation to the death of Christ, but for the moment there is just one point I am going to make – Daniel prophesied the destruction of the city of Jerusalem and the temple: 'And the people of the prince who is to come shall destroy the city and the sanctuary'.

We have already shown that Daniel's prophecy was written just when it claims to be, so, in the sixth century BC, Daniel was writing about events that would take place hundreds of years in the future and hundreds of miles away. When Daniel wrote, Solomon's glorious temple in Jerusalem lay in ruins. Nebuchadnezzar had wrecked it. Here was Daniel in exile implicitly prophesying that the people were going to be back in their land, a temple was going to be rebuilt in the city, priesthood, ceremonies and sacrifices restored, but then he explicitly prophesied that it was going to be demolished by invading forces again.

Now it was one thing to prophesy the rebuilding of the temple, but it must have been a stunning thing to predict that it would be tumbled again. God had guaranteed the protection of His people based on their faithfulness to Him (as Lev. 26 and Deut. 28 state). In Leviticus chapter 26 verse 31 God says to the nation that, as a result of national disobedience, 'I will lay your cities waste and bring your sanctuaries to desolation' NKJV. Linked with that, He says, 'I will scatter you among the nations', v. 33, NKJV. So Daniel was prophesying not only the destruction of the city and sanctuary but, as a cause of that, another national apostasy,[41] and, as a consequence, another exile from the land.

Not only did Daniel make this prophecy about the fate of the city, sanctuary and nation, but he stated when it would happen as well. Daniel didn't naturally know these things, and neither did he desire them, but the God of heaven revealed them to him.

The nation of Israel is unique. At times there has been a unique protection they have enjoyed, preserving them from enemies much greater in power and number. At other times there has been a unique persecution they have experienced from the hands of their fellow-men as they have been scattered, slaughtered, rejected and hated. There is something special about this people, and they stand as a witness to the inspiration of God's word which has recorded their destiny in advance.

---

[41] It is a big question for the Christ-rejecting Jew, 'what was the national sin that amounted to national apostasy and resulted in God scattering them among the nations?' The only thing that could possibly qualify is what Daniel himself states – the nation's rejection of God's Son, their Messiah. When they were first expelled from their land, it was because of their reception of false gods; the second expulsion from the land was because of their rejection of the true God.

'Frederick the Great is said once to have asked his personal physician Zimmermann whether he [Zimmermann] could give him an absolutely certain proof of the existence of God, and to have got the laconic reply "Your Majesty, the Jews!'[42]

Prophecies relating to the Messiah

I remember listening to an atheist give a presentation and then he was asked what it would take for him to believe in God. He thought for a moment then said that if there had been some prophecy given long ago about men landing on the moon he would take that as a pretty good indication that there is a God. I must say, that wouldn't overly sway me! I'm quite sure there were people who imagined landing on the moon long before space travel was possible. I think the Bible has not only met the challenge, but exceeded it because it contains something much more impressive and useful than a prophecy about man walking on the moon – it prophesies God walking on earth.

There are prophecies relating to the birth of the Messiah, His life, miracles and teaching, but those that are particularly clear and compelling are the ones relating to His death. Consider these three:
1) The Bible prophesied *how* He would die, Psalm 22;
2) The Bible prophesied *why* He would die, Isaiah 53;
3) The Bible prophesied *when* He would die, Daniel 9. 24-27.

If these are bona fide prophecies then they not only prove that God is living but also that God is loving because they show us the price He was prepared to pay to meet our need and provide salvation for us.

How the Messiah would die, Psalm 22
Psalm 22 is a passage that Christians love because it gives insight into the feelings of the Saviour on the cross. There is no doubt that the Lord drew attention to this passage as a Messianic psalm, Matt. 27. 46.

---

[42] Karl Barth, https://karlbarth.unibas.ch/fileadmin/downloads/letter1.pdf, cited in BOA & BOWMAN, *20 Compelling Evidences that God Exists*, loc 1755.

51

Look at some of the details in verses 14 to 18:

> 'I am poured out like water,
> And all My bones are out of joint;
> My heart is like wax;
> It has melted within Me.
> My strength is dried up like a potsherd,
> And My tongue clings to My jaws;
> You have brought Me to the dust of death.
> For dogs have surrounded Me;
> The congregation of the wicked has enclosed Me.
> They pierced My hands and My feet;
> I can count all My bones. They look and stare at Me.
> They divide My garments among them,
> And for My clothing they cast lots', NKJV.

Put the pieces of this passage together and what is the picture?

- The sufferer is stripped of His garments, v. 18, and those garments are subsequently divided amongst onlookers.
- The sufferer is surrounded by dogs. This is the common Jewish epithet for Gentiles. So His suffering comes from the hands of Gentiles.
- These Gentiles pierce His hands and His feet. According to the Masoretic text of the Hebrew scriptures the rendering is 'Like a lion they are at My hands and My feet'. However, keep the following points in mind:
    > 'Actually, the Septuagint, the oldest existing Jewish translation of the Tanakh, was the first to translate the Hebrew as "they pierced my hands and feet" (using the verb *oruxan* in Greek), followed by the Syriac Peshitta version two or three centuries later (rendering with *baz'u*). Not only so, but the oldest Hebrew copy of the Psalms we possess (from the Dead Sea Scrolls, dating to the century before Yeshua [Hebrew for *Jesus*] reads the verb in this verse as

52

ka'aru (not *ka'ari*, "like a lion"), a reading also found in about a dozen medieval Masoretic manuscripts – recognised as the authoritative texts in traditional Jewish thought – where instead of *ka'ari* (found in almost all other Masoretic manuscripts) the texts say either *ka'aru* or *karu*. (Hebrew scholars believe this comes from a root meaning "to dig out" or "to bore through.") So, the oldest Jewish translation (the Septuagint) translates "they pierced"; the oldest Jewish manuscript (from the Dead Sea Scrolls) reads *ka'aru*, not *ka'ari*; and several Masoretic manuscripts read *ka'aru* or *karu* rather than *ka'ari*. This is not a Christian fabrication'.[43]

We should keep in mind as well, even if the original text did read, 'Like a lion they are at My hands and My feet', it is still an image perfectly in keeping with a crucifixion. It would be conveying the idea of a lion pinning down its prey or tearing at the victim's hands and feet. As DR BROWN points out, 'These lions are not licking the psalmist's feet!'[44] So, there is impressive evidence to retain the phrase as we have it, 'They pierced My hands and My feet', but even if the rendering is 'Like a lion' it makes no difference to the picture being painted in the Psalm – hostile Gentiles pinning the Sufferer down by, and tearing at, His hands and feet.

- His bones are out of joint, v. 14. The act of crucifying the victim, and the weight of the body pulling on the arms (like the mediaeval torture rack) would cause dislocations. What other form of execution would cause bone dislocations?
- He is exposed to burning heat, causing His strength to be dried up and His tongue to cling to His jaws, v. 15. What kind of death sentence has this long and slow aspect to it, causing the victim to experience weakness?

---

[43] MICHAEL L. BROWN, *Answering Jewish Objections to Jesus*, vol. 3, Baker Books, 2003, pp. 125-126.
[44] *Ibid.*, p. 125.

- He is gazed at by wicked onlookers who have enclosed Him, as He suffers in weakness, vv. 16-17. Is there anything other than a crucifixion that would result in such a public spectacle? Clearly the victim is able to look at those gathered, take in what is happening, think about the past, and speak to God. Can you think of another form of execution that would provide opportunity for this kind of contemplative psalm?

Going outside of these verses we see the following:

- He would suffer in daytime but it would also be in darkness, v. 2. Scripture records that there was darkness from 12:00hrs to 15:00hrs.[45] Thallus, a first-century historian, and Phlegon a second-century historian, both made reference to the darkness at the time of Christ's death, and tried to pass it off as an eclipse of the sun (which is impossible given when Christ died). Julius Africanus, the third-century church historian, had this to say:

> 'On the whole world there pressed a most fearful darkness; and the rocks were rent by an earthquake, and many places in Judea and other districts were thrown down. This darkness Thallus, in the third book of his History, calls, as appears to me without reason, an eclipse of the sun. For the Hebrews celebrate the passover on the 14th day according to the moon, and the passion of our Saviour falls on the day before the passover; but an eclipse of the sun takes place only when the moon comes under the sun. And it cannot happen at any other time but in the interval between the first day of the new moon and the last of the old, that is, at their junction: how then should an eclipse be supposed to happen when the moon is almost diametrically opposite the sun? Let opinion pass however; let it carry the majority with it; and let this portent of the world be deemed an eclipse of the sun, like others a portent only to the eye. Phlegon records

---

[45] Matt. 27. 45; Mark 15. 33; Luke 23. 44.

that, in the time of Tiberius Caesar, at full moon, there was a full eclipse of the sun from the sixth hour to the ninth — manifestly that one of which we speak. But what has an eclipse in common with an earthquake, the rending rocks, and the resurrection of the dead, and so great a perturbation throughout the universe? Surely no such event as this is recorded for a long period. But it was darkness induced by God, because the Lord happened then to suffer'.[46]

- He is being laughed at, v. 7. So the sufferer is not only suffering physically but emotionally too.
- Jewish, as well as Gentile, oppressors were there, v. 12. The bull of Bashan is a straightforward metaphor, the bull was ceremonially clean in Israel; Bashan was the place where the finest of cattle were reared, e.g., Ezek. 39. 18, and thus the bulls of Bashan would represent Jewish authority.
- This sufferer experiences a deliverance that results in universal and eternal praise to God, vv. 27-31. Is there anyone in history whose reported deliverance out of death has caused multitudes across the world and throughout the generations to turn to and praise the Lord?

There are lots more details and colours in the passage that fill out the picture and show that it is the crucifixion of Christ that is in view, and that, realistically, it can be nothing else. However, not only was this passage written about 1,000 years before Christ came, but it was also written about 500 years before crucifixion had even been invented.[47]

---

[46] *The Extant Writings of Julius Africanus*, 18.1, from the Master Christian Library.

[47] History shows that the Persians were the first to use this means of execution in the late sixth century BC,
http://www.britannica.com/topic/crucifixion-capital-punishment.
Herodotus records Darius impaling 3,000 leading men when he overcame the Babylonians in 519 BC (*The History of Herodotus*, vol. 1, iii, 159). Other ancient cultures would hang a dead body on a tree, e.g., Gen. 40. 18-19; Deut. 21. 22-23, but this is not crucifixion and certainly not what is described in Psalm 22.

This is pretty remarkable. David is writing about something that he hadn't experienced, seen, or heard about. It was beyond his ability to anticipate; it was also totally beyond anything he could have expected.[48]

> 'How difficult would it be to indicate the precise kind of death that a new, unknown religious leader would experience a thousand years from today? Could someone create and predict a new method of execution not currently known, one that wouldn't even be invented for hundreds of years? That's what King David did in 1000 BC when he wrote Psalm 22'.[49]

We will move on to our next passage.

Why the Messiah would die, Isaiah 53

'Behold, My Servant shall deal prudently;
He shall be exalted and extolled and be very high. Just as many were astonished at You,
So His visage was marred more than any man, and His form more than the sons of men;
So shall He sprinkle many nations.
Kings shall shut their mouths at Him;
For what had not been told them they shall see,
And what they had not heard they shall consider.
Who has believed our report?
And to whom has the arm of the Lord been revealed?
For He shall grow up before Him as a tender plant,
And as a root out of dry ground.
He has no form or comeliness;

---

[48] As the king of Israel, David was, in a sense, the prototype of the Messiah, yet even though this is written in the first person, it wasn't experienced by him. Thus, it indicates it is a Messianic prophecy, but it certainly wouldn't have been the expectation that the Messiah would suffer such shame.

[49] JOHN ANKERBERG & JOHN WELDON, *Fast Facts on Defending your Faith*, ATRI Publishing, 2013, loc 1011.

And when we see Him,
There is no beauty that we should desire Him.
He is despised and rejected by men,
A Man of sorrows and acquainted with grief.
And we hid, as it were, our faces from Him;
He was despised, and we did not esteem Him.
Surely He has borne our griefs
And carried our sorrows;
Yet we esteemed Him stricken,
Smitten by God, and afflicted.
But He was wounded for our transgressions,
He was bruised for our iniquities;
The chastisement for our peace was upon Him,
And by His stripes we are healed.
All we like sheep have gone astray;
We have turned, every one, to his own way;
And the Lord has laid on Him the iniquity of us all.
He was oppressed and He was afflicted,
Yet He opened not His mouth;
He was led as a lamb to the slaughter,
And as a sheep before its shearers is silent,
So He opened not His mouth.
He was taken from prison and from judgment,
And who will declare His generation?
For He was cut off from the land of the living;
For the transgressions of My people He was stricken.
And they made His grave with the wicked—
But with the rich at His death,
Because He had done no violence,
Nor was any deceit in His mouth.
Yet it pleased the Lord to bruise Him;
He has put Him to grief.
When You make His soul an offering for sin,
He shall see His seed, He shall prolong His days,
And the pleasure of the Lord shall prosper in His hand.
He shall see the labour of His soul, and be satisfied.
By His knowledge My righteous Servant shall justify many,

For He shall bear their iniquities.
Therefore I will divide Him a portion with the great,
And He shall divide the spoil with the strong,
Because He poured out His soul unto death,
And He was numbered with the transgressors,
And He bore the sin of many,
And made intercession for the transgressors', Isa. 52. 13-53. 12, NKJV.

The prophecy of Isaiah was written in the 8th century BC.[50] Let's look at some of the details here:

- This Servant is despised and rejected by His people, 53. 3. That certainly was true while Christ was here, and is still true today.
- He is condemned by an unjust trial, 53. 8. The statement of verse 8 is variously translated:
  'By oppression and judgment he was taken away', ASV, ESV, JPS.
  'He was taken from oppression and judgment', JND.
  'In his humiliation his judgment was taken away', BRENTON's LXX.
  'He was led away after an unjust trial', NET.
  The various translations all communicate the same idea, that there was an oppressive and unjust legal process. This was not a public lynching but a condemnation issued from the governing authority, so the sufferer was convicted as a criminal.

---

[50] GLEASON ARCHER examines the unity of the book of Isaiah and says, 'There is no other logical deduction to draw from the evidence of the text of Isaiah 40-66 but that it demands a pre-Exilic setting, which absolutely destroys the Deutero-Isaiah and the Trito-Isaiah theories. Such antisupernatural hypotheses can be maintained only in the teeth of the objective evidence of the Hebrew text, on which they were allegedly founded', *New International Encyclopedia of Bible Difficulties*, loc 6689.

- He is led submissively to execution, 53. 7. This verse is not demanding that the sufferer was literally speechless, but rather that He did not say anything in His own defence, nor did He call for condemnation of His oppressors. This is something that is attested to in all the Gospel accounts.[51]
- He is treated as a criminal and condemned with criminals, 53. 12. The Lord was crucified between two robbers, put on the level of the lowest and vilest of men.
- We find reference to piercing, bruising, punishment and stripes, 53. 5. The language of verse 5 is language associated with crucifixion. 'Wounded' is 'pierced through', and 'the stripe' is that which is caused by a scourge.[52] To this we could add the language of the previous Servant Song in Isaiah chapter 50 verse 6, 'I gave My back to the smiters, and My cheeks to them that plucked off the hair: I hid not My face from shame and spitting' NKJV.
- Josephus tells us this is the kind of suffering visited on one who would be crucified:

  'They were first whipped and then tormented with all sorts of tortures, before they died, and were crucified before the wall of the city . . . the soldiers, out of wrath and hatred they bore the Jews, nailed those they caught to the crosses in different postures, by way of jest'.[53]
- He was terribly disfigured, 52. 13. The appearance of the Servant in both His face and form causes horror. This is entirely consistent with what is associated with crucifixion.
- He was to be buried with criminals, but was associated with a rich man in His death, 53. 9. The word *wicked* is a plural word,

---

[51] Matt. 27. 12-14; Mark 15. 4-5; Luke 23. 9; John 19. 8-12.

[52] These are words associated with the physical suffering and crucifixion of the Lord, and yet the passage shows that they go beyond anything imposed upon Him by men, it is referring to suffering visited upon Him by God, 53. 10. But the point is that the language is associated with crucifixion.

[53] FLAVIUS JOSEPHUS, *The Wars of the Jews, Book 5*, from *The Complete Works of Flavius Josephus*, translated by William Whiston, loc 24878.

but the word *rich* is singular. It was the practice to dispose of the corpses of those who had been executed in a place reserved for such people:

> 'The executed were to be buried properly, but not in places of honour . . . This is clearly taught in the earliest writings of the rabbis: "They did not bury (the executed criminal) in the burying-place of his fathers. But two burying-places were kept in readiness by the Sanhedrin, one for them that were beheaded or strangled, and one for them that were stoned or burnt" (m. Sanhedrin 6:5). "Neither a corpse nor the bones of a corpse may be transferred from a wretched place to an honoured place." (Semahot 13.7) . . .
> The burial of the executed in "wretched places," that is, in tombs set aside for criminals, was part of the punishment'.[54]

So in this prophecy we don't just have amazing details of the trial and crucifixion, but also an accurate statement of the type of burial associated with such an execution, *all written hundreds of years before!* As the Lord's grave had been appointed with the wicked, they would have disposed of His body in the 'wretched places', but the prophecy has more to say, and we are introduced to a rich man. Matthew tells us who this rich man was:

> 'When the even was come, there came a rich man of Arimathaea, named Joseph', Matt. 27. 57.

The burial of the Lord by Joseph of Arimathaea can't be dismissed by sceptics as a Christian invention. The Gospel accounts all attest to the honourable burial by Joseph, and it is implied in Paul's message in Acts chapter 13 verses 28-29 that it was members of the Sanhedrin who were responsible for His burial. There is no competing burial account, and even the attempts of the Jews to squash the resurrection story

---

[54] Craig A. Evans in MICHAEL F. BIRD (ed.), *How God Became Jesus: The Real Origins of Belief in Jesus' Divine Nature – A Response to Bart D. Ehrman*, Zondervan, 2014, loc 1449-1456, 1463.

acknowledge that there was an empty tomb, Matt. 28. 11-15. But perhaps the most simple yet significant point is that there is no way Christians would have made this story up. The disciples don't shine too well in the burial accounts – not one of them was present to give their Master an honourable burial. Instead it is a member of the hated Sanhedrin who performed the task (witnessed by women). This is not the kind of story you would invent if you want to get a hearing and give yourself credibility. Thus, it meets the criterion of embarrassment, as well as having enemy attestation and multiple attestation; it is, therefore, very credible historically.

- His days have been prolonged, v. 10. The Servant dies, but lives again.

Acts 8 tells us about an encounter Philip the evangelist had with an Ethiopian official. This man was a spiritual seeker, and his search for reality took him to Jerusalem. He left with a copy of Isaiah's prophecy and when Philip met him he had got to chapter 53. He asked Philip, 'of whom does the prophet say this?' Acts 8. 34, NKJV. Philip knew that there was only one who fitted the description, who filled the outline and fulfilled the prophecy: 'he preached unto him Jesus', v. 35. The search was over; Jesus Christ was not only the answer to the Ethiopian's question, He was the answer to the Ethiopian's quest.

When the Messiah would die, Dan. 9. 24-27

'Seventy weeks are determined
For your people and for your holy city,
To finish the transgression,
To make an end of sins,
To make reconciliation for iniquity,
To bring in everlasting righteousness,
To seal up vision and prophecy,
And to anoint the Most Holy.
Know therefore and understand,
That from the going forth of the command
To restore and build Jerusalem
Until Messiah the Prince,
There shall be seven weeks and sixty-two weeks;

The street shall be built again, and the wall,
Even in troublesome times.
And after the sixty-two weeks
Messiah shall be cut off, but not for Himself;
And the people of the prince who is to come
Shall destroy the city and the sanctuary.
The end of it shall be with a flood,
And till the end of the war desolations are determined.
Then he shall confirm a covenant with many for one week;
But in the middle of the week
He shall bring an end to sacrifice and offering.
And on the wing of abominations shall be one who makes desolate,
Even until the consummation, which is determined,
Is poured out on the desolate', NKJV.

When you are going to pick someone up at the airport, one of the things you make sure you get right is the scheduled arrival time. You don't want to waste time sitting at the airport before the flight has landed, and you don't want to be too late and miss the person. God has kindly given us a specified period of time in which to find the person who matches the description of Psalm 22 and Isaiah chapter 53. That's what Daniel chapter 9 verses 24-27 is about.

There are many in-depth treatments of this section which go into the detail of the calculations. We are not going to do that. We are going to focus on two clear points: the Messiah would die *after* a certain time and *before* a certain event.

The prophecy is based on seventy weeks, but these are weeks of years rather than weeks of days. The clock starts running when the commandment is given to restore and build Jerusalem, and we are told that it is sixty-nine weeks (i.e., 483 years) from that commandment until Messiah the Prince, v. 24. Now there are various suggestions as to what exactly the commandment is and when exactly the commandment was given. There are also various suggestions as to how the years should be counted. But, despite the variations, the 69th week brings you right to the time of Jesus.[55]

Furthermore, the death of the Messiah is said to take place before the destruction of the city of Jerusalem and the Temple, v. 26. A prominent Messianic pretender in the first century was a man named Simon bar-Giora. He was active during the first revolt of AD 66-70. Simon fitted the picture of what Jews at that time were anticipating their Messiah to be – a freedom fighter who would triumph over pagan oppression, but he was unsuccessful in his mission. Titus destroyed Jerusalem and the temple and then took the Jewish prisoners to Rome to show them off as well as all the spoils of their victory. JOSEPHUS tells us:

> 'Now the last part of this pompous show was at the temple of Jupiter Capitolinus, whither when they were come, they stood still; for it was the Romans' ancient custom to stay till somebody brought the news that the general of the enemy was slain. This general was Simon, the son of Gioras, who had then been led in this triumph among the captives; a rope had also been put upon his head, and he had been drawn into a proper place in the forum, and had withal been tormented by those that drew him along; and the law of the Romans required that malefactors condemned to die should be slain there'.[56]

The point is that Simon is out of the running for the Messiah because his death came after the destruction of the city and the temple.[57] It's a

---

[55] See e.g., NEWMAN (ed.), *The Evidence of Prophecy* and SIR ROBERT ANDERSON, *The Coming Prince,* for different suggestions.
[56] JOSEPHUS, *The Wars of the Jews, Book 7,* from *The Complete Works of Flavius Josephus,* loc 26198.
[57] Simon's followers saw his death at the hands of the pagan Romans as the obvious disqualifier from Messianic contention. The interesting question then is why did Jesus' followers continue to insist that He was the Messiah, even though the Romans crucified Him? In the absence of His resurrection

bit like being given directions and being told if you come to a certain landmark you've gone too far. God has given directions to find the Messiah, follow the signs, and if you come to the ruined temple you've gone too far, you need to turn back.

The death of the Lord Jesus was right in the given timeframe of Daniel's prophecy. It was only one generation after the crucifixion of the Lord that the Romans came and sacked Jerusalem. The disciples thought that the death of their Master was some dead-end detour off the track to glory, but actually a timetable had been given, and the Lord was scheduled to arrive there at Calvary, and He arrived right on time: 'in due time Christ died for the ungodly', Rom. 5. 6.

Objections
The proof of inspiration shines out, bright and clear, from these Messianic prophecies, but there may be some questions or objections in your mind. I'll give you every objection I have encountered when I have presented these prophecies.

- The one book records the prophecy and the fulfilment.

On one occasion after presenting a man with the evidence of fulfilled prophecy, he told me, 'There's just one problem with that: it's all from the one book so it doesn't count'. His objection was that the prophecy and the fulfilment are in the Bible so the prophecy and/or the fulfilment could have been invented. Of course, it could be possible for someone to write a story and say that so and so prophesied an event then later in the book record the 'fulfilment', but that certainly isn't what's going on in the Bible. I told him that the Bible isn't just one book, it is a collection of books spanning about 1,600 years, so there isn't one writer recording a prophecy then telling us of its fulfilment. Rather, there are many writers prophesying events that were totally alien to their experience, contrary to their expectations and outside their ability to influence, then centuries later these very events are

---

from the dead there is no credible answer to that question. N. T. WRIGHT deals with this in *The Resurrection of the Son of God*, SPCK, 2003, pp. 557-563.

brought to pass. So if that is his 'one problem' then, once this explanation is given, there should be no problem; God, in His wisdom, revealed Himself in scripture in a way that means we can be sure the prophecies are real.

- Maybe the prophecies were written after the fulfilment.

There are two questions that need to be asked in response to this objection:

How could they?
Anyone who says that this is what happened hasn't a clue what would be involved. Think of what is being suggested here – these persecuted Christians were somehow able to gather up every single copy of the Hebrew scriptures, insert new chapters into them all, and put them back without anyone noticing! Remember too, the scriptures weren't held on a central computer, you couldn't just log in and insert a chapter – they were on scrolls; inserting anything (never mind a chapter) would be pretty obvious. These Christians were apparently able to get away with this and then quote these inserted passages as scripture without any Jewish leader catching on. Jews may have objections to these passages, but no Jew says the Christians made them up. To say it would be absolutely impossible for this to happen is no exaggeration.

Why would they?
The charge is that the Christians made up these prophecies and miraculously inserted them into the Hebrew scriptures, then proclaimed Jesus as the fulfilment, when in fact they knew full well it was all a lie. So they were guilty of deliberately tampering with the word of God, promoting a false Messiah, and leading people to leave the ceremonies and rituals of the Mosaic Law because they had supposedly been fulfilled in Jesus. If this were true then they obviously had no fear of God – they must have been atheists, because no God-fearing Jew would dare do this. Furthermore, they got nothing but persecution and trouble as a result. So if this were a Christian invention, then these Christians must have been, at the same time, the

smartest and stupidest men in the world – the smartest for managing to make up and insert the prophecies, without detection, but the stupidest because they wasted their lives promoting a story they made up.

If anyone is determined to hold on to this objection, even after being presented with these two questions, then it is clear he isn't interested in truth. However, the fact that Psalm 22 verses 13-16 and the whole of Isaiah 52 verse 13 to chapter 53 verse 12 were found preserved amongst the Dead Sea Scrolls, and are dated to before the time of Christ shows there is not the slightest possibility of the prophecies being written after the fulfilment.[58]

- Maybe Jesus fulfilled the prophecies intentionally.

The argument here is that the Lord saw that the prophets spoke of a crucified Messiah, so, since He had been born in the right town, He deliberately set about making Himself out to look like the fulfilment of these prophecies. I think the same two questions we asked about the previous objection will help us here as well.

How could He?
We recognize, of course, that there are some prophecies the Lord could and did deliberately fulfil, showing us that He did see Himself as the promised Christ and the rightful King of Israel. Anyone could, for example, get a donkey and ride into Jerusalem, but there were other things that no mere man could control. It was the Roman Governor, under pressure from the Jewish authorities (the ones denying He was the Christ), who condemned Him to be crucified.[59] It was the Roman soldiers who scourged Him, brutally disfigured Him, stripped Him and

---

[58] We will look at the subject of the Dead Sea Scrolls more in chapter 4.
[59] And the Lord made it clear He was not presenting Himself as a political rival to Caesar, John 18. 36, which would have been a capital crime. So Pilate realized there was no cause for Him to be crucified. Had a mere man wanted to engineer his crucifixion it would have been by an act of blatant rebellion against Rome.

pierced His hands and His feet. No mere man could cause darkness to occur as He was on a cross, or ensure that His burial would not be carried out in the usual manner, but instead be carried out by a rich man. No mere man would have the ability to make His name and fame spread throughout the world and down the ages. And of course, no mere man could give Himself power to perform the miraculous, which was one of the features that led people to think He was the Messiah in the first place, neither could He bring about His resurrection.

And another thing, this objection does nothing to account for the stunningly accurate details found in Psalm 22 and Isaiah chapter 53. Remember, these passages portray the details of crucifixion hundreds of years before its invention.

Why would He?
I was in a High School speaking about the fulfilment of Messianic prophecy at the crucifixion, and one of the students offered this challenge that Jesus deliberately fulfilled them so that people would think He was the Christ. So I said to him, 'Right, I've got a great plan that will get you worldwide fame and the worship and adoration of billions of people. All you have to do is let a group of soldiers savagely beat you, rip the skin from your back, and nail you alive to a cross where you will hang in unspeakable agony for six hours, then you'll die. If you do that, people will love you for generations to come. Are you interested?'

I wasn't surprised when he told me he didn't really fancy the idea. What this objection entails is that Jesus of Nazareth was not only a liar, deliberately posing as the Messiah, but also mad as well, because He was prepared to give His very life in the most agonising fashion so people would believe Him, even though He would actually gain nothing. The suggestion is ludicrous.

Some might wonder if, perhaps, Jesus genuinely thought He was the Messiah and so (maybe subconsciously) positioned Himself to fulfil the prophecies, thinking it was His destiny to be crucified. But this fails to account for the things already mentioned, that a mere man could not control. In addition, it can't explain how He, or anyone else, would have thought He was the Messiah – it would have taken more than just being born in Bethlehem to convince people. Jews at that time viewed the Messiah as a political leader and liberator; why would any think that Jesus was the Messiah when He was neither? The only reason was because of the miraculous ministry He had, which backed up the exalted claims He made, see Luke 7. 18-23. And, as we will see later, He didn't claim to be merely a human Messiah, He claimed deity and pointed to His miracles as attestation of that claim. He would have been in a fairly good position to know if that was actually true; it's not something that someone of sound mind could be genuinely mistaken about. So it is not possible that Jesus could have been sincerely mistaken about who He claimed to be.

- Maybe the disciples just said that Jesus fulfilled the prophecies.

The objector on this occasion suggests that the disciples saw that the Bible prophesied a suffering Messiah, so they just claimed that Jesus was crucified in accord with the prophecies, when in fact He wasn't at all. We can use our two questions again against this less-than-formidable objection.

How could they?
Think of what would be involved here: the disciples don't go to the far-flung regions of the empire initially to tell this story they have supposedly concocted. No, they start in the city where the fictitious story is set![60] They accuse the authorities of being guilty of the murder of the Author of life, and call on them to repent. All the while, such an execution never actually took place! Meanwhile, the real Jesus had gone into hiding somewhere while all these stories about the crucifixion are doing the rounds. It beggars belief, and is dismissed by even the most liberal scholars in the field of New Testament studies.

---

[60] Not only does the book of Acts record the gospel going out first at Jerusalem, but the epistles of Paul confirm the early presence of Christians in Jerusalem, and it is also attested to by Tacitus (*Annals* 15:44).

JOHN DOMINIC CROSSAN, a radically sceptical New Testament scholar and co-founder of the Jesus Seminar, says:

> 'That [Jesus] was crucified is as sure as anything historical can ever be'.[61]

BART EHRMAN, agnostic New Testament scholar at the University of North Carolina at Chapel Hill, and no friend of Christianity, states:

> 'One of the most certain facts of history is that Jesus was crucified on orders of the Roman prefect of Judea, Pontius Pilate'.[62]

The theory of the crucifixion being an invention is only suggested by those who are uninformed and ill thought-through.

Why would they?
This, again, is the even bigger question. If the disciples saw that the Messiah was to be crucified, and their leader had not been crucified, why would they waste their lives proclaiming this lie? What possible benefit accrued from it? Inventing Messianic fulfilments, even if it could fool the inhabitants of Jerusalem, would not fool God. A moment's reflection and a modicum of common sense will tell you there's no way they would make this up.

- Maybe the Persians got the idea of crucifixion from the Bible.

This is how desperate it can get at times! Try to take the objection seriously though. The idea is this, the Persian king is sitting reading

---

[61] JOHN DOMINIC CROSSAN, *Jesus, A Revolutionary Biography*, San Francisco, HarperCollins, 1991, p. 145, cited in JOHN C. LENNOX, *Gunning for God, Why the New Atheists are Missing the Target*, Lion Hudson, 2011, loc 3662.
[62] BART EHRMAN, *The New Testament: An Historical Introduction to the Early Christian Writings* Oxford University Press, 2011, pp. 261-262, cited at http://blogs.christianpost.com/confident-christian/the-gospel-according-to-bart-ehrman-16491/#_ftn2.

through the Hebrew scriptures, and he comes across Psalm 22, as he reads the passage he decides this would be an excellent way to execute people, so he invents crucifixion. No, you just can't take that objection seriously! Credulity has been stretched to breaking point and can take it no longer. The fact that this objection has been raised is testimony to the clarity of the prophecy, but an indictment on the clarity of the objector's thinking. When I went through this with the lady who made this objection, she said, 'Well, maybe I am prejudiced and need to be a bit more open-minded'. Maybe indeed!

- It could be talking about something other than crucifixion.

As we have seen when we examined the details of Psalm 22 and Isaiah chapter 53, every detail of what is said corresponds exactly to crucifixion, even taking in the details of the trial before and the burial after the death on the cross. These passages draw an outline that is only filled by a cross. Nothing else fills the picture; anything else goes outside the lines.

I remember one lady, who described herself as a militant atheist, studying Psalm 22 after I had read it to her. She tried to muster some sense of triumph as she proclaimed, 'It doesn't say, *They pierced My hands and feet to a cross*!' Quite true! But then the Sufferer is speaking about His sufferings – the piercing of His hands and feet, along with the fact His bones are out of joint and He is surrounded by onlookers, implies His hands and feet are pierced to something! My response was to tell her that if this omission allowed her to dismiss this evidence then it is testimony of the tenacity of her commitment to atheism, but if I were an open-minded atheist I would be troubled by this passage, and her 'answer' would do nothing to allay my fears.

On a similar level, I read an article by an unbeliever saying that Psalm 22 could portray someone in a gladiatorial arena because it speaks about bulls, lions and dogs. This is probably the most juvenile argument I've come across. The bulls, lions and dogs are clearly metaphors because no arena would have all those animals released on the same person. Furthermore, the Sufferer, using the very common method of Hebrew parallelism, identifies the dogs as 'the assembly of the wicked', and animals may be fierce, but moral terms like *wicked* cannot apply to them. And I don't think animals gamble for garments. As we have seen, the psalm pictures a Sufferer looking on His aggressors, speaking to God and contemplating the past and present. In the melee of the gladiatorial arena, such interaction and contemplation would not take place.

- Nostradamus made similar predictions.

In responding to this objection I take the approach of *Even if ... but in fact*. The *Even if* part grants, for the moment, that their point is true, and examines the consequences. The *but in fact* part shows that the objection is actually false.

I was speaking to a man who said he was an atheist, and I presented the evidence to him from Messianic prophecy. He said that Nostradamus made predictions that were just as clear. My response was, 'So what? Even if that is true, what follows from that?' He was a bit stumped because he wasn't expecting me to take that approach, so I continued, 'I'll tell you what doesn't follow, and that's atheism. If those predictions of Nostradamus were genuine prophecies then atheism certainly can't account for them'.

I then went on to point out that the predictions of Nostradamus are not nearly so clear and compelling as many people believe. He wrote in riddles that are therefore open to a very generous range of interpretations. Furthermore, some of his more high profile prophecies are made up from statements in different writings, pulled together to look like a prophecy. This, as we have seen, is totally different to the clear Biblical passages that give detailed descriptions of the events.

- Isaiah chapter 53 is speaking about the nation of Israel, or the righteous remnant within the nation.

This is not an objection I have personally encountered, but it is the standard response of Judaism to the passage. There are clear indications that the Servant of Isaiah chapter 53 cannot be the nation of Israel or a remnant within that nation. Let me list a few of them:

- The Servant is suffering for the nation – 'For the transgression of My people was He stricken', v. 8. The speaker here is either Isaiah or the Lord, but in either case *My people* can only apply to the nation of Israel.
- The Servant is blameless, vv. 9, 11. But God promised the nation of Israel that if they were righteous they would be prosperous, so the Servant cannot be the nation.
- The Servant is submissive, vv. 7, 9. But when have the Jews ever submitted themselves to those who oppressed them?
- The Servant's suffering brings blessing and peace to others, v. 5. In what sense did the suffering of the nation/remnant bring blessing to others?
- The Servant's suffering was substitutionary, vv. 4, 5, 6, 10, 11, 12. It is clear that in verses 4-6 people are contemplating the Servant's suffering and they think He got what He deserved, but then they realize He was actually getting what they deserved. When did God ever punish Israel for the sins of the nations around to bring salvation to the nations? When did God ever punish the righteous remnant for the sins of the nation, letting the nation go free? When did the nation/remnant become a guilt offering, v. 10, or bear the sins of others?
- The Servant is exalted to a position that is God's alone, 52. 13; see Isa. 6. 1. How could any in the nation ever have such a position? Scripture affirms that the Messiah will have such a position, Ps. 110. 1.

For these, and several other reasons, the suffering Servant of Isaiah chapter 53 cannot be the nation or the righteous remnant within the nation.[63]

That's it. I have given you every argument I have met in response to the evidence of Messianic prophecy. I don't think they have the slightest impact on these passages. They stand undented by all the attacks thrown at them and testify to the truth of 1 Peter chapter 1 verses 10-11:

> 'Of this salvation the prophets have inquired and searched carefully, who prophesied of the grace that would come to you, searching what, or what manner of time, the Spirit of Christ who was in them was indicating when He testified beforehand the sufferings of Christ and the glories that would follow', NKJV.

These prophecies don't just prove the Bible to be the word of God, but they also prove Jesus Christ to be the Saviour we need. A colleague and I met a lady who told us she 'had a great faith in God, but a very hard time with Jesus'. When we showed her the prophecies of the Old Testament that were fulfilled by Jesus it really shook her and showed her that she needed to change her attitude. A short time later she told us that she had received the Lord Jesus as her Saviour. Perhaps these prophecies have shown you that you need an attitude adjustment regarding the Lord Jesus Christ?

Conclusion

Humanity has always had a fascination with the future. Horoscopes in the tabloids and fortune tellers at the fair show that there is an insatiable curiosity about things to come. It is unfortunate that people go to these sources because they have done nothing to earn anyone's

---

[63] For other reasons why Isaiah 53 can only refer to the Messiah see DARRELL L. BOCK AND MITCH GLASER (ed.) *The Gospel According to Isaiah 53*, Kregel, and BROWN, *Answering Jewish Objections to Jesus*, vol. 3.

trust. The Bible is full of information about the future. This information is not given to scratch the itch of curiosity we all have; it is given for our warning and for our encouragement.

It warns us of future judgement:

> 'And as it is appointed unto men once to die, but after this the judgment', Heb. 9. 27.
>
> 'And I saw a great white throne, and him that sat on it, from whose face the earth and the heaven fled away; and there was found no place for them. And I saw the dead, small and great, stand before God; and the books were opened: and another book was opened, which is the book of life: and the dead were judged out of those things which were written in the books, according to their works. And the sea gave up the dead which were in it; and death and hell delivered up the dead which were in them: and they were judged every man according to their works. And death and hell were cast into the lake of fire. This is the second death. And whosoever was not found written in the book of life was cast into the lake of fire', Rev. 20. 11-15.

It also encourages us that there is a glorious future for all who have availed themselves of the provision of salvation through Christ:

> 'And I heard a great voice out of heaven saying, Behold, the tabernacle of God is with men, and he will dwell with them, and they shall be his people, and God himself shall be with them, and be their God. And God shall wipe away all tears from their eyes; and there shall be no more death, neither sorrow, nor crying, neither shall there be any more pain: for the former things are passed away. And he that sat upon the throne said, Behold, I make all things new. And he said unto me, Write: for these words are true and faithful', Rev. 21. 3-5.

And, unlike the astrologers, soothsayers and prognosticators, the Bible has given us good reason to trust what it says. These are not idle warnings or empty promises. The Bible has proved itself to speak with accuracy and authority about the future, and that means when it speaks about our future we can bank on it. Death is not the end, there is a God to meet, a judgement to come and an eternity to face. In light of that, every one of us needs the Saviour the Old Testament prophesied and the New Testament presents.

These prophecies can't be explained by atheism and can't be equalled by other religions. God has spoken, and you can prove it.

Chapter 2: Reality

'The entrance of Thy words giveth light; it giveth understanding unto the simple', Ps. 119. 130.
'Thy Word is truth', John 17. 17.

In the days before Internet, SatNav and Smart Phones, if you wanted to find out how to get to a specific but unfamiliar location you had to rely on someone to tell you. This person might draw you a map or give you a list of directions. As you set out on your journey you want the map to match up with what you see around you, and you want the directions to correspond to the layout of the road network. If you find that you are repeatedly being led down dead ends, or that your directions miss out key features, then you have to conclude that the person directing you doesn't know what he's talking about – he isn't a reliable guide.

As you navigate your way through life you notice that many are prepared to meander aimlessly, going wherever the notion takes them and doing whatever their heart desires, with no real goal in mind except enjoying the journey as much as possible. That may seem the way to go, but what if there are signposts warning us of danger ahead? What if there are directions to ultimate and eternal fulfilment? What if we come to cross-roads and have to choose a path? Is there a reliable road map for life, one that corresponds to the landscape around us and gives us confidence that we are on the right path? The Bible claims to be that map. In scripture we read that God's word is a lamp to our feet and a light to our path, Ps. 119. 105. But there are many religions, belief systems and worldviews that make similar claims. How can we tell who is telling the truth?

Truth is that which matches reality. Every worldview seeks to explain and account for reality, but if it fails to do so then that means it is not true. If there is one that does actually explain and correspond to reality then it is true. As we look at the teaching of the Bible we see it matches and accounts for the way the world really is.

Paul tells us in Romans chapter 1 verses 18-23 that rejecting the true God leads to foolishness, and this is exactly what we discover if we take the directions provided by other worldviews – we will find ourselves utterly lost. There are features of basic reality that aren't included in their maps; we encounter huge landmarks that, according to them, don't exist and are figments of our imagination, and we have to convince ourselves to deny the obvious. The problem is we bump into these landmarks all the time and in order to negotiate our way through life we have to treat them as if they are real.

As long as we have our eyes open to take in the landscape around us, it should only take a short journey using the maps of non-Biblical worldviews to establish that they are not reliable guides and should not be trusted. In contrast, every contour of reality fits exactly into the Biblical worldview. Consider the following subjects:

Personality

We are personal beings. We have mind, will and emotions; we interact and form relationships with other people. What worldview best accounts for this? When Paul addressed the Athenians at the Areopagus, Acts 17. 22-34, he looked at the plethora of idols and challenged his audience on this very issue – *does your worldview accurately map reality? Does it actually match the way the world is?*

> 'For in Him we live and move and have our being, as also some of your own poets have said, 'For we are also His offspring.' Therefore, since we are the offspring of God, we ought not to think that the Divine Nature is like gold or silver or stone, something shaped by art and man's devising', Acts 17. 28-29, NKJV.

Paul is saying that if we are personal, rational, relational beings, then it makes no sense to believe that what produced us does not possess those qualities.

'If as creatures we have sprung from a Creator, we can tell a great deal about our Creator from looking at ourselves. We human beings know ourselves to be personal: the Source we come from cannot be, and is not, less personal'.[64]

'The existence of personal beings constitutes evidence that they were created by a personal God, not by any non-personal cause'.[65]

This is a very pertinent and powerful point that demands some attention. Consider the naturalistic/materialistic worldview that states that nothing exists other than physical reality. In the 1980 television series, *Cosmos*, CARL SAGAN famously put it like this, 'The Cosmos is all there is, or ever was, or ever will be'. This is a bold assertion, but is it adequate to explain the way the world is? Hardly! If nothing other than physical reality exists, then how do we get consciousness, free will, rationality, personal identity or relationships?

Consciousness
The materialistic worldview states that *everything* that exists is physical, but this poses a lot of major difficulties, one of which is that matter has no consciousness. How, on an atheistic view of the universe can matter ever become conscious of itself or the world around it? Many atheists recognize this problem: Cambridge psychologist, NICHOLAS HUMPHREY, said:

'Our starting assumption as scientists ought to be that on some level consciousness has to be an illusion'.

If we dare to ask why we have to (consciously) assume this self-contradictory notion, HUMPHREY goes on to explain:

---

[64] DAVID GOODING, *True to the Faith, A Fresh Approach to the Acts of the Apostles*, Hodder & Stoughton, 1990, pp. 311, 312.
[65] NANCY PEARCEY, *Finding Truth, 5 Principles for Unmasking Atheism, Secularism, and Other God Substitutes*, Kindle edition, p. 29.

'The reason is obvious: If nothing in the physical world can have the features that consciousness seems to have, then consciousness cannot exist as a thing in the physical world'.[66]

If you want a textbook example of begging the question, then look no further! Consciousness must be an illusion because it's not physical, and we know that only physical things exist, but hold on a minute here! Who says only physical things exist? That is a presupposition that is brought to the evidence, not a conclusion drawn from the evidence. Indeed, it is shattered by the evidence – it is nonsense to say that consciousness is an illusion. If consciousness is *the state of awareness*, then how could anyone *be aware* that the state of *being aware* is an illusion?[67] It amounts to saying, *I am conscious that there is no consciousness!* It's self-defeating.

HUMPHREY's reasoning goes like this:

Only physical things exist;
Consciousness is not a physical thing;
Therefore consciousness does not exist.

So HUMPHREY recognizes that consciousness doesn't fit in a materialistic universe, but instead of abandoning his worldview he abandons consciousness (consciously)! NANCY PEARCEY puts this all in Biblical perspective and shows that this is an example of idolatry:

'If reductionism is like trying to stuff all of reality into a box, we could say the problem is that the box is always too small. Idols deify some part of the created order. But no matter which part they choose, a *part* is always too limited to explain

---

[66] Nicholas Humphrey in JOHN BROCKMAN, ed., *Intelligent Thought: Science versus the Intelligent Design Movement*, cited in PEARCEY, *Finding Truth*, p. 106.
[67] Ironically, consciousness is one thing that absolutely cannot be an illusion. The physical world could (in principle) be an illusion, but your consciousness cannot be.

80

the *whole* . . . Invariably something will stick out. Something will not fit into its restricted conceptual categories.

What then? Whatever does not fit into the box will be dismissed, devalued, or outright denied. Reductionist thinking can be summarized as saying, if my worldview does not account for X, so much the worse for X. Idols are popular precisely because they cut reality down to a size that can be stuffed into a box and controlled. They eliminate those dimensions of reality that would falsify the worldview. You can make any worldview appear successful simply by denying anything that does not fit into its box'.[68]

Therefore materialists need to repent of their idolatry, stop exalting material reality to the only and ultimate reality, and adjust their reasoning:

If only physical things existed then consciousness wouldn't exist;
Consciousness does exist;
Therefore it is false that only physical things exist.

To make the suicidal statement that we must assume consciousness is an illusion is to demonstrate the truth of Romans chapter 1 verses 21-22: when the true God is rejected and creation is elevated to ultimate reality then people become futile in their thoughts, and their foolish hearts are darkened; professing themselves to be wise, they become fools.

Reason
In March 2012 the first 'Reason Rally' took place in the National Mall in Washington, DC. This was a gathering of over 10,000 atheists who had come together for a day of speeches and performances. The name of the event could well be the biggest misnomer ever, because the atmosphere of the day was far from reasonable, the theme was one of dehumanising mockery and ridicule of those who believe in God. But

---

[68] *Ibid.*, p. 103, emphases hers.

the name is even more inappropriate for a more fundamental reason. This was a convocation of people who believe that the ultimate reality in the universe is physical reality – they believe that everything can be reduced to nothing more than material stuff, but matter doesn't think and can't reason, it just acts according to the laws of physics and chemistry.

FRANCIS CRICK, co-discoverer of the DNA molecule said:

> 'The Astonishing Hypothesis is that "You", your joys and your sorrows, your memories and your ambitions, your sense of personal identity and free will, are in fact no more than the behaviour of a vast assembly of nerve cells and their associated molecules'.[69]

If this is true then it applies to Francis Crick too, which means he didn't write the above paragraph because he rationally thought the issues through and decided to express himself in writing, but rather there was a vast assembly of nerve cells and their associated molecules unconsciously and deterministically responding to the temperature, conditions and stimuli around, and that paragraph was the result. If atheistic materialism were true, then everything is determined by physical law and can be reduced to chemical processes. That means that the atheist is not an atheist because he has thought carefully and reasoned correctly to a proper conclusion; he is an atheist just because that is the way the particular collection of chemicals in his skull is fizzing in these conditions and at this temperature, causing his brain to produce the thought and his mouth to utter the words 'There is no God'. He has no more control over the product of his brain than he does over the product of his liver or thyroid gland.

---

[69] FRANCIS CRICK, *The Astonishing Hypothesis*, Scribner, 1995, cited in FRANK TUREK, *Stealing from God, Why atheists need God to make their case*, NavPress, 2014, p. 40.

A colleague and I had a conversation with a young man who said that he had adopted a materialistic view of the universe because of logic and reason. We pointed out to him that if he was a materialist then he couldn't help himself to logic and reason – they don't exist in a materialistic world. The laws of logic are not physical, they are immaterial. Likewise, reason can't exist in a universe in which there is nothing but molecules in motion. Our beliefs would merely be the predetermined, unavoidable outcome of the reaction of the molecules within us and the environment around us.

DOUGLAS WILSON makes this point in a debate he had with atheist, Farrell Till:

> 'If there is no God, then all that exists is time and chance acting on matter. If this is true then the difference between your thoughts and mine correspond to the difference between shaking up a bottle of Mountain Dew and a bottle of Dr. Pepper. You simply fizz atheistically and I fizz theistically. This means that you do not hold to atheism because it is true, but rather because of a series of chemical reactions. Thus, your atheism destroys rationality and morality'.[70]

NANCY PEARCEY agrees:

> 'Materialism claims that my thoughts are products of physical events. What does that mean? It means that when I calculate that 5 plus 7 equals 12, or when I perceive a rose as red, or when I judge that torturing people is evil, what is really happening is that my brain is doing physical things, like producing chemical reactions and causing neurons to fire.
> As a case in point, a recent book expounding materialism claims that ideas are "physical states of matter within our brains." Thus a thought process is "a series of brain states – a

---

70

http://www.reformed.org/master/index.html?mainframe=/apologetics/credenda-agenda/wilson-till.html.

series of physical configurations of matter – each causing the next in accordance with the deterministic laws that govern the interactions of physical objects."[71] In other words, the thought produced by your brain is akin to the sweat secreted by your glands or the digestive juice produced by your stomach'.[72]

The young man we were speaking to told us that it is impossible to prove the existence of God, but we put it to him that the very fact we are debating the subject is him conceding the debate and proving that we are not just molecules in motion.

I spoke to another man who was telling me about his struggle with spiritual issues. He told me that he had his *reasons* for atheism and his *reasons* for believing in God. I tried to point out how incongruous it was to speak about having *reasons* for atheism. If atheism were true, what would that entail? Well, it would mean that we are the by-products of mindless, purposeless processes. It would mean that the only things that exist are physical things, which, of necessity, react according to the laws of physics. It is meaningless then to speak about the reasons for anything. *Reason* presupposes you can rationally think about things, but if atheism were true then there would be no reasoning going on in your mind, there would just be reactions going on in your brain. This is why atheism is unreasonable, not just in light of the reasons for believing in God's existence, but in light of the very existence of reason.

> 'It is sometimes said that a mind capable of forming an argument against God's existence constitutes evidence for His existence. That is, a conscious being with the ability to reason, weigh evidence, and argue logically must come from a source that has at least the same level of cognitive ability. 'He who planted the ear, does He not hear? He who formed the eye,

---

[71] EDWARD SLINGERLAND, *What Science Offers the Humanities: Integrating Body and Culture*, Cambridge University Press, 2008, p. 257.
[72] PEARCEY, *Finding Truth*, pp. 189-190.

does He not see?' Ps. 94. 9. The cause must be capable of producing the effect. Water does not rise above its source'.[73]

It is for this reason scripture declares, 'The fool hath said in his heart, There is no God', Ps. 14. 1. Talking about being a reasonable atheist is to saw off the branch you are sitting on.

Free will

We saw in the last section, if atheism were true then there could be no such thing as *thinking*, and, as we will see in this section, if atheism were true there could be no such thing as *freedom* – so much for atheists being the *freethinkers*!

As J. P. MORELAND says, 'If physicalism is true, then human free will does not exist. Instead, determinism is true. If I am just a physical system, there is nothing in me that has the capacity to freely choose to do something'.[74]

Molecules don't decide to act, chemicals don't choose their behaviour, and if atheism were true then we would be nothing more than chemicals – no mind distinct from the brain, no soul distinct from the body – then we have no more control over our actions than a blade of grass or a banana does. FRANK TUREK is right when he says that atheism entails that everyone is 'a biological robot whose every action is wholly determined by natural causes'.[75] One may as well condemn the grass for being green or the banana for being yellow as condemn the child-abuser for abusing children, 'DNA neither knows nor cares. DNA just is. And we dance to its music'.[76] DAWKINS wrote elsewhere that it is as ridiculous and laughable to punish a criminal as it was for

---

[73] *Ibid.*, p. 31.
[74] J. P. MORELAND, *The Soul: How we know it's real, and why it matters*, Moody, 2014, loc 1709.
[75] TUREK, *Stealing from God*, p. 92.
[76] RICHARD DAWKINS, *River Out of Eden: A Darwinian View of Life*, Basic Books, 1995, p. 133.

the famous fictional Basil Fawlty to thrash his car for not working, or for Xerxes to lash the sea for wrecking his bridge of ships.[77] He says:

> 'Retribution as a moral principle is incompatible with a scientific view of human behaviour. As scientists, we believe that human brains, though they may not work in the same way as man-made computers, are as surely governed by the laws of physics. When a computer malfunctions, we do not punish it. We track down the problem and fix it, usually by replacing a damaged component, either in hardware or software'.

But there are several problems with this. First, as we noted above, if Dawkins is right then we could never know it or rationally justify it – he holds his views because he is biologically determined to, and what he wrote was governed by the laws of physics and not the product of an intelligent mind.

Second, the criminal, on Dawkins' view is just doing what is dictated by the laws of nature, and cannot do anything else. But why, then, does Dawkins get so annoyed and angry over the actions and attitudes of certain people? Why is he so cross with young earth creationists for what he perceives as their stupidity? Why does he condemn religious people for what he judges as evil? He's the one who says that their brains are 'as surely governed by the laws of physics' as a computer is. The reason Dawkins reacts with such outrage is because he knows what he's saying is not true! He knows that people *are* responsible for their behaviour.

A third problem in his thinking is that he says that just as the car or computer shouldn't be punished, but rather fixed, so the criminal shouldn't be punished, but fixed. But wait, why should the car or computer or any man-made machine be fixed? It should be fixed because it is not serving the *purpose* for its *design*! It isn't doing what it is *meant* to do. So, on Dawkins' view of the world, was that criminal

---

[77] http://edge.org/q2006/q06_9.html#dawkins.

designed for a *purpose*? In raping, killing or stealing, is that criminal not doing what he was *meant* to do? Dawkins is the one who has told us there is no design or purpose in the universe, he is the one who says we dance to our DNA, so how can he say the criminal needs to be fixed – on atheism there is nothing 'wrong' with him. What makes Dawkins' DNA right and the criminal's faulty? After all, Dawkins did say that propagating our DNA is 'every living object's sole reason for living'.[78]

The car was made for a purpose, and the owner of the car expects the car to work according to its designed purpose. If it doesn't work then the owner can get it fixed. Dawkins seems to assume what he elsewhere vigorously denies – that we *have* been designed for a purpose, but he also seems to think that the criminal is society's property, and society has the right to 'fix' him if he goes 'wrong'.

There's a fourth problem with his statement: Dawkins talks about what we ought to do with criminals, we ought to fix them rather than punish them, but how can we get these moral imperatives? He is talking as if the criminal is a faulty car while we are rational and responsible agents, but if his view were right then we are just as determined in our behaviour as the criminal is, so the whole notion of what we ought to do is meaningless noise.

PEARCEY tells us of a time when a young man confronted Dawkins on his views on free will after a lecture:

> 'Dawkins admitted that he does not practice what he preaches. He does not treat the very idea of responsibility as nonsense. He does hold people responsible for their actions: "I blame people, I give people credit."

---

[78] *BBC Christmas Lectures Study Guide*, London, BBC 1991. If someone took that seriously, what kind of a way would that person live? What sort of things would that person do? Yet Dawkins says that *religion* is dangerous? We can be thankful that relatively few of the vast majority of people influenced by Dawkins live consistently with his preaching.

87

"But don't you see that as an inconsistency in your views?" the young man asked. Dawkins replied, "I sort of do, yes. But it is an inconsistency that we sort of have to live with, otherwise life would be intolerable"'.[79]

This is all showing us that the materialistic view of the world is unliveable. And if a worldview cannot be consistently lived out in the real world then it is not true.

Matter (i.e., physical stuff) is not conscious of itself, it does not think and reason, choose and decide, intend or desire, love and care, so if we were just material beings, 'meat all the way down' as another has said, then we could not and would not do these things either. But we recognize that we are conscious, we possess rationality, we have will and experience emotions – this proves we are not merely physical, there is literally more to us than meets the eye.

> 'It is the height of illogic to think that humans originated from anything with lower functionality than themselves – from a something instead of a Someone'.[80]

Personal identity

What is it about you that makes you *you*? When you refer to yourself, to what are you referring? You clearly aren't referring to any part of your body. You aren't even referring to your whole body, because you could lose a part of your body yet you would still be you. You could get a part of someone else's body, but you would still be you. And yet if materialism is true then you are nothing but your body, but that body is continually changing, cells are dying and are being replaced all the time. So what is it that means you are the same person you were when you were a child? It isn't your body! If you are actually the same person you were when you were a child (and you are), it means you must be more than just physical.

---

[79] PEARCEY, *Finding Truth*, p. 157.
[80] *Ibid.*, p. 29.

This problem of identity is known as *Theseus' paradox*.[81] Plutarch wrote of a ship in which Theseus travelled which had the planks replaced, and he raised the question of whether it was the same ship or not.[82] If an object is entirely physical and the physical parts get replaced then in what way does it make sense to say that it is the same object?

Former cold-case homicide detective, J. WARNER WALLACE makes the point well:

> 'If our universe is a purely physical environment, humans are nothing more than a collection of their material parts governed by natural laws and defined by physical properties.
>
> But if that's the case, how could I arrest someone for committing a crime when the person's physical properties were different than they are today? Our bodies change over time. We age and decay. If all we are is a collection of physical parts, we're not the same people we were years ago. As J. P. Moreland observed, unless there is an essential nonmaterial person surviving the process of physical change over time, "the person who committed a crime, the person brought to trial for the crime and the person serving a jail term for that same crime are all different persons"'.[83]

When you look at a photograph of yourself from your childhood, you know you are looking at *you*. You know that *you* were once a baby, yet every cell within your body has been renewed and replaced from that time. What makes you *you* is not anything physical, and that proves

---

[81] Or, in more popular culture, it is known as *George Washington's axe* or *Trigger's broom*.

[82] http://classics.mit.edu/Plutarch/theseus.html.

[83] J. WARNER WALLACE, *God's Crime Scene, A Cold-Case Detective Examines the Evidence for a Divinely Created Universe*, David C. Cook, loc 2022-2031. J. P. Moreland citation from J. P. MORELAND AND SCOTT B. RAE, *Body and Soul: Human Nature and the Crisis in Ethics*, IVP Academic, 2000, p. 232.

that *you* are more than something physical, *you* are a soul joined to a body. Any view of reality that denies that is, therefore, false.

But this chapter is intended to show that the Biblical worldview matches reality, at present all we have done is critique an atheistic worldview.

Can other faiths account for personality?
But it's not only atheism that fails to account for personality. The religions of this world can't do the job either. There are the pantheistic religions which don't believe in a personal God, so they are ruled out on the same grounds as atheism – if we are the product of an impersonal deity then that can no more ground personality than us being the product of impersonal matter.

> 'In the monistic all-is-one philosophies of the East, there are no real I-You relationships, no distinctions between the compassionate and the pitied, between good and evil. All differences are illusory (maya). And why think this impersonal 'God' is responsible for creating and sustaining the world we experience?'[84]

There are the polytheistic religions in which the gods are derived from physical reality, so they again are ruled out as providing an adequate foundation for personality. JOHN LENNOX points out that the gods of the Babylonians and Greeks were produced from and part of the physical universe.

> 'We should not think that the only difference between the Hebrew and Greek world-view is that the Hebrews reduced the number of gods to one. Hebrew monotheism is not a slimmed-down version of pagan polytheism. The God of the Hebrews is *outside the world*. This is an absolute difference in category – not a mere difference in degree. It is also why, as

---

[84] Paul Copan in PAUL COPAN & WILLIAM LANE CRAIG (ed.), *Contending with Christianity's Critics*, B & H, 2009, loc 4161-4169.

we have already noted, the God of the Hebrews gives meaning to the world, whereas the pagan gods do not. The meaning of the system will not be found in the system.[85]

But what about religions that do believe in a personal God, like Islam (or the Unitarian cults of Christianity)?

I was speaking to a 'Jehovah's Witness' and he told me that from eternity past God had been entirely on His own and was completely happy and content. Now, please think carefully about this. If God had been on His own as a single person, and was completely happy and content then it must mean that love is not an essential part of His nature, because if it were then He could not have been content without someone to love.

> 'Love is something that one person has for another person. If God was a single person, then before the world was made, He was not love'.[86]

Imagine another couple of scenarios: if love were an essential part of God's nature, and He created creatures in order to love them then that would make God a contingent being, that is, He would be dependent on His creation, and need His creation in order for Him to be fulfilled, but that would mean He isn't God.

> 'The attributes of God were active prior to creation and, if so, there must have been both agent and object then as now. To restrict the divine object to creation is to deprive God of the exercise of His qualities and characteristics during that period preceding creation. It also follows that, since creation was a matter of divine choice and thus contingent, it is to restrict the exercise of God's attributes to that which is contingent. In such a case the divine attributes might as easily have never

---

[85] JOHN C. LENNOX, *Against the Flow, The Inspiration of Daniel in an Age of Relativism*, Lion Hudson, 2015, p. 66.
[86] C. S. LEWIS, *Mere Christianity*, HarperCollins, 2002, p. 174.

been exercised at all. All this suggests the absurdity that the divine attributes were not exercised in eternity past, that they might not under certain circumstances be exercised now and that they might never be exercised at all'.[87]

Or, if love were not a part of this God's nature, and He created freely, but then found Himself loving His creation, then it would mean that He is not immutable, He is a being that has a nature that can change and be improved, and thus He wouldn't be the greatest possible being, and therefore wouldn't be God at all. Only in the scriptural revelation of the Trinity do we see that God is essentially and eternally loving, and not at all dependent on His creation to express and enjoy love.

So the God of Unitarian religions cannot be essentially loving or relational. If then we are creatures that are loving and relational it points to a God who has this as part of His own nature and being, the only candidate is the trinitarian God of scripture. *Is it not remarkable that there is only one book out of all the so-called holy books of religions that presents a God who can provide the basis for the most fundamental aspect of being human – sharing love and forming relationships?*

Let's look at another aspect of reality that only the God of scripture can account for.

Morality

We have already shown that the free will, rationality and responsibility necessary for morality to be meaningful cannot be grounded outside of a Biblical worldview, but let's briefly touch on this notion of good and evil.

It is a feature of the world we live in that we encounter evil, but what actually is evil? Typically when I ask people that question they begin giving me examples, but I have to stop them and explain I'm not asking for examples, I'm asking for a definition. Evil is a departure

---

[87] L. S. CHAFER, *Systematic Theology*, vol. 1, Kregel, 1993, p. 292.

from the way things ought to be, but if there is no God then there is no way things *ought* to be, there's only the way things *are*. C. S. LEWIS highlighted this problem of a person trying to get 'a conclusion in the imperative mood out of premises in the indicative mood: though he continues trying to all eternity he cannot succeed, for the thing is impossible'.[88]

If atheism is true then this universe didn't tumble into existence with a set of rules, and even if it did, what would be the chances of blind forces acting on mindless matter producing creatures that would discover this transcendent realm of rules, and furthermore, what would make those rules authoritative and binding on us? The idea that there is 'good' existing abstractly in the universe does nothing to account for why we are under any obligation to care. Yet we recognize that there are obligatory moral duties and objective moral standards – what worldview best accounts for that?[89] It certainly isn't atheism, or any of the other worldviews that deny a personal God.

I spoke to a man who told me he was an atheist and a follower of Richard Dawkins. He then started to complain about the evil in the world. I pointed out that Dawkins said there's no such thing as evil. The man responded by saying, 'Oh, he's definitely wrong about that, there is good and evil, there is heaven and hell!' It was astonishing that this man could say he was an atheist and yet say he believed in heaven and hell. He had these completely contradictory notions in his mind and he just had to keep them locked in separate rooms, because if they ever met each other then one would kill the other. But in holding such blatantly contradictory views he was showing himself to be a follower of Dawkins after all. DAWKINS' famous quote is worth repeating here:

---

[88] C. S. LEWIS, *The Abolition of Man*, cited in JOHN C. LENNOX, *Gunning for God, Why the New Atheists are Missing the Target*, Lion Hudson, 2011, loc 1828.
[89] Appealing to evolution doesn't ground objective morality; it would only tell us why *we think* there is objective morality. If the atheist is right then evolution doesn't explain objective morality, it explains it away.

'The universe we observe has precisely the properties we should expect if there is, at bottom, no design, no purpose, no evil and no good, nothing but blind, pitiless indifference'.[90]

Now, bear in mind, as we have noted, Dawkins is a man who condemns the wickedness of certain people and behaviours all the time. In addressing the American Humanist Association in 1996 he said, 'I think a case can be made that faith is one of the world's great evils'.[91] In *The God Delusion*,[92] he says that the God of the Old Testament is *unjust*, and says that the New Testament 'adds a new *injustice*' to the theology of the Old Testament (emphasis added).

He doesn't seem to understand that evil can't exist and not exist at the same time. He has to take his pick: either affirm that there is no evil (and then stop complaining about it!) or affirm that there is evil (and acknowledge that atheism provides no basis for it).

In theory his view is evil doesn't exist; in practice he sees the reality of it everywhere. If your theory can't survive in practice then it's time to abandon your theory. Dawkins certainly does not live as if there is no good and no evil, and we can't live that way either. Good and evil are inescapable realities of the world we live in, and any worldview that says that they don't actually exist is false.

Can other faiths ground morality?
Morality demands a personal God whose nature is good and who imposes moral demands on us. But I would argue that Unitarian religions cannot adequately ground objective morality. Morality has to do with interactions between persons, but if God were a single person then His nature could not be essentially moral. The triune God,

---

[90] DAWKINS, *River Out of Eden*, p. 133.
[91] Quoted in
http://www.forbes.com/sites/alexberezow/2013/09/30/richard-dawkins-is-wrong-about-religion/#7821b5e2d776.
[92] RICHARD DAWKINS, *The God Delusion*, Bantum Press, 2006.

revealed in scripture, exists in eternal community, thus He is essentially a moral being.

We can see another reason why only the God of scripture can be the ground of morality when we look at the way of salvation. In the Qur'an one of the main themes is that Allah is all-merciful, but the problem is that his mercy is shown at the expense of his righteousness. If someone's good deeds outweigh their bad then they enter paradise (Surah 7:8-9). But this is fudging on justice. It is unrighteous to overlook sin just because more good things were done, after all, would an absolutely righteous God not demand good works all the time (just as the Bible says, Lev. 18. 5 and Rom. 10. 5)? The God of Islam compromises on sin and thus isn't righteous. Only the God of scripture is 'a just God and a Saviour', Isa. 45. 21. He can show mercy consistent with justice because of the cross. That is why Paul said that the gospel doesn't undermine the law, it establishes it, Rom. 3. 31.

Everyone recognizes objective morality, but only one worldview can account for it – the Bible teaches there is a righteous God who has made us in His image and written the work of His law on our hearts, Rom. 2. 15.

The argument can be summarized as follows:
> *If a righteous God did not exist then good and evil would not exist;*
> *Good and evil do exist;*
> *Therefore a righteous God exists.*

Only the Bible presents such a God.
Let's move on and look at something related to the subject of morality.

The dignity/depravity of man

We recognize that human beings have intrinsic value. Intrinsic value means that they are valuable because of *what they are*, not because of *what they can do*. This is why no one apart from a psychopath believes that human life can be taken without some form of justification. Now very often the justification is not adequate, but almost everyone who takes the life of another human being does make some effort to justify their actions. Others will try to dehumanise the victim and say that they aren't really humans, but in that there is a tacit admission of the value of human beings. The question is, 'what gives humanity this value?' Only in the Bible do we read that humanity is created in God's image – this is something that separates them from the rest of creation, it elevates them above other forms of life, and confers a dignity upon them that we all can't help but recognize.

But if the atheist is correct, and we are just advanced collections of chemicals which emerged without any cause or purpose, why would we ever think there is any objective worth to humanity? Why all this talk about inalienable human rights? What makes us more valuable than any other life form on the planet? It is only because the atheist (thankfully) cannot live consistently with his professed belief that he treats human beings as if they were worthy of respect and intrinsically valuable.

Other religions may profess to ground the dignity of the human race but they really don't. The pantheistic religions say that everything is divine, but that includes the insects that annoy you, the virus that attacks you and the bacteria that afflicts you as much as it includes you, and thus provides no foundation for the uniqueness of human beings.[93] Even in Islam, mankind is not created in the image of God, and thus it seems that humans are not ends in themselves but only means to ends.

---

[93] The pantheist may profess that all of life is sacred and of equal value but they cannot live consistently with that. Real life has a way of exposing our true beliefs and values, and their reaction to seeing an animal lying dead at the side of the road would likely be different than if they saw a human lying dead at the side of the road.

So, in the rubber-hits-the-road realm of real life, we all recognize that dignity of human beings, but only one worldview can account for that – the Biblical one, which proclaims that we are image bearers of God.

However, we see that there is not only something highly dignified about humanity, we also know there is something deeply depraved; we are valuable but broken. There is something wrong with us, and we all know it. We do what we know we shouldn't, and don't have the power to live as we know we should. The Bible explains why this is – it tells us that the human race was polluted at its source:

> 'Wherefore, as by one man sin entered into the world, and death by sin; and so death passed upon all men, for that all have sinned', Rom. 5. 12.

Humanity has a bias towards sin that the Bible adequately accounts for, but does any other worldview account for it? For reasons already given, no worldview that denies a personal, righteous God can account for our recognition of our waywardness and depravity, and neither can the Muslim worldview. I had a conversation with a Muslim on one occasion and he brought up this subject of original sin; he told me he didn't believe people were born sinners. I asked him if he had children, and he told me he didn't. 'I didn't think so', I said. Anyone who has children knows that they are born sinners! Parents do not have to teach children to lie, be selfish, impatient, etc. These things come naturally to children, without any training or coercion.

So, as we look at the human race, in our dignity and depravity, we find that the Bible accounts for the way things really are, and no other worldview does.

Science and mathematics

It is the common mantra of our generation that science disproves God, but I will just point out what many thoughtful people have recognized: the bare fact that we can do science is a massive pointer to God. What kind of a universe would have to exist for us to rationally investigate and understand it? How can we account for the fact that the mathematician can sit at his desk and make calculations that actually match the way things are and predict the way things will be? What best explains what another has called 'the unreasonable effectiveness of mathematics'?[94] It certainly isn't mindless forces. Anyone who thinks that natural selection acting on random mutations would produce life-forms that can mathematically describe the universe is displaying a wonderful imagination, and nothing more.

Modern science sprang from a Christian conviction that the universe was intelligible, acted according to regular laws and could be investigated.

> 'One person who drew attention to this circumstance . . . was the eminent historian of science and mathematician Sir Alfred North Whitehead. Observing that medieval Europe in 1500 knew less than Archimedes in the third century BC and yet by 1700 Newton had written his masterpiece, *Principia Mathematica*, Whitehead asked the obvious question: How could such an explosion of knowledge have happened in such a relatively short time? His answer: "modern science must come from the medieval insistence on the rationality of God . . . My explanation is that the faith in the possibility of science, generated antecedently to the development of modern scientific theory, is an unconscious derivative from medieval theology". C. S. Lewis' succinct formulation of Whitehead's view is worth recording: "Men became scientific because they expected law in nature and they expected law in nature because they believed in a lawgiver"'.[95]

Thus the very possibility of science being done at all fits perfectly with a view of the world based on the Bible.

---

[94] EUGENE WIGNER, *The Unreasonable Effectiveness of Mathematics in the Natural Sciences*, http://www.maths.ed.ac.uk/~aar/papers/wigner.pdf.
[95] JOHN C. LENNOX, *God's Undertaker, Has Science Buried God?*, Lion, 2007, p. 20.

Conclusion

This universe is God's universe, and all people are made in God's image. That means that any view of reality which contradicts God's view cannot accurately map over real life and the real world.

When we consistently follow non-Biblical worldviews we find we get stuck in ditches of irrationality and crash into walls of contradictions. We can't explain what we are seeing around us when we look at the maps they provide.

The Lord Jesus said to His Father, 'Thy word is truth', John 17. 17; a Biblical view of the world fits the landscape of reality exactly, accounting for all the features of life we encounter, showing us that the writers of scripture were getting their information from the God who sees and says things the way they really are.

Chapter 3: Oneness

'And beginning at Moses and all the prophets, he expounded unto them in all the scriptures the things concerning himself', Luke 24. 27.
'All scripture is given by inspiration of God', 2 Tim. 3. 16.

This subject changed my life. I was 17 years old and wasting my time. Sport was a huge thing to me, but then I tore my cartilage. I hobbled along to Bible teaching meetings by Mr Malcolm Radcliffe and I was stunned. He gave teaching on the Tabernacle, Exod. 25-40, and showed how the subject threaded its way throughout scripture, how this Old Testament structure so vividly portrayed New Testament doctrine and so beautifully pictured the Lord Jesus Christ. I saw the wonder of the word of God, and realized I was wasting my time giving it to sport. I wanted to study this for myself. It started me on a journey I am still on (and will be forever), investigating how the word of God all fits together.

This subject also maintained my sanity. In my early 20's I went through a very dark period of doubt. I was exposed to arguments against the inspiration and integrity of scripture, objections I had never heard before that challenged me to the core. I eventually discovered that there were satisfying answers to all these challenges but it took me a while to find them. The thing that preserved me through that period was the truth of this subject. As I reflected on what I had learned and subsequently studied I realized that, even if I don't have answers to these questions, they must be out there, because there was no way all these parts of scripture could link up so precisely and harmonize so beautifully without a divine hand being involved. This wasn't blind faith, it was a reasonable conclusion. I didn't have all the answers to the objections to my view, but I did have evidence for my view. It is not sensible to throw out evidence you do have based on answers you don't have. I did have challenging questions, but overthrowing my belief that the Bible was God's word would have led to a much harder question – how could all of these writers have got their writings to link up in so many ways when there was no possibility of collusion? ADA HABERSHON, in writing about typology in scripture, said:

> 'This study gives us a sure antidote for the poison of the so-called "higher criticism." If we acknowledge the divine intention of every detail of the types, even though we may not understand all their teaching, and if we believe there is a lesson in every incident recorded, the attacks of modern criticism will not harm us. We may not be clever enough to understand what the critics say, or to answer their criticisms; but if our eyes have been opened to see the beauty of the types, the doubts which such writers suggest will not trouble us, and we shall have a more profitable occupation than reading their works. When so much of this destructive criticism is about, we cannot do better than urge all – even the youngest Christians – to take up the typical study of God's Word; for though He has hid these things from the wise and prudent, He reveals them unto babes.
>
> The "higher criticism" and the study of the types cannot go together; for no one who has learnt the spiritual teaching of the Old Testament pictures would believe, or try to prove, that the Bible was not what it claimed to be'.[96]

I can testify personally to the truth of this.

What changed my life and preserved my sanity was the oneness of scripture. Unity would be a better word but that would ruin my acrostic! Whatever we call it, the point is this, the Bible is a collection of books from a variety of writers over a vast span of time and distance, yet it speaks with one voice, telling one story and giving evidence of one source – a source that spans the time and distance and guided the writers.

---

[96] ADA R. HABERSHON, *Study of the Types*, Kregel, 1997, p. 21.

The Bible teaches that God is a trinity, that is, He is one being but that being is shared by three persons. Thus, there is a plurality within His unity. This is something that has no analogy in creation, but perhaps there is an analogy of it in the way God has chosen to reveal Himself in scripture. The Bible is a library of books, each one of those books is distinct from the others, yet there is a unity. We can pick any particular book and say, 'that is the word of God'. It has all the attributes of inspiration – it is perfect, authoritative and complete for the purpose for which it was given – but when we take all sixty-six books together we don't say, 'there are sixty-six words of God'. No, all of the books together are the word of God. So it is with the Godhead. We can look at each person in the Trinity and say, He is God, each one has all the attributes of deity, but when we think of the three together we don't say there are three Gods. There is only one divine being.

The unity of scripture is something that defies human ingenuity and stands as a clear signpost to the truth of inspiration. This remarkable unity can be demonstrated in a lot of different ways. Let's think of a few together.

Structural unity

The Bible gives evidence of a deliberate structure in its layout. This was not the result of an editorial committee, because the Old Testament scriptures were fixed before the New Testament came along, and the New Testament scriptures were written by a variety of men who could not have colluded to ensure they were going to coalesce with each other and correspond to the Old Testament.

The divisions of scripture
The Old Testament was composed of three parts: the Law (the Torah: Genesis to Deuteronomy), the Prophets (the Nevi'im: Joshua, Judges, the books of Samuel and Kings, Isaiah, Jeremiah, Ezekiel, and the twelve Minor Prophets) and the Writings (the Ketuvim, sometimes called the Psalms because that was the first book in that section: Psalms, Job, Proverbs, Ruth, Song of Solomon, Ecclesiastes,

Lamentations, Esther, Daniel, Ezra-Nehemiah, and the books of Chronicles).[97]

As far as the New Testament is concerned:

> 'David Trobisch has demonstrated that the New Testament in the early church was divided into four clear subsections – Gospels, Praxapostolos (Acts and Catholic Epistles), Pauline Epistles, and Revelation – as can be seen from the uniform witness of the manuscript collections themselves. Thus, the entire biblical canon (Hebrew and Greek), when viewed as a whole, contains seven sections. Given the biblical usage of the number seven as representative of completeness or wholeness, a sevenfold canonical structure would speak to the overall unity of the biblical canon and provides further reason to think that the New Testament canon we possess is the proper conclusion to the original books of the Old Testament. In addition, it should be noted that in both the first book (Genesis) and the last book (Revelation) the number seven plays a significant role'.[98]

KRUGER points out that the sections of the Old Testament are paralleled in the New Testament. The first section in each Testament (the Pentateuch and the Gospels) deals with historical narratives in which the great act of redemption is accomplished. Then the book of Acts functions in the same way as the historical books, showing how God's people progressed, took new land, and fulfilled the commission of the covenant mediator. The epistles of the New Testament perform a similar role to the prophetic books of the Old Testament 'in that they are designed to apply and uphold the terms of the covenant laid forth in the prior historical accounts'. Then the book of Revelation is

---

[97] See NORMAN L. GEISLER & WILLIAM E. NIX, *A General Introduction to the Bible,* Moody Press, 1986, p. 23.

[98] MICHAEL J. KRUGER, *Canon Revisited: Establishing the Origins and Authority of the New Testament Books,* Crossway, 2012, loc 3955.

the fitting conclusion of the New Testament, corresponding to the apocalyptic literature in the Old Testament.[99]

Moses and John

This link between the first and the last book of the Bible is worth pursuing. The book of Revelation brings closure and resolution to the problems raised by the entrance of sin in Genesis; it prophesies the restoration of humanity and creation, and the fulfilment of God's original intention. The Bible commences with a man reigning in paradise with his bride, and that is the way it ends – Christ, the last Adam, 1 Cor. 15. 45, with His bride (the church) reigning in paradise over a redeemed creation. MICHAEL KRUGER summarizes the connections:

> 'Genesis begins with the creation of the "heavens and the earth" (1:1ff.); Revelation ends with re-creation and the new "heaven and earth" (21:1). Genesis begins with the theme of paradise in the garden (2:8ff.); Revelation ends with the paradise of heaven (21:4). Genesis begins with the theme of marriage (2:18); Revelation ends with the great wedding of the Lamb (21:9). Genesis begins with a focus on the serpent's deception (3:1ff.); Revelation ends with the serpent's destruction (20:10). Genesis begins with the curse being put upon the world (3:14ff.); Revelation ends with the curse being lifted (22:3). Genesis begins by describing the creation of day, night, and the oceans (1:3, 10, 14); Revelation ends with no more need for day (sun), or night, or oceans (21:1; 22:5). Genesis begins with the "tree of life" among the people of God (2:9); Revelation ends with the "tree of life" among the people of God (22:2). Genesis begins with God dwelling with His people (2:8; 3:8); Revelation ends with God finally dwelling with His people again (21:3)'.[100]

---

[99] *Ibid.*, loc 3882-3904.
[100] *Ibid.*, loc 3964-3974.

The Old Testament commences with the writings of Moses, the New Testament concludes with the writings of John. Both of these men wrote five books. We have looked at how Genesis and Revelation link up, but that's not the end of the correspondence.

Exodus parallels John's Gospel. John presents the Lord Jesus as the fulfilment of the Passover of Exodus chapter 12 (see, for example, John 19. 36), as the fulfilment of the manna of Exodus chapter 16 (see John 6. 32-58), as the fulfilment of the rock that was smitten in Exodus chapter 17 (see John 7. 37-39), and as the fulfilment of the Tabernacle in Exodus 25-40 (see John 1. 14).

Leviticus links with 1 John. Leviticus tells us about the Day of Atonement, Lev. 16, and John tells us that Christ is the atonement, 1 John 2. 2; 4. 10. Leviticus speaks much about cleansing, e.g., chapter 14, and anointing, e.g., chapter 8; these are subjects in 1 John too, e.g., 1. 7, 9; 2. 27; 3. 3.

Numbers corresponds with 3 John. Numbers charts the journey of Israel through the wilderness, telling us about God providing for them and how they wouldn't take anything from the nations around, see, for example, 20. 17; in 3 John we read about those who have gone forth for Christ's name 'taking nothing from the Gentiles', v. 7, NKJV.

Deuteronomy fits with 2 John. Deuteronomy is the second reading of the law (the name of the book means the second law); Moses is taking them back to the commandments, telling them how to behave in the land, impressing on them the need for separation from the evil practices around them, and warning them of the consequences of compromise. This is what John is doing in his second epistle, for example:

> 'I rejoiced greatly that I found of thy children walking in truth, as we have received a commandment from the Father. And now I beseech thee, lady, not as though I wrote a new commandment unto thee, but that which we had from the beginning, that we love one another. And this is love, that we

walk after his commandments. This is the commandment, that, as ye have heard from the beginning, ye should walk in it', vv. 4-6.

The links between John's writings and the Pentateuch are too clear to be coincidental, yet too subtle to be intentional on the part of John.

Matthew and the Old Testament
The structural unity is strengthened when we look how the first book of the Old Testament links with the first book of the New Testament.

At the beginning of the Old Testament we see people going away from God to the east:

> 'So He drove out the man; and He placed at the east of the garden of Eden Cherubim, and a flaming sword which turned every way, to keep the way of the tree of life', Gen. 3. 24.
> 'And Cain went out from the presence of the Lord, and dwelt in the land of Nod, on the east of Eden', Gen. 4. 16.
> 'Then Lot chose him all the plain of Jordan; and Lot journeyed east: and they separated themselves the one from the other', Gen. 13. 11.

When we come to the commencement of the New Testament we find that there are people coming to God from the east:

> 'Now when Jesus was born in Bethlehem of Judaea in the days of Herod the king, behold, there came wise men from the east to Jerusalem, saying, Where is he that is born King of the Jews? for we have seen his star in the east, and are come to worship him', Matt. 2. 2.

How appropriate that the New Testament commences in this way. It is because of the Messiah that mankind can be brought back from their alienation caused by sin.

Matthew's Gospel not only links with the first book of the Old Testament, but also with the last. In the first century Hebrew scriptures, the books of Chronicles closed the canon. Genesis and 1 Chronicles both feature genealogies in their early chapters. Matthew commences his Gospel in the same way.

> 'Matthew's opening chapter would be a clear indication that he is intending to finish the story. He is picking up where the Old Testament ended, with a focus on David and the deliverance of Israel. Moreover, the Great Commission at the very end of Matthew's Gospel (Mt. 28:18-20) is a vivid echo of the end of 2 Chronicles (2 Chron. 36:23), leading Greg Beale to argue that "Matthew constructs his Gospel partly to reflect the beginning and ending of Chronicles"'.[101]

Designed by

Just as any structure points to a designer, so too does the structure of scripture. The designer couldn't have been any of the writers involved because none of them were able to see how their particular writings contributed to the great edifice of the Bible. This designer was engaged in a long term product: He employed the first builder in 1500 BC and laid the last one off at about AD 90. He took workers from as far east as Persia and as far west as Rome. He was present the whole time to make sure everything went according to His plan. There is only one who could have done this, and that's why we call the Bible God's word.

So far we have been standing back and seeing the shape of what has been built, but now it's time to take a closer look at the intricate details.

---

[101] MICHAEL J. KRUGER, *The Question of Canon, Challenging the status quo in the New Testament debate*, Apollos, 2013, p. 145.

Illustrative incidents

He was 96 years old (or young), strong in body and clear in mind. He had worked all his life and was telling me about all the different jobs he had done.

'And what do you do for a living?' he then asked.

I told him what I had been involved in, but that I now give all my time to spreading the gospel.

'Ah!' he nodded, 'so you spend your life telling stories?'

I told him that I spend my life telling the biggest and the best story anyone could ever hear. The Bible is a collection of (true) stories, but it is presenting one story, the gospel, and exalting one person, the Lord Jesus, and every part contributes to the whole. It is the story of God moving out in Christ to redeem fallen man and restore fallen creation for His glory. Every part of the Bible contributes to that theme. As the Lord Jesus said to the Jewish authorities:

> 'Search the scriptures; for in them ye think ye have eternal life: and they are they which testify of me', John 5. 39.

After His resurrection, He showed the two on the road to Emmaus that every part of scripture pointed to Him, Luke 24. 25-27, not only in direct prophecy but in the history it records.

MARTIN LUTHER put it this way, 'All Scripture teaches nothing but the cross'.[102]

MICHAEL KRUGER writes, 'Indeed, it can be rightly said that *the* unifying factor for all canonical books is Jesus Christ. He is what makes the

---

[102] Cited by FRANK E. GAEBELEIN, *The Unity of the Bible*, available at http://biblicalstudies.org.uk/pdf/rev-henry/24_unity_gaebelein.pdf.

Bible one book'.[103] It is for this reason that Paul referred to the scriptures as 'the word of Christ', Col. 3. 16.

Sometimes the New Testament writers, looking back at Old Testament history through the lens of the person and work of Christ, saw direct parallels and pointers and deliberately alluded to them, but we will see that there are statements in the New Testament and truths taught that match up with Old Testament pictures, seemingly without the apostles being conscious of it, and certainly in ways they could not have engineered. The best (and only viable) explanation of this remarkable unity is that 'all scripture is given by inspiration of God', 2 Tim. 3. 16.

Genesis 3

After Adam and Eve ate from the tree of the knowledge of good and evil they experienced fear and shame. They hid themselves and tried to clothe themselves with fig leaves, Gen. 3. 7. However, when God found them He clothed them in coats of skin, Gen. 3. 21. In this we see an illustration of a beautiful gospel truth:

> 'We have here, in figure, the great doctrine of divine righteousness set forth, The robe which God provided was an effectual covering, because He provided it; just as the apron [of fig leaves] was an ineffectual covering, because man had provided it. Moreover, God's coat was founded upon blood-shedding; Adam's apron was not. So also now, God's righteousness is set forth in the cross; man's righteousness is set forth in the works – the sin-stained works – of his own hands'.[104]

> 'Death provided this covering. These coats of skin owned the penalty as having come in, and those clothed with them found shelter for themselves in the death of another...How pregnant

---

[103] KRUGER, *Canon Revisited*, loc 3871, emphasis his.

[104] C. H. MACKINTOSH, *Notes on the Pentateuch, Genesis to Deuteronomy*, Loizeaux Brothers, 1980, p. 35.

with instruction as to how still man's nakedness is covered and he made fit for the presence of a righteous God! These skins were fitness, the witness of how God had maintained the righteous sentence of death, while removing that which was now his shame, and meeting the consequences of his sin. Our covering is far more, but it is such a witness also. Our righteousness is still the witness of God's righteousness, the once dead, now living One, who of God is made unto us righteousness, and in whom also we are made the righteousness of God'.[105]

Right at the beginning of the Bible we have a clear picture of what is fully taught in the gospel – our efforts can never make us right with God, we need the death of another, see Rom. 3. 20-26.[106]

Genesis 6-8 – the ark
In these chapters we are told of God's judgement in the flood. He instructed Noah to build an ark as the means of salvation for all who were sheltered in it. The judgement that would have fallen upon them fell on the ark instead. That judgement which swept away and submerged all else was borne by the ark and the ark came through it, saving all that had taken refuge in it. This illustrates the truth of substitution – all that we deserved to bear was borne by Christ, and thus, 'There is therefore now no condemnation to them which are in Christ Jesus', Rom. 8. 1.

Genesis chapter 8 in particular furnishes abundant evidence for the inspiration of scripture. The world had just gone through a period of unparalleled upheaval and tremendous unrest, and in this chapter we are entering into rest and new creation.[107] The chapter divides into

---

[105] F. W. GRANT, *Genesis in the Light of the New Testament*, Pickering & Inglis, pp. 51-52.
[106] It is difficult not to see this same point in the next chapter with Cain and Abel's sacrifices.
[107] The wind moving in chapter 8 verse 1 draws the mind back to chapter 1 verse 2 telling us that chapter 8 is a chapter of new creation.

three sections, vv. 1-5, 6-12, and 13-22, and the commencement of the second and third sections is marked by the words, 'And it came to pass', vv. 6, 13. In each section, we find rest: in the first section, the ark rests on the mountains of Ararat, v. 4; in the second section, the dove initially finds no rest for the sole of her foot, v. 9, then evidently does find rest, v. 12; then, in the third section, the Lord smells a sweet savour from Noah's offering, v. 21, or, as it literally reads, the Lord smelled 'a savour of rest'.[108] In the first section, the ark rests; in the second, the dove rests; in the third, the Lord rests, and it doesn't require any stretch of the imagination or twisting of the text to see the Trinity at rest here. The ark, as we have seen, is a picture of the Lord Jesus, the dove is a picture of the Holy Spirit, see e.g., Matt. 3. 16, and the Lord would be God the Father.

The ark came through the judgement and came to rest. Consider when the ark rested and where the ark rested: the ark came to rest on the 17th day of the seventh month. When we come to Exodus chapter 12 we find that God resets the calendar so that the seventh month becomes the first month. This means, if we go by this reset calendar, that the ark came to rest on the 17th day of the first month, which just so happens to be the day the Lord Jesus rose from the dead.[109] The resurrection is the proof that the storm of God's judgement is over, the declaration that the work is done. Christ rests.

But where did the ark come to rest? On the mountains of Ararat. BROWN-DRIVER-BRIGGS, in their Hebrew definitions, tell us that Ararat means the curse reversed.[110] So, the ark, speaking of Christ, rests on the day of resurrection on a site which means the curse reversed – can there be any doubt as to the inspiration of scripture here? It is through the work of Christ that the curse against us can be reversed and we can be brought into blessing:

---

[108] The word 'sweet' is from the same family as the words translated 'rest' in verses 4 and 9.
[109] By the Galilean way of reckoning the days, https://bible.org/article/chronology-synopsis-passion-week.
[110] *Brown-Driver-Briggs Hebrew Definitions* on e-Sword.

'Christ has redeemed us from the curse of the law, having become a curse for us (for it is written, "Cursed is everyone who hangs on a tree"), that the blessing of Abraham might come upon the Gentiles in Christ Jesus, that we might receive the promise of the Spirit through faith', Gal. 3. 13-14, NKJV.

And it is through the work of Christ that the curse on this creation will be reversed:

'For I consider that the sufferings of this present time are not worthy to be compared with the glory which shall be revealed in us. For the earnest expectation of the creation eagerly waits for the revealing of the sons of God. For the creation was subjected to futility, not willingly, but because of Him who subjected it in hope; because the creation itself also will be delivered from the bondage of corruption into the glorious liberty of the children of God', Rom. 8. 18-21, NKJV.

This pictures the truth of the gospel in a way that could not have been artificially manufactured; we can see the fingerprints of God on the page of scripture.

In the next section, Noah sent out a raven first of all. The raven was happy to land on the carrion that was floating about; it could feed on that which was dead and corrupting, but the dove couldn't do that; the dove could only rest on that which belonged to the new creation and could only feed on that which spoke of new life. This illustrates the teaching of the New Testament regarding the two natures the Christian has, see, for example, Gal. 5. 17; John 3. 6. When someone is born again he still has what the Bible calls the flesh – that sinful nature that we got from Adam, which is happy to feed on that which is corrupting; but he is also indwelt by God's Holy Spirit, which means that he can never again be comfortable in the corruption of this world; he feels at rest in God's presence.

The third section tells us about the Lord smelling a savour of rest from Noah's offering, pointing to the fact that, in the offering of Christ at Calvary, God can rest. Sin had outraged and robbed God, but, in the sacrifice of Christ, the desires of His heart and the demands of His throne have been satisfied. God rests.

The picture of the rest of the Triune God is so strikingly beautiful, and yet so obviously not something that Moses was aware of. Even if the Bible were the work of one human author, to incorporate all these features so skilfully would be a work of incomprehensible genius. It is clearly the work of one author, but not a human author; as Peter said, 'holy men of God spoke as they were moved by the Holy Spirit', 2 Pet. 1. 21, NKJV.

Genesis 22-25
There is a wonderful panorama of God's dealings with mankind in this run of chapters that testifies to the inspiration of scripture. Chapter 22 on its own is enough to show that Moses was being guided by God in what he wrote. We read about the sacrifice of a unique and beloved son, calling to mind the language of Romans chapter 8 verse 32, 'He that spared not his own Son, but delivered him up for us all'.

In Genesis chapter 22 verse 2 we have the first mention of love in the Bible, and it is the love of a father for the son who is going to be sacrificed:

> 'Take now thy son, thine only son Isaac, whom thou lovest'.

It is surely no coincidence that the first mention of love in the New Testament is the love of God the Father for His Son:

> 'This is my beloved Son, in whom I am well pleased', Matt. 3. 17.

We also encounter the Bible's first mention of a lamb in Genesis chapter 22 verse 7. As Abraham and Isaac were going to the place of sacrifice, Isaac asked, 'where is the lamb for a burnt offering?' Abraham's cryptic reply was, 'My son, God will provide himself a lamb for a burnt offering'. The first mention of lamb in the New Testament is John chapter 1 verse 29 when John the Baptist pointed to the Lord Jesus and said, 'Behold the Lamb of God'.

Isaac's question is really the theme of the Old Testament, 'where is the lamb?' Where is the sacrifice that will satisfy God's heart and meet His demands? John's response is the theme of the New Testament, 'Behold the Lamb'. He is the answer to Isaac's question and the fulfilment of Abraham's response.

When we continue the picture into the next chapter and see Abraham as a picture of God the Father, we read of the death of Sarah, which would illustrate the setting aside of the nation of Israel.[111] In the next chapter Abraham sent his servant out to get a bride for his son who had given himself as a sacrifice in chapter 22. This son then comes out to meet the bride as she is guided home by the servant. This pictures the Holy Spirit sent by the Father to get a bride, i.e., the church, see Eph. 5. 25, for the Son, who will come to meet her and bring her home, see 1 Thess. 4. 13-18. Then, in chapter 25, we read, 'Then again Abraham took a wife, and her name was Keturah'. So, after the bride has been won for Isaac, we read of a wife again for Abraham, illustrating the point the New Testament teaches that after the church has been taken to heaven, God will take up His dealings with the nation of Israel again. The picture is so clear, but two things are equally clear: (1) There's no way Moses had these future things in mind as he wrote Genesis 22-25 – he had no idea about the giving of the Son of God, the setting aside of Israel or the formation of the church; (2) There's no way the New Testament writers based their teachings on Genesis 22-25.

Joseph
> 'In scripture, there is not a more perfect and beautiful type of Christ than Joseph'.[112]

---

[111] Israel is often seen in scripture as the wife of *Yahweh*, e.g., Isa. 50. 1; Jer. 3. 1; the prophecy of Hosea, and it was through her that the Messiah came, Rom. 9. 5.

[112] MACKINTOSH, *Notes on the Pentateuch*, p. 127.

The narrative about Joseph covers Genesis chapters 37 to 50, and there are lots of features that would lead an uninformed reader to think Moses was deliberately portraying Joseph as a foreshadowing of Christ. Consider some of the details:

- A beloved son, Gen. 37. 3; Matt. 3. 17;
- Sent by his father, Gen. 37. 13; e.g., John 17. 3;
- Rejected by his own to whom he came, Gen. 37. 18-24; John 1. 11;
- Betrayed and sold, Gen. 37. 28; Matt. 26. 14-16;
- Falsely accused and condemned, Gen. 39. 16-20; Matt. 26. 59-61;
- Numbered with criminals, Gen. 40. 1-4; Luke 23. 32-33;
- Exalted to glory, given a name and people called on to bow the knee, Gen. 41. 43; Phil. 2. 9-11;
- Rescues his brethren and reveals himself to them, Gen. 45. 4; Zech. 12. 10.

There are many other details, but those are enough to show the striking parallels.[113] Obviously Moses wasn't deliberately choreographing this, but who was? Who could?

The Exodus

The Israelites were enslaved in Egypt and God was going to redeem them. The climactic plague on the land of Egypt was the death of the firstborn. God refers to the Israelites as His son and gave Pharaoh fair warning that if he didn't release His son then He would slay Pharaoh's son, Exod. 4. 22-23. Pharaoh's intransigence led to this final and fatal visitation of judgement of death on the firstborn in every home in Egypt, but God provided a way by which the firstborn could be delivered. An unblemished lamb or a goat was to be taken and slain, its blood was to be applied to the door frame of the house, and when that was done God accepted the death of the animal in the place of the death of the firstborn. Even just painting the picture with those broad

---

[113] For a list of the parallels see WILLIAM MACDONALD, *Joseph Makes Me Think of Jesus*, Gospel Folio Press, 2000.

strokes shows the vivid parallel with the gospel message – the only way we can have deliverance is by sheltering in the value of the sacrifice of Christ. But let's look at a few of the finer touches in the picture.

- This animal was to be slain on the 14th day between the evenings, which just so happens to be the day[114] and hour[115] that the Lord Jesus died.
- It was then to be roasted with fire, not raw and not boiled with water. Now this is slightly involved. Fire is a common symbol in the Bible of God's wrath and judgement.[116] The lamb being roasted with fire is symbolizing the Lord Jesus, the Lamb of God, experiencing the judgement of God. For that reason the animal wasn't to be raw – that would symbolize one who did not actually experience God's judgement; nor was the animal to be boiled, for that would signify something coming between the Lord and the judgement – not fully exposed to the fire. When we come to the passion narratives in the Gospel accounts we find that the Lord both accepted and refused a drink. The night before His death, when He was in Gethsemane, He said, 'The cup which my Father hath given me, shall I not drink it?' John 18. 11. This is the cup of divine judgement, and had the Lord refused that drink it would have been like the lamb being raw. When He came to Calvary, He was offered the vinegar mingled with gall. This was a drink that would dull the senses and deaden the pain, but we read of Christ He would not drink it, Matt. 27. 34. Had He drunk it He would be like the lamb boiled with water – He would not be fully exposed to the fire. Do we think that the Gospel writers really had these two things in mind as they wrote? Were they

---

[114] According to the Judean way of reckoning days, https://bible.org/article/chronology-synopsis-passion-week

[115] 'The interval between the sun's beginning to decline, and sunset, corresponding to our three o'clock in the afternoon', JAMIESON, FAUSSET AND BROWN, *Commentary on the whole Bible*, on e-Sword.

[116] See, for example, the first mention of fire, Gen. 19. 24, and the last mention, Rev. 21. 8.

really dropping these secret clues and giving these hidden hints? And yet, can we deny that these links are really there?

- Exodus chapter 12 verse 9 specifically mentions three parts that are to be roasted with fire: the head, the legs and the inwards. In the New Testament we have three great statements of the sinlessness of Christ, and they come from the three main apostolic writers – Paul, Peter and John. Look at what they have to say:

> 'For He made Him who knew no sin to be sin for us, that we might become the righteousness of God in Him', 2 Cor. 5. 21, NKJV.
>
> 'For even hereunto were ye called: because Christ also suffered for us, leaving us an example, that ye should follow his steps: who did no sin, neither was guile found in his mouth', 1 Pet. 2. 21-22.
>
> 'And ye know that he was manifested to take away our sins; and in him is no sin', 1 John 3. 5.

Notice these three affirmations of Christ's sinless perfection from three independent writers and set them beside the three parts mentioned in Exodus chapter 12 verse 9. The head corresponds with Paul's statement that He knew no sin; the legs fit with Peter's statement that He did no sin; the inwards link with John's statement that there is no sin in Him. Is this just luck? These three writers all see Christ as the fulfilment of the Passover[117] and they each make one great statement about His sinlessness, which combine to tie up perfectly with these three parts mentioned, Exod. 12. 9. Or, are we to believe that Peter, John and Paul got together for a chat and agreed that they each would slip a statement into their writings that corresponds with one of these three parts, then they decided, 'Peter, you take the legs; Paul, you take the head; I'll take the inwards'. Would a more simple and sensible explanation not be that this is evidence of inspiration?

---

[117] 1 Cor. 5. 7; 1 Pet. 1. 18-19; John 19. 36.

Once the Israelites left Egypt they embarked on a long wilderness journey that included some features that would have meant very little to them as far as spiritual significance or a deeper meaning was concerned, but when we view these events in the light of the gospel and through the lens of the New Testament they have an astonishing significance. Here are a few examples:

The manna
In Exodus chapter 16 the Israelites were getting hungry. God said He would meet their need by raining bread from heaven for them. The Israelites called this bread 'manna', and they came to despise this provision. But some of this manna from heaven which they despised was put into a golden pot and stored in the Ark of the Covenant. The Lord Jesus identified this manna as being a picture of Him:

> 'Then Jesus said unto them, Verily, verily, I say unto you, Moses gave you not that bread from heaven; but my Father giveth you the true bread from heaven. For the bread of God is he which cometh down from heaven, and giveth life unto the world. Then said they unto him, Lord, evermore give us this bread. And Jesus said unto them, I am the bread of life: he that cometh to me shall never hunger; and he that believeth on me shall never thirst', John 6. 32-35.

Of course, the people despised this provision God made in Christ, but God has glorified Him and received Him. The first time the phrase 'the glory of the Lord' appears in the Old Testament is in connection with the announcement of the giving of the manna, Exod. 16. 10, and the interesting thing is that the first time that phrase is used in the New Testament is in connection with the announcement of the giving of Christ:

> 'And, lo, the angel of the Lord came upon them, and the glory of the Lord shone round about them: and they were sore afraid. And the angel said unto them, Fear not: for, behold, I bring you good tidings of great joy, which shall be to all people. For unto you is born this day in the city of David a

Saviour, which is Christ the Lord. And this shall be a sign unto you; Ye shall find the babe wrapped in swaddling clothes, lying in a manger', Luke 2. 9-12.

Do you think that Luke was thinking he should employ the phrase the glory of the Lord to link up with Exodus chapter 16 verse 10? Of course not, but neither should we dismiss it as a fluke. Moses and Luke were both being guided by the same unseen hand.

Water from the rock

In Exodus chapter 17 the Israelites were gasping for water and they complained to Moses. Moses takes their complaint to the Lord, who told Moses to smite the rock with his rod (the rod used in judgement on Egypt) and God would cause water to come out. So here is a rock smitten with a rod of judgement and it causes an abundance of supply to meet the need of the people. Some thirty-eight years later, Num. 20, there was the same problem, and a similar answer, except this time Moses was told to speak to the rock, not strike it, but unfortunately Moses lost his temper and struck it. He paid for this by being forbidden to enter the Promised Land. Why such a heavy punishment for one fit of temper under intense provocation? Everyone else who did enter the land had probably done a whole lot worse than that in their day! It is tipping us off that there is a very important symbolism and significance to this whole business. But what could it be? The gospel has the answer. Christ is often pictured as a rock and indeed it is a title of the Lord. He was smitten with the rod of God's judgement at Calvary to meet our need and supply us with the 'water of life'. Having suffered, He is now exalted, never to bear the judgement again.[118] We see, then, that Moses ruined a lovely picture of the once-for-all nature of the work of Christ at Calvary. The gospel proclaims a Saviour who was smitten under the judgement of God to meet our need. He is now exalted and He meets our needs, e.g., Eph. 4. 8-16. This is the teaching of the whole of the New Testament, but it

---

[118] The word translated 'rock' in Numbers chapter 20 is different from the word in Exodus chapter 17. According to *Brown-Driver-Briggs* it comes from a root meaning 'lofty'.

certainly isn't teaching that the writers came up with based on these two incidents with Moses and the rocks. So these historical narratives just so happen to prefigure and picture the gospel reality. Coincidence? Hardly!
Having just drunk from the smitten rock the Israelites encountered Amalek. The people of Amalek were descendents of Esau, Jacob's brother, Gen. 36. 12. Esau was born first, Jacob was the second birth. Esau was the man of the flesh, a profane man, Heb. 12. 16, who was ruled by the desires of the flesh rather than spiritual desires. So here we have a newly redeemed people and their first conflict was with their close relative. Anyone who has known redemption in his own experience knows that the first battle he faces is a battle with someone very close to him – his flesh, that is, that sinful nature that he got at his first birth. Paul mentions this battle in Galatians chapter 5 verses 16-17:

> 'This I say then, Walk in the Spirit, and ye shall not fulfil the lust of the flesh. For the flesh lusteth against the Spirit, and the Spirit against the flesh: and these are contrary the one to the other: so that ye cannot do the things that ye would'.

Thus, this story of the believer's battle with the flesh is graphically portrayed in Exodus chapter 17.

The serpent of brass
Look at this incident from Numbers chapter 21 verses 4-9:

> 'And they journeyed from mount Hor by the way of the Red sea, to compass the land of Edom: and the soul of the people was much discouraged because of the way. And the people spake against God, and against Moses, Wherefore have ye brought us up out of Egypt to die in the wilderness? for there is no bread, neither is there any water; and our soul loatheth this light bread. And the Lord sent fiery serpents among the people, and they bit the people; and much people of Israel died. Therefore the people came to Moses, and said, We have sinned, for we have spoken against the Lord, and against thee;

121

pray unto the Lord, that he take away the serpents from us. And Moses prayed for the people. And the Lord said unto Moses, Make thee a fiery serpent, and set it upon a pole: and it shall come to pass, that every one that is bitten, when he looketh upon it, shall live. And Moses made a serpent of brass, and put it upon a pole, and it came to pass, that if a serpent had bitten any man, when he beheld the serpent of brass, he lived'.

The Lord Jesus drew attention to this occasion as a picture of the gospel in His conversation with Nicodemus:

'And as Moses lifted up the serpent in the wilderness, even so must the Son of man be lifted up: That whosoever believeth in him should not perish, but have eternal life', John 3. 14-15.

The people had been bitten by these serpents, the deadly poison was coursing through their veins, strength was waning and life was ebbing away, but God had an answer. The instruction was given to Moses to make a serpent of brass and lift it up on a pole, and when anyone looked to that serpent he was healed. The parallel is simple and clear:

'The whole human family have felt the serpent's deadly sting; but the God of all grace has found a remedy in the One who was lifted up on the cursed tree; and now, by the Holy Ghost sent down from heaven, He calls on all those who feel themselves bitten, to look to Jesus for life and peace. Christ is God's great ordinance, and through Him a full, free, present, and eternal salvation is proclaimed to the sinner'.[119]

The Tabernacle
As they were at Mount Sinai, God instructed Moses to build a Tabernacle and to have furniture constructed for it. This is an area full of delightful details which find their fulfilment beautifully in the Lord

---

[119] C. H. MACKINTOSH, *Notes on the Pentateuch,* p. 563.

Jesus. Books abound on this subject,[120] but we will just take a fleeting bird's eye view of it and give one example of it coming up in the New Testament.

John presents Christ as the one who is the fulfilment of the Tabernacle – the one who became flesh and tabernacled among us, and we beheld His glory, John 1. 14. In his first epistle he draws on Tabernacle themes. Look at John's first 12 verses:

> 'That which was from the beginning, which we have heard, which we have seen with our eyes, which we have looked upon, and our hands have handled, of the Word of life; (for the life was manifested, and we have seen it, and bear witness, and shew unto you that eternal life, which was with the Father, and was manifested unto us;) that which we have seen and heard declare we unto you, that ye also may have fellowship with us: and truly our fellowship is with the Father, and with his Son Jesus Christ. And these things write we unto you, that your joy may be full. This then is the message which we have heard of him, and declare unto you, that God is light, and in him is no darkness at all. If we say that we have fellowship with him, and walk in darkness, we lie, and do not the truth: But if we walk in the light, as he is in the light, we have fellowship one with another, and the blood of Jesus Christ his Son cleanseth us from all sin. If we say that we have no sin, we deceive ourselves, and the truth is not in us. If we confess our sins, he is faithful and just to forgive us our sins, and to cleanse us from all unrighteousness. If we say that we have not sinned, we make him a liar, and his word is not in us. My little children, these things write I unto you, that ye sin not. And if any man sin, we have an advocate with the Father, Jesus Christ the righteous: And he is the propitiation for our

---

[120] For example, HENRY W. SOLTAU, *The Holy Vessels and Furniture of the Tabernacle*, and *The Tabernacle, the Priesthood and the Offerings*, Kregel, and ALBERT LECKIE, *The Tabernacle and the Offerings*, Precious Seed Publications.

sins: and not for ours only, but also for the sins of the whole world', 1 John 1. 1 – 2. 2.

Think of those vessels of the Tabernacle: there's the altar, where the blood was shed. That corresponds with chapter 1 verse 7 – 'the blood of Jesus Christ . . . cleanseth . . . from all sin'. The laver was where cleansing from defilement took place, and this links with chapter 1 verse 9 – 'if we confess our sins, he . . . cleanseth us from all unrighteousness'. Moving into the holy place there is a table of showbread, speaking of fellowship. Chapter 1 verse 3 says we have 'fellowship . . . with the Father, and with his Son'. There is also the golden lampstand, and chapter 1 verse 5 tells us 'God is light'. Then, we have the golden altar, from which the fragrant incense ascended, and this seems to be the thought of us having an Advocate with the Father, 2. 1 – He is before the Father on our behalf. Finally, there is the Ark and mercy seat, and chapter 2 verse 2 tells us that Christ is the propitiation. This is the same idea as the mercy seat – divine justice satisfied. It was not John's explicit purpose here to show the spiritual significance of the items of Tabernacle furniture, but the truths are most definitely and naturally there.

The High Priest's garments
In that Tabernacle system there was a Levitical priesthood, and we get details of the garments for the priest in Exodus chapter 28. Again, there have been books written on the spiritual significance of these garments, I will lift only a couple of the most striking features.

There were three garments to be made of linen, without any other colours: there was the coat, v. 39, which was really a tunic – it was the innermost garment the priest wore; there was the mitre, v. 39, which was a turban; and there were the breeches, v. 42, which were like shorts, going from the waist to the thighs. Bear in mind that the Bible often uses linen to denote holiness, purity and righteousness, see Rev. 19. 8, and then bring in those three statements about the sinlessness of Christ that we looked at earlier: 'He did no sin', 1 Pet. 2. 22, links with the linen shorts – the legs are connected with activity; 'He knew no sin', 2 Cor. 5. 21, links with the linen turban; 'in him is no sin', 1

124

John 3. 5, links with the linen tunic – the innermost garment. These links are so clear, and yet so obviously not intentional on the part of Peter, Paul and John.[121] And, notice, we not only have Old Testament typology linking with New Testament truth, we also see Old Testament pictures linking up with other Old Testament pictures in ways that just could not be manufactured.

The high priest bore the names of the tribes of Israel in two places: on his shoulders, Exod. 28. 9-10, and on his breastplate, Exod. 28. 15-21. In having their names upon his person he was, in picture, representing them and interceding for them before God. The shoulders speak of strength, the breastplate speaks of love. Come over to the New Testament and you find two references to the Lord Jesus interceding for His people. One is Hebrews chapter 7 verse 25:

> 'Wherefore he is able also to save them to the uttermost that come unto God by him, seeing he ever liveth to make intercession for them'.

This verse is set in a context in which contrasts are being drawn between the weakness of the Levitical priesthood and the Lord's priesthood. He has none of the weaknesses the Levitical priesthood had – He is able. This corresponds to the names of His people on His strong shoulders.

The other is Romans chapter 8 verse 34:

> 'Who is he that condemneth? It is Christ that died, yea rather, that is risen again, who is even at the right hand of God, who also maketh intercession for us'.

In the very next verse Paul says, 'Who shall separate us from the love of Christ?' We are seeing the names in the breastplate – the place of affection, and they cannot be plucked out.

---

[121] I first heard this pointed out by Mr Walter Boyd.

Notice, two different writers, there is no collusion or deliberate set up here, and they are the only two writers to speak of the intercession of Christ, and what they present matches up exactly with the Old Testament picture.[122]

Consider, as well, two places where the Lord is pictured as a shepherd carrying the sheep:

> 'What man of you, having a hundred sheep, if he loses one of them, does not leave the ninety-nine in the wilderness, and go after the one which is lost until he finds it? And when he has found it, he lays it on his shoulders, rejoicing', Luke 15. 4-5, NKJV.

Here is the sheep being carried on the shoulders, the place of strength.

> 'He shall feed his flock like a shepherd: he shall gather the lambs with his arm, and carry them in his bosom, and shall gently lead those that are with young', Isa. 40. 11.

In this passage the lambs are carried in His bosom, the place of affection.

Put Luke chapter 15 verses 4-5 together with Isaiah chapter 40 verse 11 and we find an exact match with where the names of God's people were carried in Exodus chapter 28, as well as the two occasions where the Lord is said to intercede for His people. There are five different writers involved in this, but clearly one divine author.

The Levitical Offerings
Associated with the priesthood were the Levitical offerings. There are many in-depth studies of the offerings showing how they point to the

---

[122] I first heard this from Mr Jack Hay.

Lord Jesus. I refer you to them rather than repeating them,[123] but I will just pick out one of the offerings and show you a sample of their significance. Leviticus chapter 2 deals with the grain offering, and there are five ways the offering could be presented:

1) An uncooked offering;
2) An offering baked in the oven;
3) An offering baked on a flat plate;
4) An offering baked in a frying pan;
5) An offering of firstfruits.

Many have seen how this offering speaks of the life of the Lord Jesus, while the other offerings, which involve blood-shed, focus on various aspects of His death. There is a beautiful chronological portrait of the Lord's life in these five forms of grain offering. First, we have an uncooked offering; it hasn't been in the oven or through the fire. Think of the conception and birth of the Lord – is it not like the uncooked offering? He had never experienced the fire of adversity or the furnace of affliction. Thus, this is a fitting picture of the Lord entering into humanity.

Then we have the offering that was baked in the oven, in a way in which no one could see it, and, following the birth of the Lord, there were those thirty hidden years, mostly spent in obscurity in Nazareth, kept from our view in that coarse environment, but there was no coarseness in Him. He was sweet to God.

The offering baked on a flat plate was open for all to see. After those hidden years the Lord Jesus stepped into public ministry in which He was always in the public eye, under the watchful gaze of friends and the scrutinizing glare of foes. In it all there was no roughness – it was all fine flour.

---

[123] E.g., LECKIE, *The Tabernacle and the Offerings*; J. M. FLANIGAN, *Christ in the Levitical Offerings*, John Ritchie Ltd. 2011; THOMAS NEWBERRY, *Types of Levitical Offerings*, John Ritchie Ltd.

Then there was the offering in the frying pan, which was a deep dish or saucepan. It wasn't concealed like the oven, but neither was it open like the flat plate. If someone wanted to see what was in the frying pan he would have to come close to it. This is like those final hours when the Lord was with His disciples in the upper room, and then those trials before Jewish and Gentile authorities, one has to draw near to see what is going on, and in these hours a sweet savour arose to God.

Finally there was the offering of firstfruits. The firstfruit was the indication of a coming harvest, and the New Testament is clear on the significance of this:

> 'But now is Christ risen from the dead, and become the firstfruits of them that slept', 1 Cor. 15. 20.

So the firstfruit is a picture of Christ in resurrection, and, significantly, Leviticus chapter 2 verse 12 tells us that this type of grain offering was not to be burnt on the altar. The other forms of the offering were specifically said to be burned on the altar, but they all picture one who was destined for sacrifice, but in the offering of firstfruits we have pictured for us the great truth that the sacrifice is over, He is risen, never to go to the altar again.[124]

So in this one chapter we have a symbolic representation of the Lord's time on earth from conception to resurrection. The cynic can dismiss it as irrelevant, but if someone is open-minded it surely should give them pause for thought.

The crossing of the Jordan

In Joshua chapters 3-4 we have the account of the Israelites going over Jordan into the Promised Land. The whole journey from Egypt to Canaan is instructive and illustrative of Christian experience. The

---

[124] In Leviticus 2:14-16 we read of an offering of firstfruits that is to be burned as incense, but the altar is not mentioned, thus preserving the symbolic significance.

New Testament teaches that as far as the Christian's body is concerned he is in Egypt – the body has not yet been redeemed, Rom. 8. 23; as far as the Christian's soul is concerned, he is in the wilderness – needing the sustenance that God provides to get us through, see e.g., 1 Cor. 10. 1-13; as far as the Christian's spirit is concerned, he is in the Promised Land, enjoying the blessings of the land, but having to do battle with the enemies in that realm that would seek to rob us of our enjoyment of what is ours in Christ.[125]

When the Israelites come to the Jordan the ark is prominent in the narrative, and in this vessel we have a picture of the Lord Jesus: the gold speaking of His deity and the wood speaking of His humanity; it contained the tables of the law, and He was the one who could say, 'Thy law is within my heart', Ps. 40. 8; the ark had the mercy seat, which was the place where God could meet with man on the basis of sacrifice. The New Testament says Christ is the mercy seat, Rom. 3. 25.[126] The Israelites were told, 'When ye see the ark of the covenant of the Lord your God . . . then ye shall remove from your place, and go after it', Josh. 3. 3. Isn't this what we see in John chapter 1 verses 35-37?

> 'Again the next day after John stood, and two of his disciples; and looking upon Jesus as he walked, he saith, Behold the Lamb of God! And the two disciples heard him speak, and they followed Jesus'.

The one who was the fulfilment of that ark is at Jordan, and the two disciples of John the Baptist go after Him.

So we have the ark, picturing Christ, going into the Jordan. Does Jordan represent anything significant? It is clearly a picture of death – it was that which separated them from the wilderness and brought

---

[125] See, for example, Col. 2. 12; Eph. 1. 3; 2. 6; 6. 10-12.

[126] The word translated 'propitiation' in Romans chapter 3 verse 25 is the same word translated 'mercy seat' in Hebrews chapter 9 verse 5 and throughout the Greek version of the Old Testament, the Septuagint (LXX).

them into the blessings God had for them; indeed, it even went into the Dead Sea. So the ark enters into the river, and, according to verse 16, the waters stood up in a heap right back to a city called Adam, this allowed the people to enter into the inheritance God had for them. What a picture of New Testament teaching! The Lord entered into the river of death that flows down from Adam, and by His entrance into death He has provided access for all into that glorious inheritance God has prepared.

> 'All who have sought for spiritual help in this chapter have seen in the Ark standing in the midst of Jordan a type of the Lord on the cross. There He stood as our representative, and at the same time our assurance that the floods of judgement would never swamp us'.[127]

Ruth

We will pass over the other little gospel glimpses we get in Joshua and those in Judges, and come to the story of Ruth. It is a story of redemption, and a great illustration of gospel truth. Ruth was a Moabitess who had married a man named Mahlon who had come to her country from Bethlehem. Mahlon died, and Ruth went to Bethlehem with her widowed mother-in-law, Naomi. Ruth met a man named Boaz, who willingly took on the role of kinsman-redeemer to rescue Ruth from her poverty-stricken state, and from potential slavery. In order to be the redeemer, three requirements had to be met:

1) The redeemer had to have the relationship – he had to be near of kin;
2) The redeemer had to have the riches – he had to be able to purchase the land that had been lost by the poverty-stricken family member;
3) The redeemer had to have the resolve – he had to be willing to pay the price and take on the responsibility.

---

[127] A. MCSHANE, *Joshua, Possessing the Land*, John Ritchie, 1994, p. 47.

We see the Lord Jesus meets the criteria to be our redeemer uniquely. He had the relationship – He came into humanity. He had the riches – He alone could pay the great price of redemption.[128] He also had the resolve – He was not only able to pay, He was willing to do it. The story of this 'mighty man of wealth' taking a Gentile for his bride has given Christians much to enjoy as they think of their Lord paying the price so He could take a bride from the nations, Eph. 5. 25.

Esther

At this point we will take a brief look at the other book in the Old Testament which bears the name of a woman. When we put this book together with the book of Ruth we find in the one a Gentile woman who marries an Israelite, and in the other we read about a Jewish woman who marries a Gentile. But there is a more remarkable connection: Malcolm Radcliffe has pointed out that there are two books in the New Testament that bear the name of a woman – 1 & 2 Thessalonians: Thessalonica was named after Thessaloniki of Macedon, the half sister of Alexander the Great. What links these two New Testament books with the two Old Testament books? Well, what happens in Ruth? There is a woman who turns to God from idols, compare Ruth 1. 16 with 1 Thess. 1. 9, to serve, compare Ruth 2 with 1 Thess. 1. 9, and to wait, compare Ruth 3. 18 with 1 Thess. 1. 10. And what happens in Esther? There is a wicked man, see Est. 7. 6, who demands that all bow to him, see Est. 3. 1-6, and seeks to destroy the people of God, and this man is himself destroyed, and the fear and mourning is turned to joy and feasting. This is very much in line with the teaching of 2 Thessalonians chapters 1-2. Thus, there are definite links between Ruth and 1 Thessalonians, and definite links between Esther and 2 Thessalonians, and yet these links are certainly not manufactured by Paul.

David and Goliath

This is a story, found in 1 Samuel 17, that has kept Sunday School children entertained for many generations, and has afforded much material for presenting the gospel to them. The giant stood in the

---

[128] See 1 Tim. 2. 5-6; 1 Pet. 1. 18-19.

valley and for forty days he issued the challenge and none could face him and bring him down. Then there came God's chosen king from Bethlehem who defeated the giant and used his own weapon against him, delivering his people from fear and captivity. This draws the mind to the Son of David – God's chosen King. We can think of how the devil stood proud, not for forty days but for forty centuries – the whole course of human history, and none could overcome him. Then the King from Bethlehem encountered him in the wilderness, and defeated him by selecting one stone out of five as it were – He dipped into the Pentateuch and pulled out the book of Deuteronomy, and used that against the devil, see Matt. 4. 1-11. Later, the Lord would defeat the devil, and He did so by using his own weapon against him, as the writer to the Hebrews said, 'that through death he might destroy him that had the power of death, that is, the devil; and deliver them who through fear of death were all their lifetime subject to bondage', Heb. 2. 14-15.

This is a very small sample of what runs right throughout the Old Testament. The gospel was no invention of man or afterthought with God.

> 'Thus, the unity between the Old Testament books and the New Testament books is such that they are not just a collection of individual stories on a variety of topics, but combine together to form one overarching story of salvation. It is this overall unified story that shows the Old Testament and New Testament to be, in fact, one book, clearly connected by the divine origins of its constituent parts'.[129]

Recurring themes

Another indication of inspiration is the fact that throughout the Bible we see threads running through and themes coming up over and over again.

God's righteousness and holiness

---

[129] KRUGER, *Canon Revisited*, loc 3850-3860.

These attributes of God are not only taught explicitly in scripture but also pictured incidentally. Think of the two different named classes of angelic beings in the Bible – there are cherubim and seraphim. The cherubim seem to appear in the role of defending God's righteousness; after the fall in Eden, God placed cherubim and a flaming sword to guard the way to the tree of life, Gen. 3. 24. They are also found on the mercy seat looking down to see if the just claims of God have been met by the blood of a sacrifice, Exod. 25. 18-20. But the seraphim are creatures that are concerned with God's holiness; in Isaiah's temple vision the seraphim cry out 'Holy, holy, holy, is the Lord of hosts', Isa. 6. 3.

There are two main prophetic portraits of the suffering of Christ in the Old Testament scriptures: Psalm 22 and Isaiah chapter 53. In these passages we see the Lord answering to the demands of God. Because God is holy, sin must be banished from Him; that's what we see in Psalm 22, the Lord cries out, 'My God, My God, why hast thou forsaken me?' And because God is righteous, sin must be punished by Him; that's what we see in Isaiah chapter 53, 'He was wounded for our transgressions . . . Yet it pleased the Lord to bruise him'. So these two passages, written hundreds of years apart, happened to correspond to the two attributes of God that necessitated the sacrifice of Christ. This shows the overruling hand of God guiding the hands of the human authors.

The letter to the Romans is Paul's great treatise dealing with the doctrine of the gospel. In the first eight chapters of the letter, he presents the need of man in a twofold way: there is a legal problem and a moral problem. As far as the legal problem is concerned, we haven't lived the way a righteous God demands – we have broken His law and are under His condemnation. As far as the moral problem is concerned, we can't live the way a holy God demands, we are in bondage to sin and can't break free. The gospel answers both of these needs, setting us free from both the condemnation of sin and the domination of sin. This two-fold deliverance corresponds to the two great gospel doctrines of justification and sanctification. We need to be justified, because God is righteous, and we need to be sanctified, because God is holy. When the Lord's side was pierced at Calvary, blood and water flowed out, picturing the meeting of these needs – blood for our legal problem, water for our moral problem, John 19. 34. At the end of the Bible, we read of the final classifications, showing who has availed themselves of the gospel provision of justification and sanctification, and who has not:

> 'He that is unjust, let him be unjust still: and he which is filthy, let him be filthy still: and he that is righteous, let him be righteous still: and he that is holy, let him be holy still', Rev. 22. 11.

The holiness and loftiness of God

> 'For thus saith the high and lofty One that inhabiteth eternity, whose name is Holy; I dwell in the high and holy place, with him also that is of a contrite and humble spirit, to revive the spirit of the humble, and to revive the heart of the contrite ones', Isa. 57. 15.

There is a twofold description of God here: He is high and He is holy. These features of God's nature come up again and again in the book of Isaiah,[130] but also throughout scripture in subtle ways that could not realistically have been deliberately employed by the human authors.

Let me show you some examples:

When Gabriel was sent to announce to Mary that she had been chosen to be the mother of the Messiah, he told her that the child 'shall be great, and shall be called the Son of the Highest', Luke 1. 32, then he tells her that the one who would be born is 'that holy one', Luke 1. 35. So, in this section the Lord Jesus is identified as the high and holy one.

There were two recorded occasions in the Gospels when God declared the Lord Jesus to be His beloved Son: at His baptism,[131] and on the

---

[130] For example, Isa. 6:1-3.
[131] Matt. 3. 13-17; Mark 1. 9-11; Luke 3. 21-22.

Mount of Transfiguration.[132] Why should it be that God would intervene on these two occasions? At the Lord's baptism people observing would have assumed that He was a sinner repenting like everyone else – they would have concluded He was not holy, but God intervenes to declare that the one standing in Jordan can't be dragged down to the level of sinners – He is the holy one. However, at the transfiguration something different is going on; Peter sees Moses and Elijah there with the Lord and he says, 'let us make here three tabernacles; one for thee, and one for Moses, and one for Elias', Matt. 17. 4. Peter sees these two great men and seeks to bring them up to the level of Christ, but God intervenes to stop him because you can't bring any creature up to the level of Christ – He is the high and lofty one.

We have seen that the angel Gabriel testified to the Lord being the high and holy one; we have seen that God the Father testified to it, but demons did too. Christ encountered a demon in Luke chapter 4 verse 34, and Mark chapter 1 verse 24, which cried out, 'Let us alone; what have we to do with thee, thou Jesus of Nazareth? art thou come to destroy us? I know thee who thou art; the Holy One of God'. Then look at what happened when the Lord confronted Legion: 'When he saw Jesus, he cried out, and fell down before him, and with a loud voice said, What have I to do with thee, Jesus, thou Son of God most high? I beseech thee, torment me not', Luke 8. 28, see, too, Mark 5. 7. The Holy One of God, and the Son of God most high – the demons recognized Him as the high and holy one. This theme runs throughout the different books of the Bible in a way that shows a unity that the writers could not have achieved by their own ingenuity.

Our three enemies
Another theme that crops up again and again has to do with the enemies of God and of His people. The enemies that rise up against God are the devil, the world and the flesh. We see these three opponents of God and good raise their ugly heads throughout the Bible, sometimes overtly and sometimes subtly, but, as we look at

---

[132] Matt. 17. 1-5; Mark 9. 1-7; Luke 9. 28-35.

some examples, we will see evidence of divine inspiration in how they are drawn to our attention.

In the book of Genesis there are three major acts of judgement in the first eleven chapters. There is the Fall in Genesis chapter 3, the judgement of the flood in Genesis chapters 6-8 and the confusion of the languages at Babel in Genesis chapter 11. Each of these features a different enemy. The Fall was brought about by the devil tempting Eve, the flood was demanded by the unbridled expression of the flesh, and the judgement at Babel was occasioned because the people wanted to make a name for themselves in the world.

As we go through the Old Testament there are three prominent examples of young men who said 'No!' to temptation. There is Joseph, Gen. 39. 7-12, there is Moses, Heb. 11. 24-27, and there is Daniel, Dan. 1. 8. In the case of Joseph, he said no to the flesh. Potiphar's wife tried to entice him to commit adultery. With Moses, he said no to the world. All the treasures of Egypt were at his disposal, the world was at his feet but he refused them. When we come to Daniel, he said no to the devil. He was being pressured to compromise his religious purity and partake in idolatrous practices. Three great examples of refusing temptation and the three great enemies feature.

There are three occasions when Paul speaks about the need for believers to be clad in 'the armour of . . .' In Romans chapter 13 verse 12, we are to put on the armour of light; in 2 Corinthians chapter 6 verse 7 we are to put on the armour of righteousness; in Ephesians chapter 6 verse 11 we are to put on the armour of God. When you examine the context of these three statements you will find that the enemy Christians are fighting against is different. In Romans chapter 13 verses 11-14, Paul is warning them to be on their guard regarding the flesh, and he tells them not to make provision for the flesh. In 2 Corinthians chapter 6 verses 4-10, we see Paul suffering in this world and he needs the armour for the conflict he is in. In Ephesians chapter 6 verses 10-20 Paul tells us that we are in spiritual conflict with the forces of the devil.

This is just a sample of the way the recurring theme of our three enemies defies the ability of men to choreograph.

Prophet, Priest and King

The nation of Israel had three anointed offices, prophet, priest and king, and these three anointed offices combined to show what roles the Anointed, the Messiah, would undertake – He is the ultimate Prophet, bringing the full and final revelation of God; He is the ultimate Priest, offering the sufficient sacrifice for sin and ministering to the needs of His people; and He is the ultimate King, ruling in perpetual perfection. These three anointed roles address the need of the entire human personality – there is a prophet to enlighten the mind, a priest to cater to the emotions, and a king to rule the will. As we look through scripture we discover many occasions when these three offices are presented in a way that shows deliberate intention but not of the human authors; it is the deliberate intention of the one who guided the human authors. Many of the references to Christ as Prophet, Priest and King are in the space of one chapter or book, but we will look at a couple of examples of independent writers combining to present Christ in this three-fold way.

Moses was marked out by God as a unique prophet, for 'there arose not a prophet since in Israel like unto Moses', Deut. 34. 10, but this prophet prophesied that 'The Lord thy God will raise up unto thee a Prophet from the midst of thee, of thy brethren, like unto me', Deut. 18. 15. Moses was prophesying the coming of the Lord Jesus. The Lord was like Moses in many ways: both were delivered from death as infants, both refused glory and chose a path of suffering, both were involved in the redemption of God's people, both interceded for God's people, etc. But another way in which the Lord Jesus was a prophet like unto Moses is that He wasn't just a prophet: Moses fulfilled other functions too. He is called a king in Deuteronomy chapter 33 verse 5, and, while we see him carrying out priestly activities, we have to come to another writer to complete the picture and have him explicitly identified as a priest. Psalm 99 verse 6 tells us that Moses was 'among His priests'. So Moses functioned in a prophetic, priestly

137

and kingly capacity, picturing the one who would perfectly fulfil each of those roles.

Three times in the Gospel records we find Mary of Bethany at the feet of the Lord Jesus. Luke chapter 10 is the first occurrence:

> 'Now it came to pass, as they went, that he entered into a certain village: and a certain woman named Martha received him into her house. And she had a sister called Mary, which also sat at Jesus' feet, and heard his word. But Martha was cumbered about much serving, and came to him, and said, Lord, dost thou not care that my sister hath left me to serve alone? bid her therefore that she help me. And Jesus answered and said unto her, Martha, Martha, thou art careful and troubled about many things: but one thing is needful: and Mary hath chosen that good part, which shall not be taken away from her', Luke 10. 38-42.

Mary is at the feet of the great *Prophet* here listening to His word.

John chapter 11 gives the next occasion:

> 'Then when Mary was come where Jesus was, and saw him, she fell down at his feet, saying unto him, Lord, if thou hadst been here, my brother had not died. When Jesus therefore saw her weeping, and the Jews also weeping which came with her, he groaned in the spirit, and was troubled, and said, Where have ye laid him? They said unto him, Lord, come and see. Jesus wept', John 11. 32-35.

Here Mary is at the feet of the compassionate *Priest*.

John chapter 12 gives us the third instance:

> 'Then Jesus six days before the Passover came to Bethany, where Lazarus was which had been dead, whom he raised from the dead. There they made him a supper; and Martha

served: but Lazarus was one of them that sat at the table with him. Then took Mary a pound of ointment of spikenard, very costly, and anointed the feet of Jesus, and wiped his feet with her hair: and the house was filled with the odour of the ointment', John 12. 1-3.

As you consider this scene, think of the words of the Song of Solomon:

> 'While the king sitteth at his table, my spikenard sendeth forth the smell thereof', 1. 12.

Thus, in John 12, Mary is at the feet of the *King*. Three separate instances, two separate Gospels, yet the correlation between the three offices of Prophet, Priest and King, though undesigned by the writers, is undeniable.[133]

The Lord was offered a drink three times when He was at Calvary. He was offered a drink before His crucifixion:

> 'And when they were come unto a place called Golgotha, that is to say, a place of a skull, they gave him vinegar to drink mingled with gall: and when he had tasted thereof, he would not drink', Matt. 27. 33-34.

This was an act of mercy to dull the senses and deaden the pain, but He refused it. He was about to offer the great sacrifice for sin and no officiating priest could take strong drink, see Lev. 10. 9.

Luke records the second instance:

> 'And the soldiers also mocked him, coming to him, and offering him vinegar, and saying, If thou be the king of the Jews, save thyself', Luke 23. 36-37.

The soldiers here are toasting the King in mockery.

---

[133] I first heard this pointed out by Mr Jim Flanigan.

John gives us the final occurrence:

> 'After this, Jesus knowing that all things were now accomplished, that the scripture might be fulfilled, saith, I thirst. Now there was set a vessel full of vinegar: and they filled a sponge with vinegar, and put it upon hyssop, and put it to his mouth. When Jesus therefore had received the vinegar, he said, It is finished: and he bowed his head, and gave up the ghost', John 19. 28-30.

The Lord receives the drink here in fulfilment of prophecy. Thus, the first offer connects with His priestly work, the second with Him as the King, and the third links with Him as the great Prophet. There is no way Matthew, Luke and John could have conspired in this, and yet there is no way this is just coincidental.[134]

The fourfold view of Christ in the Gospels

Those who read the Bible carefully recognize that the four Gospels are not random reminiscences, nor are they mere repetitions of each other. Each writer presents Christ in a unique way. Matthew presents the Lord Jesus as the King. He commences by establishing His link with David, and majors on His discourses, the fulfilment of Old Testament scripture and the character of His Kingdom. Mark presents the Lord Jesus as the perfect servant. The genealogy is absent, the discourses aren't as prominent, but it is His busy service that is emphasized. In Luke's Gospel he is presenting the perfect humanity of the Lord Jesus. He goes right back to Adam in his genealogy and he spends time detailing the Lord's development, speaking about Him in the womb, as a new born, as a child and His growth to manhood. There is a major emphasis in the Gospel on the prayers of the Lord, showing He was a true and dependent man. Then, in John's Gospel, there is a clear presentation from beginning to end of the deity of Christ. It commences with a declaration of His deity, 1. 1, and it ends with a confession of it, 20. 28. This fourfold view of the Saviour was not a result of 'Church Fathers' looking back picking the accounts they

---

[134] I first heard this pointed out by Mr David Gilliland.

liked best. As we look into the Old Testament, we can see that God had a fourfold presentation of His Son in mind all along.

One of the titles of the Messiah in the Old Testament is the Branch. This title is used in four ways of the Messiah:[135]

> 'In that day shall the branch of the Lord be beautiful and glorious, and the fruit of the earth shall be excellent and comely for them that are escaped of Israel', Isa. 4. 2.

The expression 'the branch of the Lord' (*Yahweh*) indicates the divine nature of the Messiah and therefore corresponds to John's Gospel.

We find Jeremiah using the title twice:

> 'Behold, the days come, saith the Lord, that I will raise unto David a righteous Branch, and a King shall reign and prosper, and shall execute judgment and justice in the earth', Jer. 23. 5.

> 'In those days, and at that time, will I cause the Branch of righteousness to grow up unto David; and he shall execute judgment and righteousness in the land', Jer. 33. 15.

Jeremiah identifies the Branch as the King, and this is the theme of Matthew's Gospel.

Zechariah uses the title twice and identifies two features of the Messiah:

> 'Hear now, O Joshua the high priest, thou, and thy fellows that sit before thee: for they are men wondered at: for, behold, I will bring forth my servant the BRANCH', Zech. 3. 8.

The Branch here is God's perfect servant, and this is developed in Mark's Gospel.

---

[135] This is the Hebrew word with the Strong's number 6780, *tsemach*.

'And speak unto him, saying, Thus speaketh the Lord of hosts, saying, Behold the man whose name is The BRANCH; and he shall grow up out of his place, and he shall build the temple of the Lord', Zech. 6. 12.

The emphasis here is on 'the man', and it is Luke's Gospel that answers to this.

So we have a fourfold view of the Branch from three independent writers that marry up exactly with the fourfold presentation of Christ in the Gospels. But that's not all.
There are occasions in the prophecies of Isaiah and Zechariah when we are shown prophetic portraits of the Lord Jesus and are called on to 'Behold' Him. Here they are:

'O Zion, that bringest good tidings, get thee up into the high mountain; O Jerusalem, that bringest good tidings, lift up thy voice with strength; lift it up, be not afraid; say unto the cities of Judah, Behold your God!' Isa. 40. 9.

The context demands a Messianic interpretation of this verse, and thus the Messiah is none less than God Himself, which is the emphasis in John's Gospel.

'Behold my servant, whom I uphold; mine elect, in whom my soul delighteth; I have put my spirit upon him: he shall bring forth judgment to the Gentiles', Isa. 42. 1.

'Behold, my servant shall deal prudently, he shall be exalted and extolled, and be very high', Isa. 52. 13.

These are the opening lines of two of Isaiah's great servant songs, and they present the Lord in His lowly life and sacrificial death as God's perfect Servant. This is the theme of Mark's Gospel.

'And speak unto him, saying, Thus speaketh the Lord of hosts, saying, Behold the man whose name is The BRANCH; and he shall grow up out of his place, and he shall build the temple of the Lord', Zech. 6. 12.

Again, we have the call to behold, but this time it is 'Behold the man'. This could be the title of Luke's Gospel.

> 'Rejoice greatly, O daughter of Zion; shout, O daughter of Jerusalem: behold, thy King cometh unto thee: he is just, and having salvation; lowly, and riding upon an ass, and upon a colt the foal of an ass', Zech. 9. 9.

The call, to behold the King, is the call of Matthew's Gospel.

So here we have two writers who have no earthly idea about four Gospels that are going to be written, and yet they have these summoning shouts to behold the Messiah in this fourfold way that corresponds exactly with the theme of each of the Gospels. It's not the case that there are lots of calls to behold the Messiah with lots of different titles and offices being used to describe Him. These are the only examples of this kind of call. That is compelling proof that there was an omniscient and sovereign God guiding not only the prophets but the writers of the Gospels.

One more example will suffice:

> 'And I looked, and, behold, a whirlwind came out of the north, a great cloud, and a fire infolding itself, and a brightness was about it, and out of the midst thereof as the colour of amber, out of the midst of the fire. Also out of the midst thereof came the likeness of four living creatures. And this was their appearance; they had the likeness of a man. And every one had four faces, and every one had four wings. And their feet were straight feet; and the sole of their feet was like the sole of a calf's foot: and they sparkled like the colour of burnished brass. And they had the hands of a man under their wings on their four sides; and they four had their faces and their wings. Their wings were joined one to another; they turned not when

they went; they went every one straight forward. As for the likeness of their faces, they four had the face of a man, and the face of a lion, on the right side: and they four had the face of an ox on the left side; they four also had the face of an eagle', Ezek. 1. 4-10.

We have these four living creatures each with four faces which correspond exactly to the themes of each Gospel. The Lord in Matthew's Gospel has the face of a lion; in Mark's Gospel we have the face of the ox – the animal used for service; Luke's Gospel brings before us the face of the man; in John's Gospel we see the face of the eagle for John's Gospel takes us higher than the others.

No one could sensibly suggest that the Old Testament writers had the four Gospels in mind, neither could anyone realistically imagine that the Gospel writers had these Old Testament themes in mind when they wrote. There could not have been any collaboration between the writers,[136] yet the links are clear, and there are many more of these anticipatory glimpses of the four Gospels throughout the Old Testament.[137] It is a remarkable testimony to the unity and inspiration of all of scripture, and a proof that the four Gospels in our New Testament were not a result of a selection process by later Christians, but rather the result of a sovereign God moving men to write and guiding Christians to recognize God-breathed scripture.

There are lots more examples of themes that are woven throughout scripture that we could explore, but, hopefully, enough has been done to show how these recurring themes furnish proof that the Bible is God's word. We will move on:

---

[136] Most scholars agree that the Gospels were written in different locations outside the land of Israel.

[137] It can be seen, for example, in the life of Joseph, the colours in the Tabernacle, and the life of David.

Links between scriptures

We are not looking here at themes that run through scripture, like two attributes of God, three enemies or four Gospels, but we are looking at passages that link together in ways that point to God's involvement rather than coincidence or human intention.

Isaiah chapter 55 verse 6

> 'Seek ye the Lord while he may be found, call ye upon him while he is near'

This verse found in what many have called the Gospel of Isaiah is brought into living colour in Luke's Gospel by two incidents that he records back to back. If you want an illustration of what it means to call on the Lord while He is near then look at Bartimaeus:

> 'And it came to pass, that as he was come nigh unto Jericho, a certain blind man sat by the way side begging: and hearing the multitude pass by, he asked what it meant. And they told him, that Jesus of Nazareth passeth by. And he cried, saying, Jesus, thou Son of David, have mercy on me. And they which went before rebuked him, that he should hold his peace: but he cried so much the more, Thou Son of David, have mercy on me. And Jesus stood, and commanded him to be brought unto him: and when he was come near, he asked him, saying, What wilt thou that I shall do unto thee? And he said, Lord, that I may receive my sight. And Jesus said unto him, Receive thy sight: thy faith hath saved thee. And immediately he received his sight, and followed him, glorifying God: and all the people, when they saw it, gave praise unto God', Luke 18. 35-43.

The Lord is passing by and Bartimaeus wasn't going to let the opportunity pass him by; he called upon Him while He was near. But if you want to see 'Seek ye the Lord while He may be found' in 3D then look at the next incident Luke records:

'And Jesus entered and passed through Jericho. And, behold, there was a man named Zacchaeus, which was the chief among the publicans, and he was rich. And he sought to see Jesus who he was; and could not for the press, because he was little of stature. And he ran before, and climbed up into a sycomore tree to see him: for he was to pass that way. And when Jesus came to the place, he looked up, and saw him, and said unto him, Zacchaeus, make haste, and come down; for to day I must abide at thy house. And he made haste, and came down, and received him joyfully. And when they saw it, they all murmured, saying, That he was gone to be guest with a man that is a sinner. And Zacchaeus stood, and said unto the Lord; Behold, Lord, the half of my goods I give to the poor; and if I have taken any thing from any man by false accusation, I restore him fourfold. And Jesus said unto him, This day is salvation come to this house, forsomuch as he also is a son of Abraham. For the Son of man is come to seek and to save that which was lost', Luke 19. 1-10.

Again, the Lord was passing through, He wasn't in Jericho to stay, and Zacchaeus had to 'Seek . . . the Lord while he may be found'. I don't think Luke had Isaiah chapter 55 verse 6 in mind when he recorded these two incidents. He recorded them because they happened at Jericho, but it shows the reality of God and the unity of scripture that these incidents tie up so exactly with a scripture written seven centuries before.

Luke chapter 23 verses 39-43

'And one of the malefactors which were hanged railed on him, saying, If thou be Christ, save thyself and us. But the other answering rebuked him, saying, Dost not thou fear God, seeing thou art in the same condemnation? And we indeed justly; for we receive the due reward of our deeds: but this man hath done nothing amiss. And he said unto Jesus, Lord, remember me when thou comest into thy kingdom. And Jesus said unto him, Verily I say unto thee, To day shalt thou be with me in paradise'.

In the epistle to the Romans Paul sets out the doctrine of the gospel, but in this account of the repentant malefactor we see so many of the truths of Romans vividly portrayed.

'For the wages of sin is death; but the gift of God is eternal life through Jesus Christ our Lord', Rom. 6. 23.

The criminal on the cross certainly realized that the wages of his sin was death – he confessed that he was there on the cross justly receiving the due reward of his deeds. He then went on to receive eternal life the only way he could – as a gift.

'For when we were yet without strength, in due time Christ died for the ungodly', Rom. 5. 6.

In this verse, sinners are described in two ways: without strength and ungodly. If you were looking for two descriptions of this man crucified alongside Christ you couldn't really get two better ones. He was the epitome of helplessness. He literally couldn't move a hand or a foot to save himself, he was without strength. He could also be described as ungodly. He confessed to deserving his fate, he was a law-breaker. But this man, who was without strength and ungodly, found that the answer to his desperate plight was to be found in the man next to him, just as Paul teaches in this verse.[138]

'If you confess with your mouth Jesus is Lord and believe in your heart that God raised Him from the dead, you will be saved', Rom. 10. 9, ESV.

This verse gives a good description of how the thief was saved. When he said, 'Lord, remember me when You come into Your kingdom' he clearly confessed 'Jesus is Lord' and he obviously believed that God

---

[138] Onlookers would have thought that these two descriptions would have been true of the Lord Jesus as well, but the centurion learned the truth. He saw that the Lord certainly was not ungodly; he confessed, 'Certainly this was a righteous man', Luke 23. 47. And he also realized He was not without strength, for when He saw how the Lord cried out and voluntarily entered into death he said, 'Truly this man was the Son of God', Mark 15. 39, see too Matt. 27. 54.

was going to raise Him from the dead, and he received the assurance from the Lord that he was saved.

> 'For whosoever shall call upon the name of the Lord shall be saved', Rom. 10. 13.

The experience of the repentant thief clearly illustrates the truth of this verse. He certainly illustrates the 'whosoever' of the verse: this was a man whom many would have said was beyond redemption and past the point of no return, but there was a Saviour for this man. He also illustrates the 'shall call upon the name of the Lord' in the verse: in his helplessness he turns to the Lord and calls on Him to act on his behalf. And he also illustrates the 'shall be saved' of the verse, as he heard the Lord say, 'Verily I say unto thee, Today shalt thou be with Me in paradise'.

So, as Paul wrote Romans, was he doing so with this incident in mind and inserting verses that tie up with it? Hardly! Did Luke include this incident of the thief on the cross with the epistle to the Romans in front of him and subtly shape it to illustrate verses from Romans? Clearly not! How then do we account for the remarkable and repeated correspondence between them? The answer is that neither Paul nor Luke was writing on his own initiative, God was in control.

'Whosoever shall call upon the name of the Lord shall be saved'
Having mentioned this verse in connection with the repentant thief, let's have a look at the three places where it occurs in scripture and we will see another evidence of the unity of the Bible.

The first time the phrase occurs is Joel chapter 2 verse 32, and in that context the emphasis is on 'shall be saved'. The chapter starts with the instruction, 'Blow the trumpet in Zion, and sound an alarm in My holy mountain! Let all the inhabitants of the land tremble; for the day of the Lord is coming, for it is at hand', Joel 2. 1, NKJV. God tells His prophet to warn the people of coming judgement, which is described in vivid detail. What a relief, then, to read in verse 32 that whoever calls on the name of the Lord shall be saved.

The second time we meet this phrase is in Acts chapter 2 verse 21. Peter was preaching on the day of Pentecost, and on this occasion the stress is very definitely on the name of the Lord. Peter told them about Jesus of Nazareth, His ministry, death, resurrection and ascension, and how 'God hath made that same Jesus, whom ye have crucified, both Lord and Christ', Acts 2. 36. The point is that Jesus is Lord, and thus He is the one people need to call on.

Then we come to the third occurrence in Romans chapter 10 verse 13. The setting of the verse leaves no doubt where Paul is placing the emphasis; it is on 'whosoever shall call'. He had just said in the previous verse that 'there is no difference between the Jew and the Greek: for the same Lord over all is rich unto all that call upon him'. Paul is showing that none is excluded – it is a 'whosoever' gospel.

Three mentions, and three different emphases, that take in the whole of the verse. Did Luke and Paul conspire together to complement Joel's original quotation by repeating it in their own writings with their own emphasis? Not at all – it was the work of the God who spans the ages and was present to guide Joel, Luke and Paul in their writing and Peter in his preaching.[139]

The intermediate state
Let's go back to this malefactor of Luke chapter 23 for a moment and see, again, another link with Paul's writings. There are three prominent passages in the New Testament in which we are told about the location of believers in relation to the Lord Jesus Christ after death but before their resurrection. The first is 2 Corinthians chapter 5 verse 8:

> 'We are confident, I say, and willing rather to be absent from the body, and to be present with the Lord'.

---

[139] I am indebted to Mr Jack Hay for this insight. I heard him preach on this verse and point out the different emphases in each passage.

Paul says that when a believer is absent from the body he is at home with the Lord.

Think again of Luke chapter 23 verse 43:

> 'And Jesus said unto him, Verily I say unto thee, To day shalt thou be with me in paradise'.

It was Jesus who said 'thou shalt be with me', so the believer will be with Jesus.

Finally, Philippians chapter 1 verse 23:

> 'For I am in a strait betwixt two, having a desire to depart, and to be with Christ; which is far better'.

Paul says the believer goes to be with Christ.

With the Lord, with Jesus, with Christ – these are the three passages that deal with the believer being with his Saviour in the intermediate state, and we find that when we put them together we will be with the Lord Jesus Christ.[140] Paul and Luke certainly didn't agree that they would drop in these three passages in their documents that they were sending out to different audiences in the hope that once they were collected together students of scripture would discover this link. Is it just coincidental then, or is it intentional on the part of the God of inspiration? I think the latter option is far more sensible.

The Lord as Shepherd
One of the most delightful pictures of the Lord is that of the Shepherd. There are three different adjectives used of the Lord in this connection:

> 'I am the good shepherd: the good shepherd giveth his life for the sheep', John 10. 11.

---

[140] I first heard Mr Ian Jackson point this out.

'Now the God of peace, that brought again from the dead our Lord Jesus, that great shepherd of the sheep, through the blood of the everlasting covenant, make you perfect in every good work to do his will, working in you that which is wellpleasing in his sight, through Jesus Christ; to whom be glory for ever and ever. Amen', Heb. 13. 20-21.

'And when the chief shepherd shall appear, ye shall receive a crown of glory that fadeth not away', 1 Pet. 5. 4.

These three descriptions of the Shepherd point us in three different directions: in John chapter 10 verse 11 we are looking back to Calvary in the past; in Hebrews chapter 13 verse 20 we are looking up at a risen Christ in the present; in 1 Peter chapter 5 verse 4 we are looking on to the future to His coming again. That, in itself, is a striking indication of divine involvement, but there is more. The 22nd, 23rd and 24th Psalms form a triplet that focus our attention on the Lord Jesus and again direct us to the past, Ps. 22, the present, Ps. 23, and the future, Ps. 24. In Psalm 22 we see the Lord as the good Shepherd, giving His life for the sheep; in Psalm 23 He is the great Shepherd tending to His sheep; in Psalm 24 He is the chief Shepherd who is coming again. Only the God of inspiration can account for how these threads held in the hands of four independent writers could come together in such a beautiful tapestry.

Andrew

Andrew was a man who fished with a line rather than a net, spiritually speaking. He seemed to be a man who was adept at dealing with individuals. In John chapter 1 we see him bringing one soul to the Lord:

'One of the two which heard John speak, and followed him, was Andrew, Simon Peter's brother. He first findeth his own brother Simon, and saith unto him, We have found the Messias, which is, being interpreted, the Christ. And he brought him to Jesus', John 1. 40-42.

151

Then in John chapter 6 we find him bringing one soul to the Lord again:

> 'One of His disciples, Andrew, Simon Peter's brother, saith unto him, There is a lad here, which hath five barley loaves, and two small fishes: but what are they among so many?' John 6. 8-9.

What was the result of that one person being brought to the Lord in John chapter 6? 5,000 men, besides women and children, were blessed. What was the result of that one person being brought to the Lord in John chapter 1? Well we find that one person preaching the gospel in Acts chapters 2 and 3 and in Acts chapter 4 verse 4 we read of the result of that preaching:

> 'Howbeit many of them which heard the word believed; and the number of the men was about five thousand'.

One was brought to Christ in John chapter 6 and 5,000 men were blessed; one was brought to Christ in John chapter 1 and 5,000 men were blessed. These incidents weren't recorded by one writer to make a point, but were recorded by independent writers without their coordination. It does, however, show that God was coordinating things to work out His plan.

Two musts and two gifts
The Bible is full of instructions, imperatives and commands, but interestingly, when we come to the preaching of the gospel we find that on only two occasions are unconverted people told what they must be.

The first is John chapter 3 verse 7; the Lord says to Nicodemus, 'Ye must be born again'. The other is in Acts chapter 4 verse 12 where we hear Peter preach, 'we must be saved'.

The reason we must be born again is because of what we are – we are sinners by nature, and with a sinful nature we can never be in the presence of a holy God – we need a new nature, a new life that enables us to enjoy God and God to enjoy us. The reason we must be saved is because of what we have done – we have broken God's law and a righteous God demands our punishment.[141] So if we aren't born again we will never be in heaven, and if we aren't saved we will be forever in hell.

Corresponding to these two 'must' verses are two verses in Paul's writings where he speaks about the gift of God in a gospel context.[142] The first is Romans chapter 6 verse 23, 'the gift of God is eternal life'. This answers to the 'must' of being born again, because being born again means to receive new life, eternal life, God's life. The second is Ephesians chapter 2 verse 8, 'For by grace are ye saved through faith, and that not of yourselves, it is the gift of God'. This addresses the 'must' of Peter's preaching, Acts 4. 12.

So Paul writes to the Romans, then to the Ephesians, while Luke records the preaching of Peter and John records the words of Christ, and, without any collusion or conspiring, we discover that these different individuals all correspond beautifully. The two things humanity must have (new life and salvation) are offered to us as a gift.

Peter
Peter became the most prominent of the Lord's disciples. In the Gospels we see him being trained by the Lord for the work he was going to do after the Lord's ascension. In Ephesians chapter 4 verse 11, Paul writes about the gifts God has given to the Church. There are the two foundational gifts of apostles and prophets, see Eph. 2. 20.

---

[141] Here is another example of the theme of God's holiness and righteousness.
[142] He uses the expression 'gift of God' to refer to spiritual gifts that believers have, 1 Cor. 7. 7; 2 Tim. 1. 6, but only twice does he use it to refer to what God offers the unconverted.

These are gifts associated with new revelation, and, thus, they passed away when God's revelation in scripture finished. Then, Paul lists three gifts that continue for the whole age: evangelists, pastors and teachers. When you look at Peter in the book of Acts you see him exercise the gift of an evangelist – he is preaching the gospel and fulfilling the commission the Lord Jesus gave. In his first letter, we see him as a pastor – he is ministering to suffering Christians, giving comfort and encouragement. Then, in his second letter, he is a teacher – he is refuting the false teachers and combating wrong doctrine. This links the writings of Peter with the book of Acts and the epistle to the Ephesians in a way that only the hand of God can account for.[143]

Spiritual gifts
Just while we are on this subject of spiritual gifts we will look at the three passages in Paul's writings where he deals with them. In Romans chapter 12 Paul introduces the subject in verse 3:

> 'For I say, through the grace given unto me, to every man that is among you, not to think of himself more highly than he ought to think; but to think soberly, according as God hath dealt to every man the measure of faith. For as we have many members in one body, and all members have not the same office: so we, being many, are one body in Christ, and every one members one of another. Having then gifts differing according to the grace that is given to us, whether prophecy, let us prophesy according to the proportion of faith; or ministry, let us wait on our ministering: or he that teacheth, on teaching; or he that exhorteth, on exhortation: he that giveth, let him do it with simplicity; he that ruleth, with diligence; he that sheweth mercy, with cheerfulness', Rom. 12. 3-8.

Thus God is seen as the giver of gifts in this section.

---

[143] This strikes a fatal blow at the notion that 2 Peter wasn't written by Peter. Such scepticism collapses under the weight of the evidence of inspiration.

The next passage is 1 Corinthians chapter 12. Look at verses 7 to 11:

> 'But the manifestation of the Spirit is given to every man to profit withal. For to one is given by the Spirit the word of wisdom; to another the word of knowledge by the same Spirit; to another faith by the same Spirit; to another the gifts of healing by the same Spirit; to another the working of miracles; to another prophecy; to another discerning of spirits; to another divers kinds of tongues; to another the interpretation of tongues: but all these worketh that one and the selfsame Spirit, dividing to every man severally as He will'.

The Spirit of God is the one who gives gifts here.

Then, we have Ephesians chapter 4 verses 7-12:

> But unto every one of us is given grace according to the measure of the gift of Christ. Wherefore he saith, When he ascended up on high, he led captivity captive, and gave gifts unto men. (Now that he ascended, what is it but that he also descended first into the lower parts of the earth? he that descended is the same also that ascended up far above all heavens, that he might fill all things.) And he gave some, apostles; and some, prophets; and some, evangelists; and some, pastors and teachers; for the perfecting of the saints, for the work of the ministry, for the edifying of the body of Christ'.

Paul is telling us here that gifts come from the ascended Christ.

So he has three passages dealing with the subject of spiritual gifts, written to three different audiences at three different times. It would be ridiculous to think that he was holding in his mind the fact that he wrote to the Romans about God giving gifts, then to the Corinthians about the Spirit, and so to fill it out and complete the picture he wrote to the Ephesians about the Lord Jesus giving gifts. It wasn't in Paul's mind, but it was in the mind of the God who breathed out His word.

Paul's separation

There are three (and only three) occasions in the Bible when we read of Paul being separated for the ministry God had for him.

In Galatians chapter 1 verse 15 he wrote about 'God, who separated me from my mother's womb, and called me by His grace'. In Romans chapter 1 verse 1 he refers to himself as 'an apostle of Jesus Christ, separated unto the gospel of God'. Then in Acts chapter 13 verse 2, 'the Holy Spirit said, "Now separate to Me Barnabas and Saul for the work to which I have called them"', NKJV.

In Galatians chapter 1 verse 15, it is God the Father who separates him, in Romans chapter 1 verse 1 it is Jesus Christ, and in Acts chapter 13 verse 2 it is the Holy Spirit. The Triune God who separated Paul for gospel service is the same God who guided Paul and Luke in the recording of that threefold separation.

The inspiration of scripture

Staying with the Trinitarian theme, there are three main texts in the New Testament that deal with the subject of how the truth of the Bible got from God's mind to the page.

'All scripture is given by inspiration of God, and is profitable for doctrine, for reproof, for correction, for instruction in righteousness', 2 Tim. 3. 16

Scripture is inspired by *God*.

'Of which salvation the prophets have enquired and searched diligently, who prophesied of the grace that should come unto you: searching what, or what manner of time the Spirit of Christ which was in them did signify, when It testified beforehand the sufferings of Christ, and the glory that should follow', 1 Pet. 1. 10-11:

The prophets received testimony from the Spirit of *Christ*.

'For prophecy never came by the will of man, but holy men of God spoke as they were moved by the Holy Spirit', 2 Pet. 1. 21, NKJV.

The prophets were moved by *the Holy Spirit.*

Three passages on the subject by two writers, tying together the involvement of the Triune Godhead! These passages not only state that God was involved in the writing of scripture, but they show it – all scripture is given by inspiration of God, the Spirit of Christ was in them and they were moved by the Holy Spirit.

Conclusion

We have looked at the unity of scripture in its structure, the illustrative incidents, the recurring themes and the links between different writers and different books. There are lots of other examples and many other aspects of this subject that could be examined,[144] but I think what we have looked at is sufficient to prove the point – only God could have brought all this together. We'll close this chapter with an extended quotation from JOHN NELSON DARBY from a letter he wrote on 'the divine inspiration of the Holy Scriptures':

> 'Our attention is called to the fact that the Bible is not one book, but a collection of writings by different authors. It is precisely on this fact that I ground my argument, adding also that they were written at periods very remote from each other. In spite of this great diversity of times and of authors there is a perfect unity of design and of doctrine: a unity, the separate parts of which are so linked with each other, and so entirely adapted to each other, that the whole work is evidently that of one and the same Spirit, one and the same mind, with one purpose carried on from the beginning to the end . . . its parts are so correlative and form so harmonious a whole, that, with the least attention, one cannot fail to

---

[144] Such as the unity of the Bible's doctrine and morality.

perceive, that it is the production of one mind. Now there is but One, who lived through all the ages during which the various books of the Bible were written, and that One is the Holy Ghost.

Look at Genesis: you will find in it doctrines, promises, types, which are in perfect harmony with that which is more fully developed in the New Testament; but in this book they are related in the way of narrative with the greatest simplicity, yet in such a manner as to give the most perfect picture of things, which should happen in after ages.

Look at Exodus, and you will find the same thing. Everything is made according to the pattern seen by Moses in the mount, and furnishes us with the clearest exposition we possess of the ways of God in Christ.

Take Leviticus: the details of its sacrifices furnish a light, which throws upon the work of Christ rays so bright that nothing could replace them.

Take Numbers — the history of the journeyings of God's people through the wilderness. "These things," says the apostle, "happened to them for examples [types], and they are written for our admonition upon whom the ends of the world are come." Who was it that wrote them for us? Certainly not Moses (although he was the human instrument), but He who knoweth the end from the beginning, and who orders all things according to His good pleasure.

All this applies to the moral and to the ceremonial law; to the history of the patriarchs; to the royalties of David and of Solomon; to the sentiments expressed in the Psalms, as well as to other subjects. Is it not one mind which has done all this? Was it the mind of Moses or of Paul? Assuredly not.

I do not go through other books of the Bible to furnish proofs of this unity of design, which is manifested in a work wrought by such various instruments, and at periods so remote from each other — a unity realised in such a manner as precludes all idea of its having been intended by the persons who executed it . . . [T]o one who has any knowledge of the word of God, *it is an incontestable proof*.[145]

---

[145] J. N. DARBY, *Letter on the Divine Inspiration of the Holy Scriptures, The Collected Writings of J. N. Darby, Doctrinal*, No. 7, Vol. 23, Stow Hill Bible and Tract Depot, pp. 50-52, emphasis added.

Chapter 4: Verification

'And God said . . . and it was so', Gen. 1. 9.
'For the word of the Lord is right; and all his works are done in truth',
Ps. 33. 4.

The God of the Bible has not remained distant from His creation or His creatures. He is a God who has gotten Himself involved with real people in real places. He made statements about the world, and He has intervened in history. If this is true then there ought to be some evidence that what He said is really true and what He did actually happened, so we are going to visit the science lab and then we'll go on an archaeology field trip to see if the claims of the Bible can be verified by our observations and discoveries of the world around us.

Before we set off let me speak to those who may be reluctant to join us. If you are already a Bible-believer you may be saying that we don't need the word of God to be verified by any other source – after all, God is the supreme authority and doesn't need any other authority to confirm His claims, and these other sources of authority in the fields of science and archaeology are constantly changing and contradicting themselves.

I will say a few things in response: first, this constant flux in science and archaeology may be an exaggeration, but nonetheless we recognize that much of what is touted as the latest 'discovery' of science or archaeology is only the latest fad that will soon be refuted and forgotten. The believer in the Bible has no reason to get into a flap at the first sight of a potential problem. If we have good reason to believe the Bible is the word of God we won't abandon that confidence on the basis of a new supposed discovery. After all, one anomaly doesn't make all the evidence we have already looked at suddenly disappear. We are going to see that, very often, scientists and archaeologists have thought their findings disproved scripture, but then they had to eat their words and abandon their theories as facts came to light that disproved their stories and proved the Bible's.

That being said, there are well established facts of science and history that aren't a matter of opinion or a subject of serious debate – it is to these facts I am appealing as confirming that what the Bible says is true. So we are not basing our argument here on what scientists or archaeologists say, but on what science and archaeology show.

The second thing is this: checking the Bible's claims about history and the world around us is not submitting the Bible to a greater authority. God said to Moses He would rain manna upon the ground for the Israelites, so the next morning an Israelite comes into his tent carrying the manna and says to his wife, 'Look! God kept His promise!' That doesn't make the manna or the man a greater authority than God, and it wouldn't be a very wise wife who would say, 'I'm not looking, I don't need to see or taste the manna to know God has done it!' The Bible-believer investigates these things not in an attitude of doubt and fear but of faith and expectancy. If God says something happened or a thing is true, and we can verify it happened and show it's true then that isn't undermining God's authority, it is affirming it. Think of Jeremiah in the prison in Jeremiah chapter 32. God said to him that his cousin Hanameel would come to see him to offer him the purchase of a field. Sure enough, Hanameel came, just as the Lord had said, and Jeremiah records, 'Then I knew that this was the word of the Lord', Jer. 32. 6-8. We wouldn't say, 'Well, Jeremiah, you shouldn't have needed your cousin to come for you to know it was true!' The fact that what God said impinged on the world he lived in meant that he couldn't avoid putting the Lord's words to the test. Jeremiah was not putting Hanameel as an authority over God, but rather the supreme authority of God's word entailed that Jeremiah should be able to point to the real event of Hanameel's arrival at the prison. Similarly, for the nobleman in John chapter 4 verses 46-54: the man's son was dying and the Lord told him, 'Go thy way; thy son liveth'. John records that 'the man believed the word that Jesus had spoken unto him, and he went his way'. He didn't doubt the Lord's word, and the truthfulness of His word necessitated the man finding confirmation in the material world, which, of course, he did, for when he was on the way home his servants came to meet him with the news that his son was alive and well, and that the fever had left him at the seventh hour.

The man did the calculations and discovered that was the exact hour when the Lord said, 'Thy son liveth'. John tells us that the man 'believed, and his whole house'. He already believed, but his faith was strengthened as he saw the Lord's words verified. He was able to present this verification to his household and it led to them believing too.

The third and final thing I'll say is that we see examples in scripture of God providing verification to encourage people's faith. Think of the Lord in John chapter 5 as he spoke to the Jewish leaders. He claimed the possession of divine attributes and the right to divine prerogatives, and, of course, His hearers were having none of it. They thought that these were blasphemous claims. The Lord said to them, 'If I bear witness of myself, my witness is not true', John 5. 31. It is obvious that the Lord was not saying if He bore witness to Himself it was a lie, but rather what He was saying was that it would not be true in their estimation – they needed it confirmed, after all, the Law required the testimony of two or three witnesses. The Lord didn't resent this or just expect them to take such a massive claim without evidence, so He provided verification. They counted John as a prophet and a man carrying authority, so the Lord pointed out that John bore testimony to the truth, and He then said, 'But I receive not testimony from man: but these things I say, that ye might be saved', v. 34. He was saying that He personally didn't need John's witness but that He said it for their benefit. The Lord wasn't putting John as an authority over Himself, but they esteemed John as an authority, and the authority they esteemed pointed to a greater authority – Christ Himself, and so the Lord was prepared to appeal to John in order that His hearers might be saved. So it is with what we are going to look at – these disciplines, which many take as so authoritative, point beyond themselves to a greater authority – the God of scripture.

Another example is found in Joshua chapter 10 verse 13. This is Joshua's long day – the day the sun stood still. There had never been a day like it, and we read, 'Is not this written in the book of Jasher?' Does this put the book of Jasher on an authority with the word of God? No, but it recognizes that the book of Jasher was held as a

163

reliable source and this source confirmed what Joshua chapter 10 said, but if anyone wanted the reason for this supernatural event the book of Jasher wasn't going to help them, the book of Joshua would. We have scriptural authority then for directing people to extra-biblical evidence as a way of getting them to consider the claims of the Bible. Therefore, if we are committed to the supreme authority of scripture then we will have no problem going on this journey, so let's get started.

Science

'I'm an atheist because of science'. I couldn't begin to estimate how often I have heard that phrase or something like it. Very often it is uttered by people who know next to nothing about science, but they think it sounds smart and unchallengeable. The fact of the matter is very different. Science is no friend of atheism,[146] but rather points to the accuracy of the word of God and the reality of the God of the word.

The universe had a beginning

For centuries atheists had always said that the universe never had a beginning, it was just a brute fact existing in a steady state. This throws up big philosophical problems regarding an infinite regress,[147] but still people clung to it until it was wrestled from their grasp in the 20th century by the findings of science. The second law of thermodynamics tells us that the universe is running out of useable energy, and if this is the case then it obviously can't be eternal in the past.[148] Furthermore, the discovery of the fact that the universe is

---

[146] As we saw in chapter 2, the very possibility of science being done points to a Creator.

[147] For more on this see, for example, WILLIAM LANE CRAIG, *Reasonable Faith, Christian Truth and Apologetics*, Third Edition, Crossway, 2008, loc 1557 or his *On Guard, Defending your Faith with Reason and Precision*, David C. Cook, 2010, pp. 80-89.

[148] It's like someone's car running out of petrol but him telling you that he had been driving the car from eternity past! If the car has run out of petrol then it obviously doesn't have an infinitely big fuel tank. The Bible taught a

expanding forced scientists to realize the universe was not fixed and eternal.[149] Those who were averse to the theological implications of these scientific discoveries tried their best to find alternative explanations and develop new models.

> 'In a sense, the history of twentieth-century cosmology can be seen as a series of one failed attempt after another to avoid the absolute beginning predicted by the standard big bang model'.[150]

However, ARVIND BORDE, ALAN GUTH and ALEXANDER VILENKIN have effectively shot down any possibility of an eternal universe by proving 'that any universe that has, on average, been expanding throughout its history cannot be infinite in the past but must have a past space-time boundary'.[151]

But, of course, while scientists were wrestling with these things, and while materialists were resisting them, the Bible stated right from the outset that time and space came into being.

> 'In the beginning God created the heavens and the earth', Gen. 1. 1.

In this majestic statement we see the origin of time – 'In the beginning'; we have the input of energy – 'God created'; and we have the origin of matter and space – 'the heavens and the earth'.[152]

---

wearing out and a running down of creation long before scientists discovered it, e.g. Ps. 102. 25-26.

[149] For other scientific confirmations of the beginning of the universe see NORMAN L. GEISLER & FRANK TUREK, *I Don't Have Enough Faith to be an Atheist*, Crossway, 2004, pp. 74-92, or J. WARNER WALLACE, *God's Crime Scene, A Cold-Case Detective Examines the Evidence for a Divinely Created Universe*, David C. Cook, loc 262-327.

[150] CRAIG, *On Guard*, p. 93.

[151] *Ibid.*, p. 93. This applies to the much vaunted multiverse as well, which seems to serve as a substitute God to the materialist.

[152] This is a Hebrew expression denoting the whole universe.

Interestingly, while the expansion of the universe was a discovery of 20th Century science, it was also repeatedly hinted at in the Old Testament Scriptures:

'Which alone spreadeth out the heavens, and treadeth upon the waves of the sea', Job 9. 8.

'Who coverest thyself with light as with a garment: who stretchest out the heavens like a curtain', Ps. 104. 2.

'It is he that sitteth upon the circle of the earth, and the inhabitants thereof are as grasshoppers; that stretcheth out the heavens as a curtain, and spreadeth them out as a tent to dwell in', Isa. 40. 22.

'Thus saith God the Lord, he that created the heavens, and stretched them out; he that spread forth the earth, and that which cometh out of it; he that giveth breath unto the people upon it, and spirit to them that walk therein', Isa. 42. 5.

'Thus saith the Lord, thy redeemer, and he that formed thee from the womb, I am the Lord that maketh all things; that stretcheth forth the heavens alone; that spreadeth abroad the earth by myself', Isa. 44. 24.

'I have made the earth, and created man upon it: I, even my hands, have stretched out the heavens, and all their host have I commanded', Isa. 45. 12.

'Mine hand also hath laid the foundation of the earth, and my right hand hath spanned the heavens: when I call unto them, they stand up together', Isa. 48. 13.

And forgettest the Lord thy maker, that hath stretched forth the heavens, and laid the foundations of the earth; and hast feared continually every day because of the fury of the oppressor, as if he were ready to destroy? and where is the fury of the oppressor?' Isa. 51. 13.

'He hath made the earth by his power, he hath established the world by his wisdom, and hath stretched out the heavens by his discretion', Jer. 10. 12.

'The burden of the word of the Lord for Israel, saith the Lord, which stretcheth forth the heavens, and layeth the foundation of the earth, and formeth the spirit of man within him', Zech. 12. 1.

When we look at what other worldviews teach about the universe it makes the Bible stand out all the more.[153] It certainly isn't the case that there were lots of religions claiming an absolute beginning to space/time – the Bible was unique in that regard.

The earth

The theories about what the earth was and where the earth was ranged from good guesses to weird imaginations. There was a story that prevailed in many ancient cultures that the earth was resting on a giant animal. Now whether this was taken as a serious explanation or just a myth, I don't know, but the point is that there was no way that these primitive people could get an accurate idea of what the world was like, given how limited their perspective and knowledge was. However, in what is probably the oldest book in the Bible – the book of Job, we have an insight that shows us that he was not speaking on his own initiative, but was getting information from one who could see the way things really were: Job says about God that He hangs the earth on nothing, 26. 7.

---

[153]For example, Hinduism tells us our universe has been preceded by an infinite number of universes and will be succeeded by an infinite number of universes. Buddha put the question of whether the universe came into existence amongst his fourteen unanswered questions. Confucianism doesn't weigh in on the question.

Other passages may also indicate details about the earth that wouldn't have been accessible to or known by the writers at the time. For example, Isaiah chapter 40 verse 22 refers to God as He who sits above the circle of the earth; it can be argued that this is describing the spherical shape of the earth.[154] In addition, when speaking about His return, the Lord said that it will be day and night at the same time:

> 'I tell you, in that night there will be two in one bed. One will be taken and the other left. There will be two women grinding together. One will be taken and the other left', Luke 17. 34-35, ESV.

This implies that the earth is a rotating globe. Some may respond with alternate explanations about what these verses mean, but they certainly do fit in with what we now know from science.

The stars
The number of the stars
In Genesis chapter 22 verse 17 God said that He would make Abraham's offspring as numerous as the stars in the sky and the sand of the shore. The Bible similarly equates the number of stars with the sand in Jeremiah chapter 33 verse 22. But up until relatively recently that would have been seen as a massive inequality. The number of stars visible to the naked eye apparently amounts to about 3,000-5,000. To put such a number in the same sentence as the number of grains of sand is something nobody would have done at that time. However, according to the Biblical record, the one who used the number of stars alongside the number of grains of sand was God Himself, the one of whom it is said, 'He telleth the number of the stars; He calleth them all by their names', Ps. 147. 4. Scientists today put estimates of the total number of stars up in the hundreds of septillions! The number of grains of sand is estimated to be about 7.5 quintillion.[155] Only one who knew the vast number of the stars would

---

[154] See http://creation.com/isaiah-40-22-circle-sphere.
[155] One septillion is 1 followed by 24 zeroes. One quintillion is 1 followed by 18 zeroes. See

ever have made such a comparison, and the point is that at the time these passages were written only one did know the vast number of the stars, only one could – the God who created them.

The constellations
Another scriptural insight about the stars is found in Job chapter 38 verses 31-32:

'Canst thou bind the sweet influences of Pleiades, or loose the bands of Orion? Canst thou bring forth Mazzaroth in his season? or canst thou guide Arcturus with his sons?'

J. WARNER WALLACE has this to say:

'The text refers to three constellations, Pleiades, Orion and Arcturus (the fourth, Mazzaroth, is still unknown to us). In the first part of the verse, God challenged Job's ability to "bind the sweet influences of Pleiades." It's as if He was saying, "Hey Job, you think you can keep Pleiades together? Well, I can!" As it turns out, the Pleiades (also known as the Seven Sisters) is an open star cluster in the constellation of Taurus. It is classified as an open cluster because it is a group of hundreds of stars formed from the same cosmic cloud. They are approximately the same age and have roughly the same chemical composition. Most importantly, they are bound to one another by mutual gravitational attraction. Isabel Lewis of the United States Naval Observatory (quoted by Phillip L. Knox in Wonder Worlds) said, "Astronomers have identified 250 stars as actual members of this group, all sharing in a common motion and drifting through space in the same direction." Lewis said they are "journeying onward together through the immensity of space." Dr. Robert J. Trumpler (quoted in the same book) said, "Over 25,000 individual measures of the Pleiades stars are now available, and their study led to the

http://www.npr.org/sections/krulwich/2012/09/17/161096233/which-is-greater-the-number-of-sand-grains-on-earth-or-stars-in-the-sky.

important discovery that the whole cluster is moving in a south-easterly direction. The Pleiades stars may thus be compared to a swarm of birds, flying together to a distant goal. This leaves no doubt that the Pleiades are not a temporary or accidental agglomeration of stars, but a system in which the stars are bound together by a close kinship." From our perspective on Earth, the Pleiades will not change in appearance; these stars are marching together in formation toward the same destination, bound in unison, just as God described them.

The next section of the verse describes the Orion constellation. God once again challenged Job, this time to "loose the bands of Orion." God was referencing the "belt" of Orion; the three stars forming the linear "band" at Orion's waist. God appeared to be challenging Job in just the opposite way he had in the first portion of the verse. Rather than bind the Pleiades, God challenged Job to loosen Orion. It's as if He was saying, "Hey Job, you think you can loosen Orion's belt? Well, I can!" Orion's belt is formed by two stars (Alnilam, and Mintaka) and one star cluster (Alnitak). Alnitak is actually a triple star system at the eastern edge of Orion's belt. These stars (along with all the other stars forming Orion) are not gravitationally bound like those in Pleiades. Instead, the stars of Orion's belt are heading in different directions. Garrett P. Serviss, a noted astronomer, wrote about the bands of Orion in his book, Curiosities of the Sky: "The great figure of Orion appears to be more lasting, not because its stars are physically connected, but because of their great distance, which renders their movements too deliberate to be exactly ascertained. Two of the greatest of its stars, Betelgeuse and Rigel, possess, as far as has been ascertained, no perceptible motion across the line of sight, but there is a little movement perceptible in the 'Belt.' At the present time this consists of an almost perfect straight line, a row of second-magnitude stars about equally spaced and of the most striking beauty. In the course of time, however, the two right-hand stars, Mintaka and Alnilam (how

170

fine are these Arabic star names!) will approach each other and form a naked-eye double, but the third, Alnita, will drift away eastward, so that the 'Belt' will no longer exist." Unlike the Pleiades clusters, the stars in the band of Orion do not share a common trajectory. In the course of time, Orion's belt will be loosened just as God told Job.

In the last section of the verse, God described Arcturus, one of the brightest stars in the night sky. God challenged Job to "guide Arcturus with his sons." With this challenge, God appeared to be saying, "Hey Job, you think you can direct Arcturus anywhere you want? Well, I can!" While Arcturus certainly appeared in antiquity to be a single star, in 1971 astronomers discovered there were 52 additional stars connected directionally with Arcturus (known now as the Arcturus stream). Interestingly, God described Arcturus as having "sons" and Charles Burckhalter, of the Chabot Observatory, (again quoted in Wonder Worlds) said "these stars are a law unto themselves." Serviss added, "Arcturus is one of the greatest suns in the universe, is a runaway whose speed of flight is 257 miles per second. Arcturus, we have every reason to believe, possesses thousands of times the mass of our sun... Our sun is traveling only 12 ½ miles a second, but Arcturus is traveling 257 miles a second..." Burckhalter affirmed this description of Arcturus, saying, "This high velocity places Arcturus in that very small class of stars that apparently are a law unto themselves. He is an outsider, a visitor, a stranger within the gates; to speak plainly, Arcturus is a runaway. Newton gives the velocity of a star under control as not more than 25 miles a second, and Arcturus is going 257 miles a second. Therefore, combined attraction of all the stars we know cannot stop him or even turn him in his path." Arcturus and "his sons" are on a course all their own. Only God has the power to guide them, just as described in the ancient book of Job'.[156]

The details of these heavenly bodies could not have been known by any observer on earth without the aid of very advanced technology, or without the aid of the all-knowing Creator. Clearly the writer of Job didn't have the former, it follows therefore that he had the latter.

The Star of Bethlehem
The 'Christmas Story' of wise men following a star is considered by many to be no more than folklore, and it is considered by others to be no less than a miracle. To say that it is legendary is to fail to take into account the genre of Matthew's Gospel, and the fact that he is clearly attempting to write honest history. To say that the star was a miraculous occurrence doesn't really do justice to the details of Matthew's account. If it was just a miraculous event then why didn't the star lead them straight to Bethlehem? Why did they go first to Jerusalem? Why did the star seemingly disappear then reappear? Is there another option? There certainly is. A groundbreaking and painstaking study by COLIN NICHOLL offers the suggestion that the star of Bethlehem was a comet.[157] NICHOLL goes through the text of scripture, then looks at the data of astronomy, and, without sacrificing any of the details of either, he documents a complete correspondence – the biblical and astronomical facts converge on a great comet. This ought to make the sceptic very slow to dismiss the biblical account of the nativity.

The water cycle
The water cycle was 'discovered' by Bernard Palissy in 1580 and refined and advanced by Edme Mariotte and Pierre Perrault. But it was Solomon who first wrote about it:

---

[156] http://coldcasechristianity.com/2013/is-the-astronomy-in-the-book-of-job-scientifically-consistent/
[157] COLIN R. NICHOLL, *The Great Christ Comet, Revealing the True Star of Bethlehem*, Crossway, 2015.

'All the rivers run into the sea; yet the sea is not full; unto the place from whence the rivers come, thither they return again', Eccles. 1. 7.

Notice that Solomon says that the rivers run into the sea and that they return to the place from which they had come.

How does the water from the sea get back to the source of the rivers? Amos tells us:

'He that calleth for the waters of the sea, and poureth them out upon the face of the earth: The Lord is his name', Amos 9. 6.[158]

The picture of water coming from the sea and falling on the earth is clearly implied in scripture well over 2,000 years before mankind discovered it.

Oceanography
Matthew Fontaine Maury (1806-1873) was brought up in a God-fearing home in which the Psalms were read daily. It was one phrase from Psalm 8 that set him on a journey of discovery and resulted in him being called the Pathfinder of the Seas. It was the expression in verse 8:

'The fowl of the air, and the fish of the sea, and whatsoever passeth through *the paths of the seas*'. (emphasis added.)

In addition to this, the statement of Solomon in Ecclesiastes chapter 1 verse 6 that 'The wind goeth toward the south, and turneth about unto the north; it whirleth about continually, and the wind returneth again according to his circuits', informed him that there is such a thing as atmospheric circulation. Believing the Creator had given mankind insight into the nature of reality he set off in that direction, and his investigations to find the paths of the seas gave rise to many

---

[158] See also Ps. 135. 7 and Jer. 10. 13.

important and useful discoveries about ocean currents and ocean lanes. He wrote several books including *Physical Geography of the Seas and its Meteorology*, which remains a standard book on the subject, and he helped launch the American Association for the Advancement of Science in 1848.[159]

It was said of him, 'He saw so much because he knew the Bible, believed it, and saw the harmony between what it taught and the natural sciences'.[160]

Isn't it ironic that this man, who was so passionate for the advancement of science, and who made so many groundbreaking discoveries, was inspired by his knowledge of and trust in the Bible? There is a widespread but historically ignorant view that if one accepts the authority of scripture then he won't bother to do science, but it was completely the opposite with Maury, as well as with many who came before and after him.

Air has weight

In the 17th century Evagilista Torricelli discovered that air has weight. Job chapter 28 verse 25 had revealed it a long time before that:

> 'To make the weight for the winds; and He weigheth the waters by measure'.

Job is discoursing on how all of creation displays the wisdom of God, everything is finely tuned and precisely balanced, and this includes the weight of the winds. If someone has a scriptural worldview it

---

[159] An organisation which sadly now seems scared of the direction science is advancing since it passed a resolution urging 'citizens across the nation to oppose the establishment of policies that would permit the teaching of "intelligent design theory" as part of the science curricula of the public schools' and appealing for its members to understand 'the inappropriateness of "intelligent design theory" as subject matter for science education'. *AAAS Board Resolution on Intelligent Design Theory*, 18/10/2002.
[160] STEPHEN MCDOWELL, *Matthew Fontaine Maury, the Pathfinder of the Seas*, loc 144.

leads to a scientific worldview because it would encourage the investigation of God's creation to discover His wisdom. God has given signposts in His Word that, if followed, lead the scientist to treasures of discovery.

Noah's ark

In all likelihood Noah was ridiculed for building the ark, and the biblical account of the ark has been ridiculed ever since. However, when people lay aside their ridicule and investigate what the Bible says they find that it's not so funny after all.

Masters students in the Physics and Astronomy Departments at the University of Leicester were given the task of studying the dimensions set out in scripture to see if such a vessel could float with the weight of 70,000 animals onboard. The Telegraph reported, 'they were astonished to find out that the Ark would have floated . . . Student Thomas Morris, 22, from Chelmsford, said: "You don't think of the Bible necessarily as a scientifically accurate source of information, so I guess we were quite surprised when we discovered it would work. We're not proving that it's true, but the concept would definitely work'".[161] Their work was published in a peer-reviewed journal, The Journal of Physics Special Topics.[162]

I don't think Noah knew about Archimedes' principle of buoyancy, neither do I suppose he had access to the technology available at Leicester University's Physics and Astronomy Department, nor could he have constructed a few different arks, filling each with 70,000 animals to see which one floated. So how did he happen upon the right dimensions? The Bible provides the only sensible answer:

---

[161]http://www.telegraph.co.uk/news/science/science-news/10740451/Noahs-Ark-would-have-floated...even-with-70000-animals.html

[162]

https://physics.le.ac.uk/journals/index.php/pst/article/viewFile/676/475

'**And God said to Noah,** "The end of all flesh has come before Me, for the earth is filled with violence through them; and behold, I will destroy them with the earth. Make yourself an ark of gopherwood; make rooms in the ark, and cover it inside and outside with pitch. **And this is how you shall make it**: the length of the ark shall be three hundred cubits, its width fifty cubits, and its height thirty cubits"', Gen. 6. 13-15, NKJV, emphases added.

Thomas Morris is correct when he says that most people don't think of the Bible as a source of scientifically accurate information, but hopefully he, and many others, will be led to think again.

There are several ancient flood legends (more on this below), but these other accounts either don't give any dimensions for the ark or else they don't give the dimensions that the Bible gives. For example, the Gilgamesh flood epic tells us that the boat Ut-napishti built was a cube of 120 cubits,[163] and a tablet dated between 1900 BC and 1700 BC speaks of a circular ark with a diameter of about 230 feet with walls 20 feet high.[164] Only the biblical design could survive the flood.[165]

The ratio of the dimensions of the ark (30:5:3) has been employed by engineers in their ship designs. For example, one of the heroes of mechanical and civil engineering, Isambard Kingdom Brunel, designed the SS Great Britain with a length of 322 feet, a beam of 51 feet and a height from keel to main deck of 32 feet – almost exactly the same ratio as the ark.[166] How do we account for the 'spot on' dimensions? Luck? Noah's genius? Or would it not be a lot more

---

[163] http://www.ancienttexts.org/library/mesopotamian/gilgamesh/tab11.htm. The oldest copy dates to 2000-1600 BC, the most complete version is from about 650 BC.

[164] http://www.biblicalarchaeology.org/daily/biblical-topics/hebrew-bible/the-animals-went-in-two-by-two-according-to-babylonian-ark-tablet/

[165] http://www.icr.org/article/cuneiform-reed-ark-story-doesnt-float/

[166] http://www.nationalhistoricships.org.uk/register/76/ss-great-britain

reasonable to believe that Noah got his information from the Supreme Engineer and Master Builder – God Himself?

Many critics of the Bible are keen to proclaim that the writers of the Bible were ignorant peasants who had nowhere near the knowledge we have today about anything scientific. If that is the case then it only serves to underscore the point that they were being guided by one who did know – the God of creation.

The agnostic astronomer, physicist and cosmologist, ROBERT JASTROW, faced up to this, and had to confess:

> 'For the scientist who has lived by his faith in the power of reason, the story ends like a bad dream. He has scaled the mountain of ignorance; he is about to conquer the highest peak; as he pulls himself over the final rock, he is greeted by a band of theologians who have been sitting there for centuries'.[167]

The scientist shouts with triumph at the magnitude of his discoveries, while the simple Bible believer says about many of them, 'Yes, I knew that, it says that in my Bible!'

Archaeology

Many a criminal has been caught because of footprints or fingerprints left behind at the scene of the crime. Many children have been caught because of crumbs in the bed which match the bun missing from the box. These silent witnesses can confirm a theory, disprove a story, place a person at the scene of a crime, and help us in understanding what went on in the past. This applies to the ancient past as well. If the events the Bible records as real history actually happened we would expect to find some evidence for them in the real world. The archaeologist is the person we turn to for help in this matter. Now

---

[167] ROBERT JASTROW, *God and the Astronomers*, cited in GEISLER & TUREK in *I don't have enough Faith to be an Atheist*, p. 94.

archaeological discoveries may be sufficient to confirm the historicity of an event, but they are not always necessary. We can have confidence that certain events occurred, even if there are no archaeological evidences of them, provided we have other evidence that is reliable, so absence of evidence isn't necessarily evidence of absence. There could be other factors explaining why certain historical data doesn't show up on archaeological digs, e.g., we are looking in the wrong place, we are looking for the wrong thing, another event that we are ignorant of has taken place and obscured or destroyed the evidence, etc. So an archaeological find can confirm an event has taken place, but the absence of a find, generally speaking, cannot confirm it did not take place.[168]

We are going to look at some of the archaeological discoveries that confirm Biblical accounts, and we are going to confine ourselves to those findings that confirm events that demand divine intervention.

The Flood
The Biblical account of the flood has been dismissed as a mere Hebrew myth. However, if you get disparate ancient groups in every continent of the world telling a similar story it makes it a whole lot more difficult to ignore – it indicates a real historical event took place. A primeval catastrophic flood is well embedded in the traditions of nations across the world, including Iran, Egypt, Russia, China, India, Mexico, Peru and Hawaii.[169]

Several of these flood legends are extremely ancient. Consider the following:

---

[168] On certain occasions the absence of evidence can serve to disconfirm a theory, if that theory entails that there should be a lot of readily accessible evidence. For example, the complete lack of any archaeological confirmation of accounts in the Book of Mormon, or the lack of transitional fossils supporting Darwinism.
[169] CLIVE ANDERSON & BRIAN EDWARDS, *Evidence for the Bible*, Day One Publications, 2015, p. 3.

The Gilgamesh Epic
The earliest extant manuscript of the Gilgamesh Epic goes back to 2000-1600 BC[170] but the most complete version dates to about 650 BC. The 11th tablet (apparently originating in the 12th century BC)[171] tells the story of Ut-napishti who is warned by one of the gods about a flood that the gods are going to inflict:

> 'Tear down the house and build a boat!
> Abandon wealth and seek living beings!
> Spurn possessions and keep alive living beings!
> Make all living beings go up into the boat.
> The boat which you are to build,
> Its dimensions must measure equal to each other:
> Its length must correspond to its width'.[172]

So he built it, pitched it, and 'had all my kith and kin go up into the boat, all the beasts and animals of the field and the craftsmen I had go up'. The flood came (which only lasted seven days and actually frightened the gods!). He then sent out a dove which came back to him having found nowhere to land, after which he sent out a swallow and a raven. When they got out they offered sacrifices.

The Weld-Blundell Prism
The Weld-Blundell Prism was discovered in 1922 and dates back to the 18th century BC. It gives a list of Sumerian kings and tells us of those who reigned before and after 'the flood swept over'. The reigns of the kings before the flood are incredibly long (e.g. 43,200 years!), and after the flood they are a whole lot shorter (the longest post-flood reign is listed as 1,200 years).[173]

---

[170] See http://bmcr.brynmawr.edu/2004/2004-04-21.html.
[171] *Exploring Genesis, The Bible's Ancient Traditions in Context*, Biblical Archaeology Society, 2013, p. 23.
[172]

http://www.ancienttexts.org/library/mesopotamian/gilgamesh/tab11.htm
[173] http://etcsl.orinst.ox.ac.uk/section2/tr211.htm

The Atrahasis Epic

This story, discovered in the 1880s, dates back to the 17th century BC. It tells of a flood coming to destroy humanity because their noise was annoying the gods. Atrahasis is warned of this and builds a boat, saves his family and some animals, and offers sacrifices to the gods when he gets out.[174]

A flood, a big boat to take humans and animals, birds released and sacrifices offered, and these features are found in a wide range of cultures. As time passes, the story in each culture changes and develops, but there is still a common historical core. So the question is, 'how do we know the Bible hasn't changed and added its own details?' Well, we look back to our previous section in which we find the perfectly designed dimensions of the biblical ark as opposed to all the other stories which have many unworkable features and obviously legendary details.[175]

The Destruction of Sodom and Gomorrah

The idea of God raining fire and brimstone down upon the wicked is seen by many as nothing more than a joke. However, the evidence suggests it is no joke. It seems to be the case that this fiery intervention of God in judgement has left its mark. Excavations are ongoing at Tall-el-Hammam which lies at the northern end of the Dead Sea on the Jordanian side, east of Bethel and Ai. In its geography and topography it appears to match the Biblical description of the cities of the plain. ANDERSON AND EDWARDS summarize the pertinent findings:[176]

---

[174] http://www.livius.org/as-at/atrahasis/atrahasis.html; ANDERSON AND EDWARDS, *Evidence for the Bible*, p. 3; DOUG POWELL, *iWitness Biblical Archaeology*, available as an app or paperback (Apologia Educational Ministries, 2014).

[175] The flood legends have finite and fleshly gods. The biblical worldview stands apart from all other ancient worldviews in that it presents God as distinct from matter rather than derived from it. See JOHN C. LENNOX, *Against the Flow, The Inspiration of Daniel in an Age of Relativism*, Lion Hudson, 2015, pp. 64-67.

[176] ANDERSON & EDWARDS, *Evidence for the Bible*, p. 5.

- When Lot made his choice of the best land, he was between Bethel and Ai, Gen. 13. 3.
- The Hebrew word for 'plain', Gen. 13. 10, is *kikkar* or 'disk shaped'. A disk-shaped alluvial plain in this area meets the Genesis chapter 13 verse 10 [criterion] of 'Well watered like the garden of the Lord'. The area is richly fertile even today.
- On the 100 acre mound in this plain, the remains of a large fortified city have been found dated to the Middle Bronze Age – the time of Abraham and Lot.
- Scorched walls and floors were buried beneath three feet of 'dark grey ash', and pottery shards had been subject to searing temperatures exceeding 2,000 degrees Fahrenheit. Yet there is no geological evidence of volcanic activity in this area.
- The whole area was left abandoned for around seven hundred years.

This evidence of the destruction of the cities of the plain is not just a matter of the historical reliability of the Bible but a matter of personal relevance to us all, for Jude tells us that these cities serve as a warning to all who 'turn the grace of our God into lewdness', Jude 4, NKJV:

'as Sodom and Gomorrah, and the cities around them in a similar manner to these, having given themselves over to sexual immorality and gone after strange flesh, are set forth as an example, suffering the vengeance of eternal fire', Jude 7, NKJV.

The Exodus
Throughout the history of the nation of Israel, God pointed back, and the people looked back, to the Exodus from Egypt as a proof of God's power, love and faithfulness.[177] It is vital, then, that this event actually happened. As we follow the trail the Bible charts from Egypt to Canaan, we find clues that the Israelites really did take that journey.

---

[177] For example: Josh. 24. 6; Judg. 2. 1; 1 Sam. 10. 18; 1 Chr. 17. 21; Hos. 11. 1.

Internal evidence

We noted in our chapter on prophecy that GLEASON ARCHER proves that the writer of the Pentateuch had firsthand knowledge of Egypt and the Sinai Peninsula, but no firsthand acquaintance with Palestine.[178] This is seen in the following features ARCHER lists:

- The writer displays knowledge of the Egyptian crop sequence, Exod. 9. 31-32.
- The animals listed in Leviticus chapter 11 and Deuteronomy chapter 14 include some that are peculiar to the Sinai Peninsula. As ARCHER states, 'It is difficult to imagine how a list of this sort could have been made up nine hundred years later, after the Hebrew people had been living in a country not possessing any of these beasts'.
- The writer uses an Egyptian region as a way of describing the Jordan Valley, Gen. 13. 10, and shows his familiarity with the founding of Zoan, Num. 13. 22. Writing about Shechem, he says it is in the land of Canaan, which would have been redundant to people who lived there, but a perfectly normal way of describing it if it was written by one who hadn't been in the land.
- There are many Egyptian names and loan words in the Pentateuch, far more than in any other section of scripture.

These features show that the writer knew Egypt and the Sinai Peninsula personally, but only the Promised Land only from reports passed on to him. This accords exactly with the biblical account that the children of Israel left Canaan, went into Egypt, came out and journeyed through the wilderness to Canaan again, and this was recorded by Moses.

A repeated theme in the account of the plagues is the hardening of Pharaoh's heart. This statement has particular significance when set against an Egyptian background. In the *Book of the Dead*, an ancient

---

[178] GLEASON L. ARCHER, *New International Encyclopedia of Bible Difficulties*, Zondervan. The points listed are all taken from Archer, loc 1015-1046.

Egyptian funerary text, we find that after death the heart of the Pharaoh is 'weighed against the feather of truth and righteousness. If the heart is too heavy, Ani will be adjudged a sinner and cast to the voracious Amemit'.[179] The hardening of the heart in such a context is a further confirmation of Mosaic authorship.

Furthermore, there are incidents of failure on the part of the nation, and Moses, Aaron and Miriam, which are difficult to account for unless the events actually happened. There are details such as the numbers from each tribes, e.g., Num. 1; 26, and the particular quantities for the offerings, e.g., Num. 7, which just don't seem like the kind of things one would include if the story was an invention.

External evidence
The plagues wrought utter devastation in Egypt and humiliated their vaunted power, so it is no surprise that they would not be officially chronicled. However, there is a convincing case to be made that they are being referred to in the Ipuwer Papyrus. This dates back to 13th century BC and talks about the river Nile becoming blood, the crops and trees being destroyed, darkness in the land, 'he that lays his brother in the ground is everywhere', and the poor become rich and the rich are made poor.[180]

In the late 19th and early 20th century, FLINDERS PETRIE excavated a site near the pyramid of Senusret II. This site, named Kahun by Petrie, contains some interesting features, most noticeably boxes buried under the floors containing the skeletons of infants. PETRIE recorded:

---

[179] JOHN D. CURRID, *Ancient Egypt and the Old Testament*, Baker Books, 1999, p. 97. See too TED WRIGHT, *Who was the Pharaoh of the Exodus?*, http://crossexamined.org/ancient-israel-myth-or-history-part-3c/.

[180] http://www.reshafim.org.il/ad/egypt/texts/ipuwer.htm. The comment is made on this website that it is a leap to suppose that the Ipuwer Papyrus is speaking about the Egyptian plagues. This is merely asserted with no evidence given. It certainly does not appear to be a leap to me – it is a very small and very sensible step. Maybe the commentator recognizes the implications of admitting the truthfulness of the Exodus account – it entails the God of Israel is the true God.

'Many boxes were thus found in which babies had been buried. The boxes were evidently intended for domestic uses, to hold clothes, tools, etc., but babies were put in them, sometimes two or three together, and buried in the rooms'.[181]

DR ROSALIE DAVID of the University of Manchester remarks that 'the quantity, range and type of articles of everyday use which were left behind in the houses may indeed suggest that the departure was sudden and unpremeditated'.[182]

History shows that in the ninth year of the reign of Amenhotep II (whom many historians take to be the Pharaoh in 1446 BC) there were a number of crises. The city of Avaris was abandoned and an order was given to destroy the images of the gods, one of the gods singled out for special mention was Amun-Re. The significance of this is that Amenhotep II had previously ascribed praise to Amun-Re for military victories. When we remember that the plagues were not only a judgement on the Egyptians but a statement of *Yahweh*'s superiority over the gods of the Egyptians we can see why this drastic step was taken. The gods of the Egyptians had failed:

> 'For the Egyptians buried all their firstborn, which the Lord had smitten among them: upon their gods also the Lord executed judgments', Num. 33. 4.

According to independent lines of evidence, the Pharaoh who succeeded Amenhotep II was not actually his firstborn son.

> 'For the exodus-pharaoh, the worst part of God's prediction of judgement was that his own firstborn son would die. If

---

[181] W. M. FLINDERS PETRIE, *Kahun, Gurob, and Hawara*, p. 24, available at http://www3.lib.uchicago.edu/cgi-bin/eos/eos_title.pl?callnum=DT73.K3P5_cop1.

[182] A. R. DAVID, *Pyramid Builders of Ancient Egypt*, Routledge & Kegan Paul, 1986.

Amenhotep II was the exodus-pharaoh, his firstborn son had to die without the chance to rule, which the historical record should confirm. The son who succeeded Amenhotep II was Thutmose IV (ca. 1418–1408 BC), whose Dream Stele—located between the paws of the Great Sphinx—reveals that he was not the original heir to the throne. Moreover, inscriptional and papyritious evidence confirms that Thutmose IV was not the eldest son of Amenhotep II'.[183]

There is a potential conflict though. The Bible does seem to tell us that the Pharaoh was drowned in the Red Sea:

'But overthrew Pharaoh and his host in the Red sea: for his mercy endureth for ever', Ps. 136. 15.

But Amenhotep II's body is mummified. There are a couple of different ways this apparent discrepancy can be resolved. The first is a suggestion by DOUG PETROVICH:

'However, the Hebrew verb וְנִעֵר (n'r, "he shook off") shows that God actually "shook off" the powerful pharaoh and his army, who were bothersome pests that God—whose might is far greater than theirs—merely brushed away. The same Hebrew verb is used in Ps. 109:23, where David laments, "I am gone like a shadow when it lengthens; I am shaken off like the locust." Here, he describes the sad condition of his suffering, as both lines of this synonymous parallelism indicate his feeling of being cast away, or discarded. The picture painted by the verb is that David has become as a locust that is casually flicked away from a man's garment. Surely David was not describing his own demise and death! The context of Ps. 136, which states that God "brought Israel out from their midst...with a strong hand and an outstretched arm" (Ps.

---

[183] DOUG PETROVICH, *Amenhotep II and the Historicity of the Exodus Pharaoh*, http://www.biblearchaeology.org/post/2010/02/04/Amenhotep-II-and-the-Historicity-of-the-Exodus-Pharaoh.aspx.

136:11–12), confirms that the unequalled might of God is the thrust of the passage, thus accentuating the ease with which He shook off Israel's adversary: the mighty Egyptian army.[184]

Given that the Pharaoh would probably not have headed the charge, it could be that all his army was destroyed without necessitating his death. Perhaps he went in at the rear of the company and retreated back to shore before being submerged.

The second option is given by WILLIAM SHEA.[185] He says there is evidence that after the death of Amenhotep II there was a new Pharaoh who actually took his title without making the transition evident to the general population. Now this might sound too conspiratorial, but just hear him out.

There are two texts from the reign of Amenhotep II which refer to his 'first victorious campaign', but they are different campaigns from different times. The first of his 'first victorious' campaigns took place in the third year of his reign. However, there is a text that says the seventh year of his reign was the year of 'his first campaign of victory'. Also, there are two different accession dates given: his father, Thutmose III died on the 30th of the seventh month, so Amenhotep II's accession date should have been the first day of the eighth month, but in the account of a campaign in the ninth year of his reign the anniversary of his coronation was said to be at the end of the eleventh month. There have been efforts to iron out these difficulties by inserting co-regencies, but all these efforts have failed.

If we take the view that there was a replacement Amenhotep II to save face for the Egyptians then:

---

[184] *Ibid.*

[185] WILLIAM SHEA, *Amenhotep II as Pharaoh of the Exodus*, http://www.biblearchaeology.org/post/2008/02/22/Amenhotep-II-as-Pharaoh-of-the-Exodus.aspx.

'The chronological correlation here fits very well. The Biblical date for the Exodus falls right between the two first campaigns of victory for the king named Amenhotep II. If the king of the first campaign died at the time of the Exodus, then the king of the new first campaign . . . should be a new king who also took the same nomen and prenomen of Amenhotep II. This could have resulted from an attempt to cover up the disaster that had taken place. Instead of taking a new set of throne names, the king who came to the throne after the first Amenhotep took the same set of throne names. But the attempt to cover up the disaster was not complete or perfect. A hint of it was left behind by the king or the scribes who either forgot or intentionally did not take into account the first victorious campaign of the first king by that name. Hence the conflict arose, both in terms of numbering his campaigns and in terms of identifying his accession date.[186]

Having gathered up the evidence, it seems a very strong case has been made for Amenhotep II being the Pharaoh at the time of the Exodus. TED WRIGHT says:

'What we do see in Amenhotep II, however, is a radical change in his foreign policy (which was very much unlike him), a re-alignment of his Naval forces which he used to launch military forays into Asia, and a religious "crisis" which led to the defacement of many Egyptian "gods" in the 9th year of his reign. Hmm . . . I wonder what that crisis could have been?'[187]

The Bible gives a very plausible answer to the question WRIGHT leaves hanging.

The critics say that something as monumental as the ten plagues and the mass exodus of thousands and thousands of slaves would have

---

[186] *Ibid.*
[187] TED WRIGHT, *Was there an Exodus and Conquest?*, http://crossexamined.org/was-there-an-exodus-conquest/

been recorded in Egyptian history. This shows a naivety on the part of the critic. History was recorded by nations then to highlight their victories and enhance their glory.[188] The devastation of the land of Egypt and the humiliation of the gods of Egypt certainly would not have been recorded. But while we don't have official, explicit references to the plagues and the Exodus, we do have multiple lines of independent evidence which all fit in neatly around the biblical account. The God of Abraham had said to Moses, 'Wherefore say unto the children of Israel, I am the Lord, and I will bring you out from under the burdens of the Egyptians, and I will rid you out of their bondage, and I will redeem you with a stretched out arm, and with great judgments', Exod. 6. 6. Moses records the fulfilment of that promise, and archaeology adds its Amen.

The Conquest of Canaan

The Exodus from Egypt is one side of a very valuable coin in Israel's history, the other side being the conquest of Canaan. The Bible records that they experienced mighty divine interventions that gave them victory over the evil inhabitants of the land. Excavations have confirmed the biblical account.

> 'During the 1930s John Garstang, from the University of Liverpool in England, discovered huge walls in the ruins of the old city of Jericho that had collapsed and been burned with fire; he dated the destruction at around 1407 BC – the time of the Israelite conquest'.[189]

Garstang's dating was challenged in the 1950s by the work of Dame Kathleen Kenyon. She concluded that the city had actually been destroyed in 1550 BC, meaning that when the Israelites arrived there was no walled city, but her work has been challenged and answered by a number of archaeologists.

---

[188] This is one of the areas in which biblical history stands apart and its integrity shines out – the failures are not glossed over or left out. The facts are recorded, even if they reflect badly on the nation of Israel.
[189] ANDERSON & EDWARDS, *Evidence for the Bible*, p. 27.

'[I]n 1978 John Bimson from Sheffield University argued comprehensively against Kenyon's dating and supported Garstang'.[190]

In the early 1990s DR BRYANT WOOD from the University of Toronto also took a fresh look at the whole subject. WOOD found several major problems with Kenyon's methodology as well as highlighting discoveries that strongly confirm the biblical account and disprove Kenyon's theory about the city being destroyed by the Egyptians. For example:

'Moreover, Jericho itself has produced evidence that militates against a destruction of City IV by the Egyptians. In the burnt debris of City IV both Garstang and Kenyon found many store jars full of grain, indicating that when the city met its end there was an ample food supply. This flies in the face of what we know about Egyptian military tactics. Egyptian campaigns were customarily mounted just prior to harvest time – food supplies stored inside the cities would be at their lowest level then; the Egyptians themselves could use the produce in the fields to feed their army; and what the Egyptians did not want for their own use they could destroy, thereby placing a further hardship on the indigenous population. This was clearly not the case at Jericho'.[191]

WOOD points out that the discovery of many jars full of grain is particularly significant because it shows that not only did the city

---

[190] *Ibid.*, p. 27.
[191] BRYANT G. WOOD, *Did the Israelites Conquer Jericho? A New Look at the Archaeological Evidence*, http://www.biblearchaeology.org/post/2008/05/Did-the-Israelites-Conquer-Jericho-A-New-Look-at-the-Archaeological-Evidence.aspx. See too WOOD's brief article dealing with the issue of Carbon 14 dating (which critics cite as evidence that Jericho was destroyed earlier than the Bible would allow for): http://www.biblearchaeology.org/post/2008/08/Carbon-14-Dating-at-Jericho.aspx.

189

meet a swift end (the people weren't starved as in other sieges, e.g., 2 Kgs. 6. 24-29), but also that the city fell shortly after harvest, just when the Bible states it happened, Josh. 5. 10. A third conclusion we can draw from the full jars is that the city wasn't plundered. Given how valuable grain was at that time (it was even used as a form of currency), it is remarkable that the grain wasn't taken and used. What explanation can there be for this? Joshua chapter 6 verses 17-18 tells us: God had given instructions that nothing in the city was to be taken for the Israelites.

> 'In short, Wood maintains that Garstang's original dating of Jericho was correct and that Kenyon was wrong. Wood based his conclusions not on his opinion or his ideas about the Bible, but on the evidence of the pottery itself! If the dating of archaeological sites should be based on pottery and other historical considerations (such as the chronology of Egypt's pharaohs), then all of the evidence from Tell Jericho argues for its destruction and burning around 1401-1406 BC. All of the evidence from Jericho at this time (ca. 1401-6 BC) fits the biblical record in an amazing way, from the details about the city being burned along with everything in it [offered to God as a burnt offering] (see Joshua 6), to the walls having dwelling places [houses] where Rahab helped the Jewish spies enter the city to spy its defences (Joshua 2)'.[192]

Given the fortifications of the city and the evident swiftness of the victory, the conquest of Jericho requires the intervention of divine power. So the archaeological evidence points to the reliability of a historical account but also to the reality of the transcendent cause – Israel's God, the God of scripture.

The Overthrow of Nineveh

We have already dealt with this in our section on prophecy. There won't be much more to say here. As we saw, writing sometime between 663 and 654 BC, Nahum prophesied the destruction of the

---

[192] WRIGHT, *Was there an Exodus and Conquest?*

city of Nineveh. In the 19th century there were those who doubted if Nineveh had ever existed. However, in 1847 all doubts were removed as Austen Henry Layard discovered the palace of Sargon II. The massive sculptures and miles of wall reliefs 'demonstrated to many people that the Assyrian Empire was as big and mighty as the Bible implied'.[193]

As Layard excavated, 'The fire-blackened walls recovered from the palace at Nineveh revealed just how accurate Nahum's prophecy was'.[194]

The charred remains of a once-glorious and formerly mighty city show the reality of the ever-glorious and almighty God who spelt out its doom decades before.

The Existence of Belshazzar
For centuries scholars thought that Belshazzar was a legend and that the writer of Daniel must have been far removed chronologically from the events because no ancient historians referred to this character, but rather spoke of how Nabonidus was the King of Babylon at the end of the Babylonian empire. Many thought it was a pretty straightforward proof that the Bible was in error.

But that's not the end of the story. It was well established by historical sources, such as the Nabonidus Chronicle, that Nabonidus was in North Arabia when Cyrus invaded Babylon, and thus there would have been a viceroy in charge during his absence. I wonder who that could have been?

Excavations at Ur (Iraq) in 1854 by J. G. Taylor uncovered four cylinders which are known as the Nabonidus Cylinders. The cylinders

---

[193] KATHERINE EUGENIA JONES, *Backward Glances: Americans at Nippur*, in *From Babylon to Baghdad, Ancient Iraq and the Modern West*, Biblical Archaeology Society, 2009, p. 11.
[194] ANDERSON & EDWARDS, *Evidence for the Bible*, p. 79.

contain prayers of Nabonidus for himself in his reign, and also for his firstborn son, whose name is ... Belshazzar.

> 'As for me, Nabonidus, king of Babylon, save me from sinning against your great godhead and grant me as a present a lifelong of days, and as for Belshazzar, the eldest son – my offspring – instil reverence for your great godhead in his heart and may he not commit any cultic mistake, may he be sated with a life of plenitude'.[195]

The fact that prayers are included for Belshazzar indicates that he was in a position of authority too. This explains why, in Daniel chapter 5 verse 7, Belshazzar said, 'Whosoever shall read this writing, and show me the interpretation thereof, shall be clothed with scarlet, and have a chain of gold about his neck, and shall be the third ruler in the kingdom'. The reason he offered the third place in the kingdom was because he was number two.

As we said in chapter two, due to the stunning accuracy of the prophecies in Daniel, unbelievers had concluded that it must have been written well into the time of the Greek empire. Due to their naturalistic presuppositions they ruled out the option that someone writing in the time of the Babylonian or Medo-Persian empires could have prophesied about Alexander the Great and Antiochus Epiphanes etc. But we know that Belshazzar was not known by Greek historians such as Herodotus (approximately 450 BC) and Xenophon (early fourth century BC). If Belshazzar had been forgotten by history and was unknown to historians, how did someone writing in the mid second century BC know about him?

CLYDE BILLINGTON writes:

> 'Incidentally, Daniel 5 is a better historical source on the fall of Babylon to Cyrus the Great in 539 BC than is either Herodotus (fifth century BC) or Xenephon (early fourth century BC).

---

[195] http://www.livius.org/sources/content/nabonidus-cylinder-from-ur/

Daniel knew the name of the last king ruling in Babylon, Belshazzar, and he also knew that a co-regency existed between Belshazzar and his father Nabonidus. Both of these facts are missing from Herodotus and Xenephon. Herodotus even incorrectly states in his Histories that the Babylonian king killed by Cyrus was named "Labonidas." Belshazzar's father Nabonidus, in fact, survived the fall of Babylon and eventually died of old age. How is it that, centuries after the fall of Babylon in 539 BC, the author of Daniel writing in 165 BC had better historical information than the Greek historians Herodotus and Xenephon? I once asked this question of Jonathan Goldstein, the translator and author of I Maccabees and II Maccabees in the Anchor Bible series. His response to me was that somehow the author of Daniel in 165 BC got his hands on some very good historical sources!'[196]

This is nothing but a desperate (and feeble) attempt to deny the obvious because of the theological ramifications and worldview issues at stake.

The discovery of the Nabonidus cylinders not only confirms the historical accuracy of Daniel, but also its prophetic accuracy and divine inspiration.

The Dead Sea Scrolls
We have already mentioned the Dead Sea Scrolls in our prophecy chapter, but since the scrolls stand out as one of the most significant archaeological finds ever made in relation to the Bible, the subject does merit a mention in this chapter. The story of the initial discovery of the scrolls is like something from a children's novel: a Bedouin shepherd boy was looking for one of his goats that had strayed from the flock. He came to the caves at Qumran and threw a rock into one of them. He heard the sound of pottery breaking and when he and his

---

[196] CLYDE E. BILLINGTON, The Curious History of the "Editor" in Biblical Criticism, http://www.biblearchaeology.org/post/2010/07/01/The-Curious-History-of-the-e2809cEditore2809d-in-Biblical-Criticism.aspx.

friend went in to investigate they found several broken jars and some scrolls and fragments of scrolls. They had apparently been hoping to find gold but they had stumbled across a far more valuable treasure trove.

Subsequent investigations led to the discovery of almost one thousand scrolls and about seventeen thousand fragments representing every book of the Old Testament, with the exception of Esther.[197]

There are two points that I have previously made but need to repeat for the purposes of this chapter. First, the great Isaiah scroll (a complete copy of Isaiah, given the label 1QIsa) found in the first cave at Qumran was dated to 100 BC. W. F. ALBRIGHT wrote:

> 'There is no doubt in my mind that the script is more archaic than the Nash papyrus . . . I should prefer a date around 100 BC . . . What an absolutely incredible find! And there can happily not be the slightest doubt in the world about the genuineness of the manuscript'.[198]

This proves that the prophecy of the Lord Jesus in Isaiah chapter 53 is not a Christian invention and has not been subjected to tampering by Christians. It is a passage that pre-dates Christ and yet reads like an eye-witness report of His trial, execution and burial. The same is true for Psalm 22.[199]

The second point is that the presence of the book of Daniel, dating back to the late second century BC, amongst the sacred scriptures, eliminates any possibility that it was written mid-second century BC.

---

[197] ANDERSON & EDWARDS, *Evidence for the Bible*, p. 112.

[198] Cited in NORMAN L. GEISLER & WILLIAM E. NIX, *A General Introduction to the Bible*, Moody Press, 1986, p. 366.

[199] See F. M. CROSS JR, *The Ancient Library of Qumran and Modern Biblical Studies*, Gerald Duckworth & Co., 1958, p. 122, or PETER W. FLINT in WILLIAM P. BROWN (ed.), *The Oxford Handbook of the Psalms*, Oxford University Press, 2014, p. 241.

The fact that the book of Daniel is there, copied and preserved, shows that it must have been written much earlier or it would never have been accepted as scripture.

> 'It had long been assumed by critics that the book of Daniel was written sometime in the 2nd century BC because of its many detailed prophecies. Yet the Dead Sea Scrolls, written in the 2nd century, include texts of Daniel and they are unquestionably part of the Jewish Canon of Scripture predating the 2nd century'.[200]

This means that the stunningly accurate details of chapter 11 (and the other prophetic passages) were indeed written before they took place.

There are loads more archaeological discoveries that have been made that confirm Old Testament and New Testament history. I haven't included them here for two reasons: first, it would make this book far too big, and second, my aim is not merely to show the historical accuracy of the Bible but the divine inspiration of the Bible. In theory, the Bible could be accurate in all the history it records and yet not be given by inspiration of God, but we have focussed on archaeological confirmation of events that:
- demand divine intervention, and
- prove divine inspiration.

We have seen that the archaeological confirmations of the Flood, the Exodus and the conquest of Canaan show us that God has intervened in history, exactly in the way the Bible says He has. It gives us good grounds, then, for believing that these records of His actions are what they claim to be and carry His authority.

We also pointed out that the archaeological confirmations of the overthrow of Nineveh and the existence of Belshazzar, and the discovery of the Dead Sea Scrolls all have massive implications. Nineveh's demise points to Nahum being prophetic. Belshazzar's

---

[200] ANDERSON & EDWARDS, *Evidence for the Bible*, p. 215.

existence puts the writer of the book of Daniel at the scene and in the time of the events he records, showing that he truly was a prophet. And the discovery of the Dead Sea Scrolls proves that the Messianic prophecies predate the coming of Christ and were not invented or edited by Christians.

This expedition into the dirt and dust of history has unearthed the unearthly, and points to the heavenly source of the volume we call the Bible.[201]

The ultimate verification

The witness of science and archaeology is compelling on its own, but what if God Himself actually came and stated unambiguously that the Bible is the word of God? Well, that is precisely what happened.

The Christian position is that Jesus of Nazareth is none less than God Himself, and He affirmed the Old Testament which we have as God's word, and, as we shall see, He anticipated the writings of the New Testament as given by the Holy Spirit of God. Now, you might be saying, *Wait a minute! You are pointing to the authority of Jesus to*

---

[201] Some readers may be wondering about the issue of the transmission of the text (i.e., do we have today what was originally written?). It is not really within the remit of this book to go into that issue, but the evidence for the integrity of the text of scripture is overwhelming. It has been said that as far as the Old Testament is concerned, the integrity of the text is guaranteed by the quality of the copies – there were professional scribes who took their responsibilities seriously and made the copies meticulously, while as far as the New Testament is concerned, the integrity of the text is guaranteed by the quantity of the copies – the books of the New Testament were copied rapidly and spread widely showing there was no individual or group that had the ability or the authority to gather them all up and make changes. Due to the wide and rapid geographical spread, textual critics can identify which manuscripts contain errors or have been altered. In the approximately 5,800 Greek New Testament manuscripts, we have preserved for us the original writings of the New Testament. For more information see GEISLER & NIX, *A General Introduction to the Bible*, pp. 321-489.

prove the authority of the Bible, but if I ask you to prove the authority of Jesus you are going to point to the authority of the Bible! This is circular reasoning! Not at all, let me explain.

I can take two approaches to the issue of the Bible's authority. I can take a top-down approach, or a bottom-up approach. The top-down approach is what we have been up to thus far in this book – we have been saying, 'Here is evidence for God's involvement in the scriptures'. We see the marks of inspiration in many places so we have good reason to believe it in all places. This whole story we see in scripture has God's fingerprints on it so we can say: I believe in Christ because of the Bible – there's compelling evidence that the Bible is God's word, and it says Jesus is God's Son. The bottom-up approach approaches the text of scripture as any other text of antiquity and looks at what can be established using the historian's tools and by applying the criteria for historicity. When we do that with the New Testament accounts we see that Jesus was someone who proclaimed Himself to be the divine Son of God – the full and final revelation of God to man. His disciples proclaimed Him as such and said that following His death He had appeared to them as the risen Christ. The best explanation of these facts is that Jesus really is who He claimed to be, and thus what He said comes with divine authority, and He proclaimed the Bible to be God's word. So in the bottom-up approach we can say I believe in the Bible because of Christ – there's compelling evidence that Jesus is God's Son, and He says the Bible is God's word.[202]

We will look at some of the details relating to Christ that even the most liberal critics grant and show that when we start right at the bottom we can still get all the way up to the top.

Let's start by showing that *Jesus claimed to be God's Son*.

---

[202] The bottom-up approach is certainly sufficient to prove the Bible is God's word, but it is not necessary, because the Lord Jesus held the Jews of His day accountable for not obeying the word of God. There was sufficient evidence before Christ came that the Hebrew Scriptures were from God.

Matthew chapter 11 verse 27
> 'All things have been delivered to Me by My Father, and no
> one knows the Son except the Father. Nor does anyone know
> the Father except the Son, and the one to whom the Son wills
> to reveal Him', NKJV.

Without going into too much detail, scholars of all theological stripes accept that this is a genuine statement of Jesus. It is recorded in Luke chapter 10 verse 22, which means it is a *Q* saying of Jesus. New Testament scholars have sought to explain the commonalities in the Synoptic Gospels (Matthew, Mark and Luke) by saying that if there is material common to Mark and one or both of the others it comes from Mark (because he is reckoned to be the earliest), but the material absent from Mark and included by Matthew and Luke is from an earlier source, labelled *Q*. So these academics think that when we get a *Q* saying we are getting right back to the most primitive source, right back to 'the historical Jesus' free from legendary development. The thing is that in this supposed *Q* we have a very high Christology.

Scholars have pointed out that this is not the kind of a statement that is likely to be a Christian invention, and they give a number of reasons for this.[203] One reason is that it says that knowing the Father depends on the Son choosing to reveal Him whereas in the epistles the teaching is that knowing the Son is dependent on the Father revealing Him.

So when we look at this statement, who did Jesus think He was? He refers to Himself as the unique Son of God who has unique knowledge of the Father and has the authority to reveal the Father to others. These are audacious claims, but the biggest shock of the statement is that He says that He is more incomprehensible than the Father Himself! He doesn't say, 'no one knows the Son except the Father, and the one to whom the Father wills to reveal Him'. He says that people can know the Father but no one can know the Son. Why is this? The only explanation for the Son being inscrutable is that He possesses

---

[203] See, for example, CRAIG, *Reasonable Faith*, loc 5505.

two natures: the union of humanity and deity in one person means that there are mysteries about His person that none but God can understand.

Mark chapter 12 verses 1-12

'And he began to speak unto them by parables. A certain man planted a vineyard, and set an hedge about it, and digged a place for the winefat, and built a tower, and let it out to husbandmen, and went into a far country. And at the season he sent to the husbandmen a servant, that he might receive from the husbandmen of the fruit of the vineyard. And they caught him, and beat him, and sent him away empty. And again he sent unto them another servant; and at him they cast stones, and wounded him in the head, and sent him away shamefully handled. And again he sent another; and him they killed, and many others; beating some, and killing some. Having yet therefore one son, his wellbeloved, he sent him also last unto them, saying, They will reverence my son. But those husbandmen said among themselves, This is the heir; come, let us kill him, and the inheritance shall be ours. And they took him, and killed him, and cast him out of the vineyard. What shall therefore the lord of the vineyard do? he will come and destroy the husbandmen, and will give the vineyard unto others. And have ye not read this scripture; The stone which the builders rejected is become the head of the corner: This was the Lord's doing, and it is marvellous in our eyes? And they sought to lay hold on him, but feared the people: for they knew that he had spoken the parable against them: and they left him, and went their way'.

This parable is recognized as an authentic utterance of Christ by all, even the most sceptical of scholars (it is in their beloved Gospel of Thomas). It is in what most New Testament historians take to be the earliest Gospel (Mark), and '[t]he parable also contains interpretative nuances rooted in the Aramaic paraphrases of Isaiah 5, which were in use in Jesus' day'.[204] It is also unlikely to be a Christian invention based on the fact that the lord of the vineyard sends the son with the expectation of him being received and reverenced. If Christians were making up a parable they wouldn't have attributed ignorance to the character in the parable who represents God.

From the parable we can see that the Lord pictures the prophets as servants sent by the lord of the vineyard, but how does He portray Himself? Is it as the greatest of the servants? No, it is as the only and well-beloved son of the master, the heir of the vineyard. This is light-years away from the Messiah being a mere man who brings political deliverance and turns people to the true God. This is a relationship of intimacy that can only find its answer in the fact that Jesus was portraying Himself as the Son who had been with the Father in the enjoyment of His love before He was sent.

Mark chapter 13 verse 32
> 'But of that day and that hour knoweth no man, no, not the angels which are in heaven, neither the Son, but the Father'.

This passage would certainly not have been put into the mouth of Jesus by the early Christians because He said He didn't know the day or hour of His return. If Christians wanted to invent and present a divine Messiah they certainly wouldn't have made up such a statement.[205] The criterion of embarrassment establishes this as an

---

[204] CRAIG, On Guard, p. 205. CRAIG gives other reasons why scholars affirm the authenticity of this parable.

[205] It's not that there is no answer to this conundrum, the point is that Mark does not provide the answer – he tells us that this was said but doesn't explain how this fits with the deity of Christ. The reason he records Christ saying it is because Christ really said it! The answer can be found in a New Testament analogy and an Old Testament prophecy. In 1 Corinthians chapter 2 verse 2 Paul says he determined not to know anything among the Christians except Jesus Christ and Him crucified. Paul was not saying he was literally ignorant of everything else, he was saying that nothing else was his concern – he was focussed on his mission. This is seen in the Messianic prophecy of Isaiah chapter 42 verses 19-21 – the Servant is blind to

authentic utterance of Christ. But look at what this statement shows – Christ is superior to mere men and even to mighty angels, He is of a different order to both.

> 'Jesus' sense of being God's Son involved a sense of proximity to the Father that transcended that of any human being (such as a king or a prophet) or even any angelic being'.[206]

Mark chapter 14 verses 60-64

> 'And the high priest stood up in the midst, and asked Jesus, saying, Answerest thou nothing? what is it which these witness against thee? But he held his peace, and answered nothing. Again the high priest asked him, and said unto him, Art thou the Christ, the Son of the Blessed? And Jesus said, I am: and ye shall see the Son of man sitting on the right hand of power, and coming in the clouds of heaven. Then the high priest rent his clothes, and saith, What need we any further witnesses? Ye have heard the blasphemy: what think ye? And they all condemned him to be guilty of death'.

Using historical criteria, this incident has to be accepted as genuine. WILLIAM LANE CRAIG (citing from ROBERT GUNDRY) provides an impressive list of reasons that establish the historicity of this event.[207] For example, the indirect way of referring to God (i.e., calling Him 'the Blessed' and 'the Power' rather than just 'God') was a Jewish custom rather than a Christian one, and thus would not be how a Christian would tell the story had he been making it up. And the prediction about them seeing the Son of man sitting on the right hand of power and coming in the clouds of heaven certainly would not have been invented because there is no account of this being fulfilled.

---

everything but the will of God and deaf to everything but the word of God. In that sense the Lord Jesus did not know the day and hour of His coming – it was not the purpose of His mission to get into such things.

[206] *Ibid.*, p. 208.
[207] See CRAIG, *Reasonable Faith*, loc 5613-5637.

What then did Jesus claim about Himself here? He affirmed He was the Christ, the Son of God, and also the Son of man prophesied in Daniel chapter 7 verses 13-14 who receives universal dominion and the worship due to God alone:

> 'I saw in the night visions, and, behold, one like the Son of man came with the clouds of heaven, and came to the Ancient of days, and they brought him near before him. And there was given him dominion, and glory, and a kingdom, that all people, nations, and languages, should serve him: his dominion is an everlasting dominion, which shall not pass away, and his kingdom that which shall not be destroyed'.

He also claimed to be the one who shares God's throne in Psalm 110 verse 1:

> 'The Lord said unto my Lord, Sit thou at my right hand, until I make thine enemies thy footstool'.

The high priest and Sanhedrin got the full force of what the Lord was saying and accused Him of blasphemy, condemning Him to death. It wasn't blasphemous for someone to claim to be the Messiah – there were many before and since Jesus who claimed that; nor was it blasphemous to claim to be a pre-existent, exalted being – that would just have been considered barmy, not blasphemy. But to claim equality with God, yes, that definitely qualifies as blasphemy, and that is why the Sanhedrin condemned Him.

Having established that Jesus really claimed deity, the question is, 'was He right or wrong?' These are the only two options. If He was wrong then that opens up only two avenues: either He thought He was right and made a mistake, or He knew He was wrong and was telling lies, but neither of these is even remotely possible.

If He were deluded, think of the extent of the delusion. He thought He was the divine, pre-existent Son of God, the full and final revelation of God to man, the one with the authority to forgive sins and save sinners, who will judge all mankind and rule over all of creation. If He sincerely but mistakenly thought these things were true then this is extreme madness. Yet no honest assessment of the life and legacy of Jesus of Nazareth could ever lead to the conclusion that He was deluded.

> 'Is such an intellect – clear as the sky, bracing as the mountain air, sharp and penetrating as a sword, thoroughly healthy and vigorous, always ready and always self-possessed – liable to a radical and most serious delusion concerning His own character and mission? Preposterous imagination!'[208]

If He were deceptive, think of the extent of the deception. He told people their eternal destiny hinged on their response to Him. He called on people to follow Him no matter the cost. If He was deliberately lying then He was not a good man, He was wicked. But someone who lived as He lived, loved as He loved, taught as He taught and suffered as He suffered could not be an evil person.

C. S. LEWIS's famous quote is worth repeating:

> 'I am trying here to prevent anyone saying the really foolish thing that people often say about Him: "I'm ready to accept Jesus as a great moral teacher, but I don't accept His claim to be God." That is the one thing we must not say. A man who was merely a man and said the sort of things Jesus said would not be a great moral teacher. He would either be a lunatic – on a level with the man who says he is a poached egg – or else he would be the devil of hell. You must make your choice. Either this man was, and is, the Son of God: or else a madman or something worse. You can shut Him up for a fool, you can spit at Him and kill Him as a demon; or you can fall at His feet and call Him Lord and God. But let us not come with any

---

[208] PHILIP SCHAFF, *The Person of Christ: The Perfection of His Humanity Viewed as a Proof of His Deity*, Granted Ministries Press, 2013, loc 1608.

patronising nonsense about His being a great human teacher. He has not left that open to us. He did not intend to'.[209]

We will now spend a few moments showing *the disciples proclaimed Jesus to be God's Son.*

It is a popular notion that the doctrine of the deity of Christ was a legendary development that reached full bloom at the Council of Nicaea. Nothing could be further from the truth – in the very earliest texts of the New Testament we have the very highest Christology. Within the New Testament epistles there are sections that bear the hallmarks of being earlier, well-known confessions, prayers and hymns. We will look at one of each:

A Confession, 1 Corinthians chapter 8 verse 6

'But to us there is but one God, the Father, of whom are all things, and we in Him; and one Lord Jesus Christ, by whom are all things, and we by Him'.

In the context of idolatry, Paul introduces a statement which may well have been well-known to his readers (the introductory "But to us" may have been Paul reminding them of a confession in common currency amongst them).[210] This confession draws on the great Hebrew affirmation of absolute monotheism, the Shema:

'Hear, O Israel: The Lord our God is one Lord', Deut. 6. 4.

Writing about 1 Corinthians 8:6, CHRIS TILLING comments:

'For many, this verse is a clincher, showcasing a "Christological monotheism," including Christ in the Shema. All the Greek words of the Shema in the Greek translation of

---

[209] C. S. LEWIS, *Mere Christianity*, HarperCollins, 2002, p. 52.
[210] CRISPIN FLETCHER-LOUIS says this verse reflects 'traditional pre-Pauline liturgical language', *Jesus Monotheism: Volume 1: Christological Origins: The Emerging Consensus and Beyond*, Cascade Books, 2015, p. 24.

the Bible used by the earliest Christians are repeated by Paul in 8:6. The "God" and "Lord" of the Shema which both identify the one God of Israel are now split between "God" the Father and the "Lord" Jesus Christ'.[211]

Paul takes all the elements of this confession in the Septuagint and incorporates both the Father and the Lord Jesus. So Paul is teaching monotheism but showing that monotheism does not mean unitarianism. The Father and Jesus Christ are both included in the identity of the one true God of Israel – *Yahweh*.

If this is a confession that pre-dates the writing of 1 Corinthians then it shows how early and widespread belief in the deity of Christ was – it was not late and it was not local.

> That Paul might have been able to draw on these types of materials in his correspondence with the churches under his jurisdiction would attest to the early nature of Christians' worship of Jesus as God and exalted Lord.[212]

A Prayer, 1 Corinthians chapter 16 verse 22
> 'If any man love not the Lord Jesus Christ, let him be Anathema; Maranatha'.

Paul includes two Aramaic words in the closing paragraph of his letter – *Anathema*, which means 'accursed', and *Maranatha* which means 'Our Lord, come'.

> 'That Paul uses this Aramaic expression in a letter to the Corinthian Christians, most of whom were Gentile converts

---

[211] MICHAEL F. BIRD (ed.), *How God Became Jesus: The Real Origins of Belief in Jesus' Divine Nature – A Response to Bart D. Ehrman*, Zondervan, 2014, loc 2607-2615.

[212] ANDREAS J. KOSTENBERGER & MICHAEL J. KRUGER, *The Heresy of Orthodoxy, How Contemporary Culture's Fascination with Diversity Has Reshaped Our Understanding of Early Christianity*, Apollos, 2010, p. 78.

and did not speak Aramaic, shows that *maranatha* was already widely established in Christian use in the mid-fifties, when Paul wrote the epistle . . . R. T. France helpfully compares the Corinthian church's familiarity with maranatha to our easy use of such Hebrew prayers as hosanna and hallelujah. Thus, we are looking at an expression that the early, Aramaic-speaking church was using as a prayer to Jesus – probably in some sort of corporate Christian worship setting. The epistle of 1 Corinthians, therefore, begins (1:2) and ends (16:22) with indications that the early church prayed to Jesus'.[213]

For this expression to gain such familiarity so as to be left untranslated in a letter to a Gentile assembly shows it had been part of Christian terminology for a long time. Right from the beginning, prayer was offered to the Lord Jesus.[214]

A hymn, Philippians chapter 2 verses 6-11

'Who, being in the form of God, thought it not robbery to be equal with God: but made himself of no reputation, and took upon him the form of a servant, and was made in the likeness of men: and being found in fashion as a man, he humbled himself, and became obedient unto death, even the death of the cross. Wherefore God also hath highly exalted him, and given him a name which is above every name: that at the name of Jesus every knee should bow, of things in heaven, and things in earth, and things under the earth; and that every tongue should confess that Jesus Christ is Lord, to the glory of God the Father'.

---

[213] ROBERT M. BOWMAN JR & J. ED KOMOSZEWSKI, *Putting Jesus in His Place: The Case for the Deity of Christ*, Kregel Publications, 2007, p. 53.

[214] The first prayer recorded in Acts is to the Lord Jesus (Acts 1. 24-25). See *Putting Jesus in His Place*, p. 48, for evidence that the prayer is directed to the Lord Jesus.

This majestic passage has come to be known as the *Carmen Christi*, or the Hymn to Christ. It contains a hymnic structure and this has led many to believe it was meant to be sung and was well known in the Christian assemblies. It identifies Christ as possessing the nature of God ('in the form of God'), and pre-existing in a position of equality with God, which position He voluntarily relinquished. God then exalts Him to that position again and gives to Him the name that is above every name, which can only be the name of *Yahweh*, and all creation will acknowledge this as they bow to Him and confess Him as Lord.

> 'In the Christ hymn of Philippians 2, which I take to be pre-Pauline, the words of YHWH about His sovereignty found in Isa. 45:23 ("Before Me every knee will bow; by Me every tongue will swear") are nonchalantly applied to Jesus with these words: "at the name of Jesus every knee should bow, in heaven and on earth and under the earth" (Phil. 2:10). In another Christ hymn, this time from Colossians, we are told that "in Him all things were created: things in heaven and on earth, visible and invisible, whether thrones or powers or rulers or authorities; all things have been created through Him and for Him" (Col. 1:16)'.[215]

Paul's words to the Ephesians in chapter 5 verse 19 show that singing praise to the Lord Jesus was expected:

> 'Speaking to yourselves in psalms and hymns and spiritual songs, singing and making melody in your heart to the Lord'.

Confessions, prayers, hymns, predating the writing of any of the New Testament documents prove that belief in the deity of Christ was not a later, legendary development but that from the birth of Christianity Christians treated Jesus as God alone should be treated.

> 'Paul's Christology, and perhaps also that which was expressed in credal formulae before he was writing the extant

---

[215] Michael F. Bird in BIRD (ed.), *How God Became Jesus*, loc 480.

letters, indicates that very early on in the Christian movement this God and this Jesus were being referred to as "Father" and "Son" within contexts that clearly put them together on the "divine" side of the equation'.[216]

The facts show not that Jesus became God over time, but that God became Jesus in time.

The significance of this is that all the first Christians were Jews, God-fearing, Torah-observing, monotheistic Jews, and yet they were proclaiming this crucified Nazarene to be equal with God and worthy of worship. This is not something they would have done lightly.

'While the Jews had lapsed into the worship of other deities in the period prior to the exiles, post-exilic Judaism, including that of the first century AD, was committed to monotheism and monolatry. In fact, this became an important distinguishing characteristic of Jewish religion in a polytheistic environment and was recognized as a hallmark of Jewish faith by Greco-Roman historians such as Tacitus, who wrote, "The Jews conceive of one God only" (Hist. 5.5)'.[217]

These early Christians would never have dared invent such a doctrine as the deity of Christ. The only explanation for how they would have believed it is that Jesus Christ claimed it and there was overwhelming evidence that He was right. He was condemned by the Sanhedrin for His claim, and consequently crucified by the Romans. That would have extinguished any notion in the mind of a Jew that His claim was true, but God vindicated Him by raising Him from the dead, and thus He was 'declared to be the Son of God with power . . . by the resurrection from the dead', Rom. 1. 4.

[216] N. T. WRIGHT, *The Resurrection of the Son of God*, SPCK, 2003, pp. 731-732.
[217] ANDREAS J. KOSTENBERGER & SCOTT R. SWAIN, *Father, Son and Spirit, The Trinity and John's Gospel*, Apollos, 2008, pp. 34-35.

Since Christ is the Son of God then what He says comes with divine authority, and we find that He affirmed the Old Testament and He anticipated the New Testament.

He affirmed the Old Testament

The Lord Jesus Christ believed in the historical reliability of the Old Testament. He affirmed the historicity of Adam and Eve, Matt. 19. 4, Cain and Abel, Matt. 23. 35, Noah's flood, Matt. 24. 37-39, the destruction of Sodom and Gomorrah, Matt. 11. 23-24; Luke 17. 28-32, the call of Moses, Mark 12. 26, the Exodus, John 6. 32, 49, the history of David, Mark 2. 25-26, and his psalms, Matt. 22. 41-45, the Queen of Sheba coming to Solomon, Matt. 12. 42, Isaiah's prophecy, Matt. 13. 14-15, the story of Jonah, Matt. 12. 39-41, Daniel's prophecy, Matt. 24. 15, etc. But He did not just view the Hebrew Scriptures as historically reliable, He said they were divinely inspired.[218]

Matthew chapter 4 verse 1-11

'Then was Jesus led up of the Spirit into the wilderness to be tempted of the devil. And when he had fasted forty days and forty nights, he was afterward an hungred. And when the tempter came to him, he said, If thou be the Son of God, command that these stones be made bread. But he answered and said, It is written, Man shall not live by bread alone, but by every word that proceedeth out of the mouth of God. Then the devil taketh him up into the holy city, and setteth him on a pinnacle of the temple, And saith unto him, If thou be the Son of God, cast thyself down: for it is written, he shall give his angels charge concerning thee: and in their hands they shall

---

[218] Assessing the Gospel accounts on purely historical grounds, it is not a point of controversy that Christ believed in the inspiration of the Hebrew Scriptures. Gary Habermas cites critical New Testament scholars such as Bart Ehrman (an agnostic) to prove this. Historians point out that there is multiple, independent attestation to Christ's view of the authority of scripture, and the fact that the early church believed the Hebrew Scriptures were God's word proved that their leader did too. See http://www.garyhabermas.com/articles/areopagus_jesusinspirationscriptu re/areopagus_jesusinspirationscripture.htm.

bear thee up, lest at any time thou dash thy foot against a stone. Jesus said unto him, It is written again, Thou shalt not tempt the Lord thy God. Again, the devil taketh him up into an exceeding high mountain, and sheweth him all the kingdoms of the world, and the glory of them; and saith unto him, All these things will I give thee, if thou wilt fall down and worship me. Then saith Jesus unto him, Get thee hence, Satan: for it is written, Thou shalt worship the Lord thy God, and him only shalt thou serve. Then the devil leaveth him, and, behold, angels came and ministered unto him'.

The Lord encounters the temptations of the devil by quoting scripture. It is evident that He took the Bible to be authoritative, decisive and the final word on the matter. ANDREW WILSON comments:

'He has the resources of heaven available, yet He fights by using the authority of the Scriptures. Not as a one-off, or as a change of tactics, but each and every time. 'It is written . . . it is written . . . it is written' He repeatedly emphasises. His position is unequivocal: "You're trying to tempt Me, but the Scriptures have spoken. That's the end of the conversation"'.[219]

Matthew chapter 5 verses 17-18
'Think not that I am come to destroy the law, or the prophets: I am not come to destroy, but to fulfil. For verily I say unto you, Till heaven and earth pass, one jot or one tittle shall in no wise pass from the law, till all be fulfilled'.

The Lord underscores the authority of all the Old Testament scriptures, the law and the prophets, in their most minute details. The jot is the smallest Hebrew letter, and the tittle is 'one of those little

---

[219] ANDREW WILSON, *Unbreakable: What the Son of God Said About the Word of God*, 10Publishing, 2014, loc 140 (emphasis his).

strokes by which alone some of the Hebrew letters are distinguished from others like them'.[220]

Matthew chapter 15 verses 1-9
> 'Then came to Jesus scribes and Pharisees, which were of Jerusalem, saying, Why do thy disciples transgress the tradition of the elders? for they wash not their hands when they eat bread. But he answered and said unto them, Why do ye also transgress the commandment of God by your tradition? For God commanded, saying, Honour thy father and mother: and, He that curseth father or mother, let him die the death. But ye say, Whosoever shall say to his father or his mother, It is a gift, by whatsoever thou mightest be profited by me; and honour not his father or his mother, he shall be free. Thus have ye made the commandment of God of none effect by your tradition. Ye hypocrites, well did Esaias prophesy of you, saying, This people draweth nigh unto me with their mouth, and honoureth me with their lips; but their heart is far from me. But in vain they do worship me, teaching for doctrines the commandments of men'.

Twice in the section the Lord refers to the fifth commandment as 'the commandment of God' in contrast to the 'traditions of the elders' and the 'commandments of men'. In the parallel section in Mark chapter 7 verse 13, Christ accused them of 'making the word of God of no effect through your tradition', NKJV. The Pharisees and scribes were disobeying 'the commandments of God' and disregarding 'the word of God' – that's how the Son of God viewed the law.

Matthew chapter 19 verses 3-6
> 'The Pharisees also came unto him, tempting him, and saying unto him, Is it lawful for a man to put away his wife for every cause? And he answered and said unto them, Have ye not read, that he which made them at the beginning made them male and female, and said, For this cause shall a man leave

---

[220] *Jamieson, Fausset and Brown Commentary*, e-Sword.

father and mother, and shall cleave to his wife: and they twain shall be one flesh? Wherefore they are no more twain, but one flesh. What therefore God hath joined together, let not man put asunder'.

On the issue of divorce, the Lord went back to Genesis and tells them what God said and what God did.

Who said, 'Therefore a man shall leave his father and mother'? Answer: 'He who created them . . . said'. That is, God said. But in Genesis chapter 2 verses 24, God is not being quoted. The verse that Jesus quotes, Gen. 2. 24, is simply part of the narrative that Moses wrote, 'Therefore a man shall leave his father and his mother and hold fast to his wife, and they shall become one flesh'.

> 'What this means is that Jesus saw the narratives of Moses as what God himself said. He did not think that we have God's word only in those places where Moses quotes the voice of God. All the Scripture that Moses wrote was the voice of God'.[221]

He viewed Genesis not as the musings of Moses or the folklore of the Jews but as the word of God.

Matthew chapter 22 verses 23-33
> 'The same day came to him the Sadducees, which say that there is no resurrection, and asked him, saying, Master, Moses said, If a man die, having no children, his brother shall marry his wife, and raise up seed unto his brother. Now there were with us seven brethren: and the first, when he had married a wife, deceased, and, having no issue, left his wife unto his brother: likewise the second also, and the third, unto the seventh. And last of all the woman died also. Therefore in the resurrection whose wife shall she be of the seven? for they all

---

[221] JOHN PIPER, *A Peculiar Glory, How the Christian Scriptures reveal their complete truthfulness*, IVP, 2016, p. 102.

had her. Jesus answered and said unto them, Ye do err, not knowing the scriptures, nor the power of God. For in the resurrection they neither marry, nor are given in marriage, but are as the angels of God in heaven. But as touching the resurrection of the dead, have ye not read that which was spoken unto you by God, saying, I am the God of Abraham, and the God of Isaac, and the God of Jacob? God is not the God of the dead, but of the living. And when the multitude heard this, they were astonished at his doctrine'.

The Sadducees tried to disprove the doctrine of resurrection by using *reductio ad absurdum*, that is, seeking to show a belief is false by showing it has absurd results. The Lord counters the argument by pointing out their mistaken premise, their argument was based on a mistaken belief that the doctrine of resurrection meant marriage was eternal, then He advances a scriptural proof for resurrection based on that which was spoken unto them by God. There are two things to note here: first, the Lord teaches that what was written by Moses is what was spoken by God; second, what was spoken by God was spoken to them – the teaching of scripture was binding on them even though they were living 1,500 years later. According to Christ we are responsible to hear and heed the teaching of the Bible.

The scriptural argument He gave was based on the tense that God used when He spoke to Moses, 'I am' rather than 'I was'. Thus, in the estimation of the Son of God, we can depend not only on every letter and part of a letter, the jot and tittle of Matthew chapter 5 verse 18, but on the tense of every verb.

Matthew chapter 22 verses 41-46
    'While the Pharisees were gathered together, Jesus asked them saying, "What do you think about the Christ? Whose Son is He?" They said to Him, "The Son of David." He said to them, "How then does David in the Spirit call Him 'Lord,' saying: 'The Lord said to my Lord, Sit at My right hand, Till I make Your enemies Your footstool'"? If David then calls Him 'Lord,' how is He his Son?" And no one was able to

answer Him a word, nor from that day on did anyone dare question Him anymore', NKJV.

The Lord refers to Psalm 110 as the words of David, but they weren't just the words of David. According to Christ, David was speaking 'in the Spirit', meaning in the power of the Spirit. The Spirit of God was guiding David so that what he wrote was exactly what the Spirit wanted.

Matthew chapter 23 verses 34-35
> 'Therefore, indeed, I send you prophets, wise men, and scribes: some of them you will kill and crucify, and some of them you will scourge in your synagogues and persecute from city to city, that on you may come all the righteous blood shed on the earth from the blood of righteous Abel to the blood of Zechariah, son of Berechiah, whom you murdered between the temple and the altar', NKJV.

In condemning the scribes and the Pharisees, the Lord warned them of impending doom, saying that there would be recompense meted out for all the righteous who had been slain. The significant point is that He spoke of Abel and Zechariah. Abel was the first person to be murdered in the Old Testament, Zechariah's murder is recorded in 2 Chronicles chapter 24 verses 20-22. In the Hebrew canon of scripture at the time of Christ, 2 Chronicles was the last book.[222] Furthermore, that canon contained all, and only, the books we have in our Old Testament today. So in referencing Abel and Zechariah, the Lord was talking about all the righteous martyrs from the beginning of the Bible to the end, in the same way Christians today would say from Genesis to Revelation. This shows us the Lord affirmed the divine authority of everything from Genesis to Chronicles (Genesis to Malachi in the order we have), and everything outside it was excluded.

---

[222] See GEISLER & NIX, *A General Introduction to the Bible*, pp. 22-24.

'Jesus answered them, "Is it not written in your law, 'I said, "You are gods"'? If He called them gods, to whom the word of God came (and the Scripture cannot be broken), do you say of Him whom the Father sanctified and sent into the world, 'You are blaspheming,' because I said, 'I am the Son of God'? If I do not do the works of My Father, do not believe Me; but if I do, though you do not believe Me, believe the works, that you may know and believe that the Father is in Me, and I in Him''', NKJV.

The two points to be noticed here are that Christ refers to the Old Testament as 'the word of God' and then says that 'the Scripture cannot be broken'. He was pointing out the impossibility of the Bible being incorrect. He didn't say that the writers were fallible men who were just products of their own times but had special insight. He asserted that there was an infallible God who communicated His word and it stands forever.

These are only some of the many occasions when Jesus made reference to the scriptures. He always asserted or assumed their absolute authority and divine origin. He believed the Old Testament was God's word, and since He is God we can believe Him.

He anticipated the New Testament
The Lord Jesus looked back to the Old Testament and gave it His divine seal of approval, but He also looked forward to the New Testament writings as well. We can see this implied in His final discourse.

'But the Helper, the Holy Spirit, whom the Father will send in My name, He will teach you all things, and bring to your remembrance all things that I said to you', John 14. 26, NKJV.

'I still have many things to say to you, but you cannot bear them now. However, when He, the Spirit of truth, has come, He will guide you into all truth; for He will not speak on His own authority, but whatever He hears He will speak; and He will tell you things to come', John 16. 12-13, NKJV.

The Spirit bringing all things Christ said to their remembrance covers the Gospels.

The Spirit guiding them into all truth covers the epistles.

The Spirit telling them things to come covers the book of Revelation.

The Lord was teaching His disciples that the Spirit of God would not only empower them but would also reveal truth to them. As the gospel spread and the years passed, it was natural that this truth would be written down so that all the churches would have access to apostolic teaching.

KOSTENBERGER AND KRUGER counter the view that the early Christians would have had no concept of New Testament scriptures, and have laid out three reasons why such scriptures would have been anticipated. The first reason has to do with the nature of covenants. The fact that the Lord inaugurated the New Covenant would have made new scriptures necessary and expected. They point out that the covenants of scripture are based on the treaty covenants of the ancient near east which are always accompanied by written texts.

Thus, there would have been clear expectations that this new covenant, like the old covenant, would be accompanied by the appropriate written texts to testify to the terms of the new arrangement that God was establishing with His people:

> 'Just as the ancient extrabiblical treaty covenants would not have a covenant without a written document as a witness to the relationship between the two parties, so the biblical covenants would not exist without a written witness to the

relationship between God and His people. Canon, therefore, is *the inevitable result of covenant*.[223]

The second reason is to do with redemptive history.

Scripture was given after God's great act of redemption in the Old Testament – the deliverance of His people from Egypt. It would have been expected that the act of redemption which the Exodus prefigured would have led to further scripture being given.

> 'So, just as covenant documents were delivered to Israel after the deliverance from Egypt by Moses, so it would seem natural to early Christians that new covenant documents would be delivered to the church after deliverance from sin by the second Moses, Jesus Christ. If Israel received written covenant documents to attest to their deliverance from Egypt, how much more would the church expect to receive written covenant documents to attest to their deliverance through Christ? Thus, it is the dawning of God's long-awaited redemptive triumph in the person of Jesus that is the foundation for the giving of canonical documents, and not later fourth-century ecclesiastical politics. As D. Moody Smith declared, "The early Christian claim that the narrative and prophecies of old are fulfilled and continued in Jesus and the church prefigures, perhaps even demands, *the production of more scripture*"'.[224]

Their third reason is community.

When God establishes a covenant He gives instructions relating to how a community is to function under it. Scripture not only records redemptive history but it shapes a community within which God is going to dwell. After redeeming His people from bondage in Egypt and making a covenant with them at Sinai, God gave them

---

[223] KOSTENBERGER & KRUGER, *The Heresy of Orthodoxy*, p. 112, emphasis theirs.
[224] *Ibid.*, pp. 114-115. Emphasis added by Kostenberger/Kruger.

instructions about His dwelling place. It is inconceivable that God would fulfil these pictures in Christ and the church and yet not give instructions about His dwelling place.

> 'Thus, according to the earliest Christian conceptions, canonical documents, God's word, are understood as God's building plan, the means by which He structures and molds the community of faith to be His dwelling. If so, then it is clear that they would have viewed *the community of faith to be, in some sense, the result of the canon, rather than the canon being the result of the community of faith'*.[225]

Covenant, redemptive history and community thus demanded new scripture. The next question is how would we know what constitutes scripture?

The answer to this lies in the office of the apostle. The Lord personally chose apostles to whom He revealed truth and through whom that truth was to be spread. These men had miraculous abilities granted to them by the Spirit to attest to the fact that they were recipients of new revelation, see 2 Cor. 12. 12; Heb. 2. 3-4. The spread of Christianity in distance and time from the epicentre of this new revelation demanded that those who had this unique authority have their teaching written down so that they could be effectively communicated and accurately preserved.

Writings that would be considered scripture would have to come with apostolic authority or have apostolic association. Luke was a close associate or Paul, and Mark was a close associate of Peter.

> 'The function of the apostolate was to make sure that the message of Christ was firmly and accurately preserved for future generations through the help of the Holy Spirit, whether written by its members directly or through a close follower of theirs. In the end, the New Testament canon is not

---

[225] *Ibid.*, pp. 120-121. Emphasis theirs.

so much a collection of writings by apostles, but rather a collection of apostolic writings – writings that bear the authoritative message of the apostles and derive from the foundational apostolic era (even if not directly from their hand)'.[226]

So not only was there a requirement for apostolic authority/association, but the document needed to come from the apostolic age. The apostles were the recipients and guardians of new revelation, so once they passed away so too did the period of new revelation.

To conclude this section on the ultimate verification, we have looked at the evidence for Christ's divine identity: there is no doubt He claimed it and His Jewish followers proclaimed it, and the only sensible conclusion is that Jesus really was and is who He and His disciples said He was. This means we can't dismiss what He says as just another opinion. Everything He said comes with divine authority, and He assumed and affirmed, implicitly and explicitly, the inspiration and inerrancy of the Old Testament. Furthermore, by Him inaugurating the new covenant, performing the great act of redemption and forming the Church, He gave the expectation of new scriptures. By selecting apostles who would be channels of new revelation, He gave us the means of knowing objectively which writings carried His divine authority. This means then that we have it on the highest authority that the Bible is God's word.

Conclusion

Many unbelievers have complained about the hiddenness of God, If He's there, why doesn't He make it more obvious? When we open our eyes and look at how scripture anticipates science it is clear He is there. If we dig a little we can literally trip over the evidence of His existence and interventions. He even came personally to earth and left proof of it for us to examine. God has not hidden Himself – He has

---

[226] *Ibid.*, p. 117.

revealed Himself in the Bible. Science, archaeology and (supremely) Christ verify it.

Chapter 5: Experience

'For the word of God is living and powerful, and sharper than any two-edged sword', Heb. 4, 12, NKJV.
'How sweet are thy words unto my taste! yea, sweeter than honey to my mouth!' Ps. 119. 103.

In this final proof we are dealing with the one which is the most simple to encounter but the most difficult to explain. As the Scots might say, *It's better felt than telt*. It is the argument that you can experience the reality of God in scripture yourself apart from arguments. It was in this way that the majority of people were won to Christ during His ministry – there was just something about the way He spoke, His teaching had the ring of truth, His word came with a unique authority, what He said hit home, reached the heart and changed the life. It has been in this way that the majority of people have been won to Christ ever since. People have been confronted by God through His word in a way they cannot deny. This is what is meant when people say that scripture is *self-authenticating*.

We will examine three ways in which you can experience God through His word.

You can experience God's power in His word

The writer to the Hebrews tells us that the word of God is living and powerful, and sharper than any two-edged sword, 4. 12. This power is seen in how it transforms *sinners* and how it transforms *societies*.

The word of God transforms sinners
HARRY IRONSIDE was preaching the gospel at an open air meeting in San Francisco. A well-known agnostic challenged him to a debate the next week on Agnosticism versus Christianity. Here's how he responded:

"'I am very much interested in this challenge. Frankly, I am already announced for another meeting next Lord's Day afternoon at three o'clock, but I think it will be possible for me to get through with that in time to reach the Academy of Science by four, or if necessary I could arrange to have another speaker substitute for me at the meeting already advertised. Therefore I will be glad to agree to this debate on the following conditions: namely, that in order to prove that Mr.—— has something worth fighting for and worth debating about, he will promise to bring with him to the Hall next Sunday two people, whose qualifications I will give in a moment, as proof that agnosticism is of real value in changing human lives and building true character. First, he must promise to bring with him one man who was for years what we commonly call a "down-and-outer." I am not particular as to the exact nature of the sins that had wrecked his life and made him an outcast from society — whether a drunkard, or a criminal of some kind, or a victim of any sensual appetite — but a man who for years was under the power of evil habits from which he could not deliver himself, but who on some occasion entered one of Mr.——'s meetings and heard his glorification of agnosticism and his denunciations of the Bible and Christianity, and whose heart and mind as he listened to such an address were so deeply stirred that he went away from that meeting saying, 'Henceforth, I too am an agnostic!' and as a result of imbibing that particular philosophy he found that a new power had come into his life. The sins he once loved, now he hated, and righteousness and goodness were henceforth the ideals of his life. He is now an entirely new man, a credit to himself and an asset to society — all because he is an agnostic.

Secondly, I would like Mr.—— to promise to bring with him one woman — and I think he may have more difficulty in finding the woman than the man — who was once a poor, wrecked, characterless outcast, the slave of evil passions, and the victim of man's corrupt living". As I spoke I was within perhaps a stone's throw of San Francisco's infamous Barbary Coast, where so many young lives have been shipwrecked; and so I added, "Perhaps one who had lived for years in some evil resort on Pacific Street, or in some other nearby hell-hole, utterly lost, ruined and wretched because of her life of sin. But this woman also entered a hall where Mr.—— was loudly proclaiming his agnosticism and ridiculing the message of the Holy Scriptures. As she listened, hope was born in her heart, and she said, "This is just what I need to deliver me from the slavery of sin!" She followed the teaching until she became an intelligent agnostic or infidel. As a result, her whole being revolted against the degradation of the life she had been living. She fled from the den of iniquity where she had been held captive so long; and today, rehabilitated, she has won her way back to an honoured position in society and is living a clean, virtuous, happy life — all because she is an agnostic.

"Now, Mr.——," I exclaimed, "if you will promise to bring these two people with you as examples of what agnosticism will do, I will promise to meet you at the Hall at the hour appointed next Sunday, and I will bring with me at the very least one hundred men and women who for years lived in just such sinful degradation as I have tried to depict, but who have been gloriously saved through believing the message of the gospel which you ridicule. I will have these men and women with me on the platform as witnesses to the miraculous saving power of Jesus Christ, and as present-day proof of the truth of the Bible."

Turning to the little Salvation Army captain, I said, "Captain, have you any who could go with me to such a meeting?" She exclaimed with enthusiasm, "We can give you forty at least, just from this one corps, and we will give you a brass band to lead the procession!"

"Fine!" I answered. "Now, Mr.——, I will have no difficulty in picking up sixty others from various Missions, Gospel Halls,

223

and evangelical churches of the city, and if you promise faithfully to bring two such exhibits as I have described, I will come marching in at the head of such a procession, with the band playing 'Onward, Christian Soldiers,' and I will be ready for the debate."

I think Mr.—— had quite a sense of humour, for he smiled rather sardonically, waved his hand in a deprecating kind of way as much as to say, "Nothing doing!" and edging through the crowd he left the scene, while that great crowd clapped the Salvation Army and the street-preacher to the echo, for they well knew that in all the annals of unbelief no one ever heard of a philosophy of negation, such as agnosticism, making bad men and women good, and they also knew that this is what Christianity has been doing all down through the centuries.

Our gospel proves itself by what it accomplishes, as redeemed people from every walk of life, delivered from every type of sin, prove the regenerating and keeping power of the Christ of whom the Bible speaks'.[227]

IRONSIDE was certainly not exaggerating. Hundreds and hundreds of stories can be told of lives positively, powerfully and permanently transformed, not through religion, will-power or therapy, but through accepting the message of the gospel.[228] Atheism can't account for this, religion does not offer it. The only explanation that fits all the data is that the gospel is 'the power of God to salvation for everyone who believes', Rom. 1. 16, NKJV.

This is one of the many unique things about the biblical gospel; it doesn't just say if you trust Christ as your Saviour you will go to

---

[227] http://www.wholesomewords.org/etexts/ironside/irsrem4.html
[228] For more examples of these stories of conversion see, for example, WILLIAM MACDONALD's *The Wonders of God*, and *Our God is Wonderful*, both Gospel Folio Press, or LEE STROBEL's *The Case for Grace*, Zondervan.

heaven when you die. It says if you trust Christ as your Saviour you will get new life *now*. That's what it means to be born again. Look at some of the Bible promises:

> 'For God so loved the world that He gave His only begotten Son, that whoever believes in Him should not perish but have everlasting life', John 3. 16, NKJV.
> 'He who believes in the Son has everlasting life; and he who does not believe the Son shall not see life, but the wrath of God abides on him', John 3. 36, NKJV.
> 'Most assuredly, I say to you, he who hears My word and believes in Him who sent Me has everlasting life, and shall not come into judgment, but has passed from death into life', John 5. 24, NKJV.
> 'He who has the Son has life; he who does not have the Son of God does not have life. These things I have written to you who believe in the name of the Son of God, that you may know that you have eternal life', 1 John 5. 12-13, NKJV.

Eternal life is the life of God, and it is communicated to the believer at conversion. This results in the Christian having new appetites, abilities and aims in life. Things that previously she had no interest in or desire for, she now has the capacity to enjoy. Things that once he thought he couldn't live without, lose their sparkle and he can no longer feel comfortable engaging in. What has happened? The new birth!

When I was concerned about salvation I got down on my knees at the side of the bed and opened my Bible to John chapter 3 verse 16. I saw that the Lord Himself was making me a promise that if I would trust Him to save me I would never perish. I took Him at His word and jumped up off my knees with the wonderful joy of knowing I was saved. But there was something I didn't take much notice of when I was on my knees, and that was that He also promised that upon believing I would have everlasting life. It was only as time went by that I came to see that I had a desire for things that once held no appeal; I had an interest in things that none of my non-Christian friends had an interest in. I didn't read the Bible and pray because I had to, I did it because there was that within me that craved it. I had received eternal life. As Paul said to the Thessalonians, the word of God 'effectively works in you who believe', 1 Thess. 2. 13, NKJV.

This is similar to how we finished our previous chapter –we can trust the gospel because we can prove the Bible, or we can trust the Bible because we can prove the gospel. In presenting the evidence for Christianity, I often give people evidence that the Bible is God's word and thus they can believe the gospel, but in the experience of the vast majority of people, they believe the Bible because they have proved the gospel. They have seen in their own lives that the message of the gospel delivers on its promises.

This is a perfectly reasonable step. The Bible contains the message of the gospel, it is illustrated in narratives, it is anticipated in prophecies, it is preached in sermons, it is explained in epistles. If someone finds that this message does indeed have life-changing power and brings someone into a real relationship with God, then that is a good reason for believing that the book which contains this obviously divine message is a divine book.

When BILLY GRAHAM was faced with intellectual doubts about the inerrancy of scripture he reflected on what happened when he preached the Bible as the word of God:

> 'The Word became a hammer, breaking up stony hearts and shaping men into the likeness of God. Did not God say, "I will make My words in thy mouth fire" (Jer. 5:14), and "Is not My word like as a fire? Saith the LORD; and like a hammer that breaketh the rock in pieces (Jer. 23:29).
> I found that I could take a simple outline, then put a number of Scripture quotations under each point, and God would use it mightily to cause men to make full commitment to Christ'.[229]

---

[229] BILLY GRAHAM, "The Authority of the Scriptures," *Decision* (June 1963), cited in JOHN F. MACARTHUR, *Why Believe the Bible?*, Regal, 2007, p. 19.

His personal experience of knowing and seeing the power of God through the Bible in his own life and in the lives of others was sufficient grounds for a sensible faith that the Bible is the word of God.

An electrical appliance is useless unless it is plugged in to a source of power. Once it is plugged in and switched on, it works in a way it couldn't have done on its own. So it is with the Christian – at the moment of conversion we are plugged in to a power source that enables us to do things we never could do before. The power source is the Saviour revealed in scripture.

The Biblical gospel isn't calling on you to take a gamble on something you can't prove. You can, today, now, be 'born again . . . by the word of God which lives and abides forever', 1 Pet. 1. 23, NKJV.

The word of God transforms societies
What has the influence of the Bible been on societies? Some would like to paint it as a dark picture of oppression and tyranny, crusades and witch trials.[230] That would be a very inaccurate and unfair portrait of the impact of Biblical Christianity on history. It is inaccurate because of the massive good that Biblical teaching has brought to our world and it is unfair because no worldview should be blamed for those who live in violation of it. Yes, there have been sad examples of so-called Christianity being spread by the sword, but the very nature of the gospel shows that such efforts are not only wicked but useless – the gospel calls on people to repent and believe, and while you can make someone *say* 'I repent and believe', you cannot *make* someone repent and believe.

---

[230] It is worth noting that atheist dictators were responsible for more deaths in the twentieth century than all religions combined in all the previous nineteen centuries combined, see for example: https://www.str.org/articles/the-real-murderers-atheism-or-christianity#.WBN1LdQrKt8.

D. JAMES KENNEDY wrote:

> 'Christianity has been a boon to mankind . . . (and) has had a beneficent effect upon the human race . . . Most people today who live in an ostensibly Christian environment with Christian ethics do not realise how much we owe Jesus of Nazareth . . . What goodness and mercy there is in this world has come in large measure from him.[231]

That is quite a claim, and I will briefly present some of the evidence that backs it up. It will be a very small sample from a very large pool, because, as JOHN BLANCHARD said regarding the Bible's positive impact, 'The difficulty here is not in beginning to answer the question, but in knowing when to stop'.[232]

A moral revolution took place as biblical Christianity spread. For the first time meekness and humility were seen as virtues.

> 'For Aristotle and the Greek philosophers generally, the "worth" of a human being could be ranked; some people were simply worth more than others – notably the intelligent, the beautiful, the proud, and so forth. Moreover, after philosophy, or intelligence, pride was the core virtue of the classical philosophical outlook, the "crown of the virtues"'.[233]

Into this moral milieu came the message of the gospel centring on the one who, although in the form of God, made Himself of no reputation, and humbled Himself to the extent of death on a cross, Phil. 2. 5-8. PATRICK GLYNN states that, even though meekness and humility might have been prized and practiced by some preceding the advent of

---

[231] D. JAMES KENNEDY, *Why I Believe*, Word, 1980, pp. 118, 121, cited in LEE STROBEL, *The Case for Faith, A Journalist Investigates the Toughest Objections to Christianity*, Zondervan, 2000, p. 271.

[232] JOHN BLANCHARD, *Does God Believe in Atheists?*, Evangelical Press, 2000, p. 412.

[233] PATRICK GLYNN, *God: The Evidence, The Reconciliation of Faith and Reason in a Postsecular World*, Prima Publishing, 1999, p. 155.

Christianity, 'as a purely historical matter, the New Testament is the point where these values entered the bloodstream of human history, where the vision appeared with a wholeness and emphasis capable of transforming the nature of human societies'''.[234]

Historian, TOM HOLLAND, had his mind changed on the impact of Christianity on the world as he studied the moral landscape that preceded it:

> 'The longer I spent immersed in the study of classical antiquity, the more alien and unsettling I came to find it. The values of Leonidas, whose people had practised a peculiarly murderous form of eugenics, and trained their young to kill uppity *Untermenschen* by night, were nothing that I recognised as my own; nor were those of Caesar, who was reported to have killed a million Gauls and enslaved a million more. It was not just the extremes of callousness that I came to find shocking, but the lack of a sense that the poor or the weak might have any intrinsic value'.[235]

The doctrine that transformed the ethical atmosphere, according to Holland, was, 'We preach Christ crucified', 1 Cor. 1. 23. This message of God condescending to suffer for His creatures transformed individuals and revolutionised humanity generally, so that,

> 'Today, even as belief in God fades across the West, the countries that were once collectively known as Christendom continue to bear the stamp of the two-millennia-old revolution that Christianity represents. It is the principal reason why, by and large, most of us who live in post-Christian societies still take for granted that it is nobler to suffer than to inflict suffering. It is why we generally assume that every human life is of equal value. In my morals and

---

[234] *Ibid.*, p. 156.
[235] http://www.newstatesman.com/politics/religion/2016/09/tom-holland-why-i-was-wrong-about-christianity

ethics, I have learned to accept that I am not Greek or Roman at all, but thoroughly and proudly Christian'.[236]

TERTULLIAN, writing at the end of the second century, commented about 'the brand' those around put on the Christians, "'See" they say, "how they love one another . . . how they are ready even to die for one another"'.[237] This was said about them with a sneer – it was perceived as soft, weak and unworthy. The gospel totally revolutionized what morality looked like and enthroned love as the supreme virtue.

The love of the early Christians extended beyond their own community. For example, they opposed the widespread practice of infanticide. In the Greek and Roman world 'infanticide was infamously universal',[238] especially if the child was deformed, or if the parents didn't want a large family.[239] The Christians preached and wrote against such cruel and selfish behaviour.

They also looked after the children who were callously and frequently abandoned. ALVIN SCHMIDT documents examples of how the early Christians 'provided protection and nourishment for abandoned children, some of whom were deformed as a result of failed abortions'. He says, 'Christian writings are replete with examples of Christians adopting throw-away children'. This ultimately led to Emperor Valentinian outlawing infanticide and criminalizing child abandonment in AD 374.[240]

And they opposed the gladiatorial contests. W. E. H. LECKY stated that 'There is scarcely any single reform so important in the moral history

---

[236] *Ibid.*
[237] TERTULLIAN, *Apology*, ch. 39, Master Christian Library.
[238] FREDERIC FARRAR, *The Early Days of Christianity*, A. L. Burt Publishers, 1882, cited in ALVIN J. SCHMIDT, *How Christianity Changed the World*, Zondervan, 2004, loc 939.
[239] *Ibid.*, loc 939. How sadly familiar this sounds. The 'pro-choice' movement is not a movement forward, but backward into a cruel, pagan culture that the gospel took humanity out of.
[240] *Ibid.*, loc 1014-1023.

of mankind as the suppression of the gladiatorial shows, a feat that must be almost exclusively ascribed to the Christian church'.[241]

This counter-cultural belief that everyone, including the deformed child and the despised slave, was valuable, was sourced exclusively in the Bible, and it was this belief that made such a massive difference in the world.

These are just some of the examples of the way society was impacted in the early dawn of Christianity. To borrow from and adapt Hebrews chapter 11 verses 32-38:

> *'And what shall I more say? For the time would fail me to tell of Barnardo, Guthrie, Muller, Carey, Carmichael, Dunant, Howard, Fry, Booth, Nightingale and Wilberforce, who through faith in the Bible subdued kingdoms, wrought righteousness, obtained promises, filled the mouths and minds of the poor, quenched the violence of the fires of widow-burning, caused many to escape the sword of Gladiators and human sacrifice, out of weakness were made strong to support the weak, waxed valiant in the fight against slavery, turned to flight the oppressive laws of nations. Women received their dignity again, and others faithfully served, not accepting an easy life. And others had trial of cruel mocking and scourging, yea, moreover of bonds and imprisonments: they were stoned, they were sawn asunder, were tempted, were slain with the sword: they wandered about in poverty; being destitute, afflicted, tormented, all for the blessing and betterment of their fellowmen, and all based on their confidence in and commitment to the Bible. We can say of them, "of whom the world was not worthy"'.*

What about other worldviews? Can they put up a similar record? Quite simply there is no competition. No other worldview has had such a powerful and positive effect on the lives of so many.

---

[241] W. E. H. LECKY, *History of European Morals*, cited in Schmidt, *How Christianity Changed the World*, loc 1232-1241.

MATTHEW PARRIS testified to the positive effect of not just *Christians* but *Christianity* in the land of his boyhood, Malawi:

> 'Now a confirmed atheist, I've become convinced of the enormous contribution that Christian evangelism makes in Africa: sharply distinct from the work of secular NGOs, government projects and international aid efforts. These alone will not do. Education and training alone will not do. In Africa Christianity changes people's hearts. It brings a spiritual transformation. The rebirth is real. The change is good.
>
> I used to avoid this truth by applauding – as you can – the practical work of mission churches in Africa. It's a pity, I would say, that salvation is part of the package, but Christians black and white, working in Africa, do heal the sick, do teach people to read and write; and only the severest kind of secularist could see a mission hospital or school and say the world would be better without it. I would allow that if faith was needed to motivate missionaries to help, then, fine: but what counted was the help, not the faith.
>
> But this doesn't fit the facts. Faith does more than support the missionary; it is also transferred to his flock. This is the effect that matters so immensely, and which I cannot help observing'.[242]

This is why LECKY called Christianity 'the most powerful moral lever that has ever been applied to the affairs of man'.[243]

The world has truly felt the power of God through the Bible, sadly so many never bother to thank Him.

---

[242] MATTHEW PARRIS, *As an atheist, I truly believe Africa needs God*, *The Times*, 27th December 2008.
[243] LECKY, *History of European Morals*, available at http://leporollak.hu/egyhtori/LECKY3.HTM.

You can experience God's perfection in His word

How would you go about convincing someone of the beauty of a piece of music, or what would you do to prove to them that a particular food was delicious? You would probably sit them down and make them listen to the music or taste the food. But if your friend happened to be tone deaf, or had lost his ability to taste food, that wouldn't cause you to doubt the reality of what you have enjoyed. His inability to hear or taste doesn't invalidate your experience of the beauty of the music or the deliciousness of the food.

It is like that with the Bible. Millions of us have been captivated by the beauty and delighted by the sweetness of the scriptures. We have seen divine glory shine from its pages and it convinces us over and over again that it is the very revelation of God. But many people have looked at the Bible and are utterly unimpressed. They hear no melody, they taste no sweetness. But what if they are spiritually tone deaf or there is something wrong with their spiritual taste buds?

You may think this is an unfair, and very convenient, way to argue, but we need to recognize that the Bible itself says that its beauties cannot be appreciated apart from the miracle of regeneration and the impartation of the Holy Spirit of God. The unconverted person is spiritually blind to the glory of God; when he says 'I've read the Bible and I don't see anything glorious in it!' he is only confirming what the Bible teaches.

> 'But the natural man does not receive the things of the Spirit of God, for they are foolishness to him; nor can he know them, because they are spiritually discerned', 1 Cor. 2. 14, NKJV.

> 'But even if our gospel is veiled, it is veiled to those who are perishing, whose minds the god of this age has blinded, who do not believe, lest the light of the gospel of the glory of Christ, who is the image of God, should shine on them. For we do not preach ourselves, but Christ Jesus the Lord, and ourselves your bondservants for Jesus' sake. For it is the God who

233

commanded light to shine out of darkness, who has shone in our hearts to give the light of the knowledge of the glory of God in the face of Jesus Christ', 2 Cor. 4. 3-6, NKJV.

If the Bible is the word of God then its beauty and perfections cannot be appreciated by those who have not had their spiritual eyes opened. MICHAEL KRUGER writes:

> 'It is here, then, that we come to the crux of the matter. Should Christians abandon their commitment to the canon's authority because biblical critics, who view scriptural interpretation as merely a human enterprise, claim to have discovered theological incongruities? No, because Christians have no grounds for thinking that those without the Spirit can rightly discern such things – indeed, Christians have good grounds for thinking they cannot. One might as well ask whether Joshua Bell, world-renowned violinist, should abandon his musical career because his concert in a Washington, DC metro station (on a 3.5-million-dollar Stradivarius) was met with disinterest and boredom. The answer depends on whether we have reason to think that the average pedestrians in the DC metro station can identify musical genius when they hear it. Apparently they cannot. When all was done, Bell had not drawn a crowd, was never given a single instance of applause, and left with a paltry $32.17'.[244]

The claim the Bible makes is that God's glory shines through its teachings, but the warmth of that glory will not be felt in the soul of one who is 'dead in trespasses and in sins', Eph. 2. 1, and the light of that glory will not be seen by one who is 'blinded' by 'the god of this age', 2 Cor. 4. 4, NKJV.

This thesis has been confirmed in real life experience. Those who have never been born again don't see the glory of God in the text,

---

[244] MICHAEL J. KRUGER, *Canon Revisited: Establishing the Origins and Authority of the New Testament Books*, Crossway, 2012, loc 3820-3830.

which is exactly what the Bible anticipates. But on the other hand, there have been multitudes who once yawned, shrugged or scoffed at the Bible, it held no appeal to us, but then something happened; suddenly, we found ourselves enthralled by it – we could see beauty we never saw before, we had an appetite for it that we never had before. This book that once seemed as dry as dust and as dull as ditchwater came alive to us, or rather we came alive to it. This is what we would expect to happen if the Bible is God's word.

> 'Things of the Spirit are spiritually discerned. For him who is spiritual, divine perfection shines forth in every page; and the unity of the whole, the perfect connection of its several parts, the relation of these parts to each other and to all the ways of God, to the Person of Christ, to the Old Testament, to the heart of the renewed man, to the necessities of sinful man, to the dangers and difficulties which have sprung up in the church — all combine to crown with divine glory the demonstration of the origin and the authorship of the book which contains these things'.[245]

This sight of divine glory ensures that the simplest believer, without access to apologetics, has good reason for believing the Bible is from God. JONATHAN EDWARDS was greatly concerned that the uneducated to whom he ministered would have accessible and adequate reasons for believing the Bible to be the word of God. To him it was unthinkable that the vast majority of Christians would have to wade into the academic world or just take the word of scholars in order to be justified in believing in the inspiration of scripture:

> 'Miserable is the condition of the Houssatunnuck Indians and others, who have lately manifested a desire to be instructed in Christianity, if they can come at no evidence of the truth of

---

[245] J. N. DARBY, *Letter on the Divine Inspiration of the Holy Scriptures*, http://www.stempublishing.com/authors/darby/DOCTRINE/23001F.html.

Christianity, sufficient to induce them to sell all for Christ, in any other way but this [path of historical reasoning]'.[246]
JOHN PIPER shows that Edwards pointed to the divine glory of Scripture as the means by which believers can have a well-grounded faith.[247]

So, unless the unbeliever is presuming the Bible is not God's word, he will need to acknowledge the possibility that the reason he sees no perfection in scripture is because of a spiritual problem.

The psalmist prayed, 'Open thou mine eyes, that I may behold wondrous things out of thy law', Ps. 119. 18. Make it your prayer too as we look at ways the perfections of the scriptures are seen.

Its perfection in regard to apparent contradictions
David was a real sceptic, and when I met him he took the opportunity to give me a page filled on both sides with 'contradictions' in what the Bible teaches. He told me in a sarcastic tone to come back to him when I had them all sorted out . . . so I did. I told him that rather than his list denting my confidence in the Bible it actually fortified it, because the supposed contradictions can be cleared up just by reading carefully and contextually. The more closely someone reads the Bible the more the difficulties disappear and the perfection is apparent. The fact that all of these apparent contradictions end up harmonizing so beautifully shows that the Bible isn't just a human work. I will give you a few of the issues he raised.

How to be saved
My sceptical friend said that the Bible presents two ways of salvation. The rich young ruler of Matthew chapter 19 was told to keep the law, while the Philippian jailor of Acts chapter 16 was told to believe on

---

[246] JONATHAN EDWARDS, *A Treatise Concerning Religious Affections*, vol. 2, *The Works of Jonathan Edwards*, ed. John Smith, Yale University Press, 1957, p. 304, cited in JOHN PIPER, *A Peculiar Glory, How the Christian Scriptures reveal their complete truthfulness*, IVP, 2016, pp. 133-134, inclusion his.
[247] *Ibid.*, pp. 138, 142.

the Lord Jesus Christ. He added that Paul seemed confused on the matter too. In Romans chapter 2 verse 13 he said, 'For not the hearers of the law are just before God, but the doers of the law shall be justified'. Then in chapter 3 verse 20 he said, 'Therefore by the deeds of the law there shall no flesh be justified in His sight'.

I pointed out to David that, although he didn't believe Paul was writing under the influence of the Holy Spirit, he would have to admit that Paul wasn't stupid. Did he really think that a man who could write a letter like Romans would contradict himself within the space of a page, and be confused in his own mind on how to be justified? Perhaps David was the one confused and not Paul. The answer to the supposed conflict between Romans chapter 2 verse 13 and chapter 3 verse 20 lies in reading what comes between those two verses! Paul is mounting an argument. He is showing in the first three chapters that the human race needs the gospel. He is saying in chapter 2 verse 13 that hearing the law doesn't justify anyone; if someone wants to be declared righteous based on how good he is, then he has to be a doer of the law, that is, he has to obey the law continually and completely. Paul goes on to show that no one has done that – the whole world is guilty before God, '*Therefore* by the deeds of the law there shall no flesh be justified in His sight: *for by the law is the knowledge of sin*', Rom. 3. 20, emphasis added. If someone was completely blameless then he would be declared righteous, but none has kept the law in its entirety, and that is why no one will be justified by his efforts at law-keeping; the law shows us our guilt.

This sorts out why the Lord gave the answer He did to the rich young ruler. Look at the incident:

> 'Now behold, one came and said to Him, "Good Teacher, what good thing shall I do that I may have eternal life?" So He said to him, "Why do you call Me good? No one is good but One, that is, God. But if you want to enter into life, keep the commandments." He said to Him, "Which ones?" Jesus said, "'You shall not murder,' 'You shall not commit adultery,' 'You shall not steal,' 'You shall not bear false witness,' 'Honor your

father and your mother,' and, 'You shall love your neighbor as yourself.'" The young man said to Him, "All these things I have kept from my youth. What do I still lack?" Jesus said to him, "If you want to be perfect, go, sell what you have and give to the poor, and you will have treasure in heaven; and come, follow Me." But when the young man heard that saying, he went away sorrowful, for he had great possessions', Matt. 19. 16-22, NKJV.

The Lord was pulling this young man up on his loose use of the word *good*. He called the Lord a good teacher, then wanted to know what good thing he could do to have eternal life (notice, he did not ask how to be *saved*). He thought eternal life was achieved by doing good, so the Lord says that if he wants to go down that route then he will have to keep the commandments. The young man gets a bit uncomfortable and asks which commandments he has to keep. Christ lists several of the ones to do with our responsibilities to others. The young ruler claims to have kept them; he still harbours a hope of being good enough. So the Lord put to Him what the entire law demands (i.e., we are to love the Lord our God with all our heart, soul and mind, and to love our neighbour as ourselves, Matt. 22. 37-40.

So, if this man claims he has kept those ones relating to loving his neighbour as himself, he won't be reluctant to sell all that he has and give to the poor. If he really is keeping God's law he won't be content to let the poor languish while he has an abundance. And furthermore, if he's going to do what the law requires in relation to loving God then he will 'come, take up the cross, and follow Me'.

The Lord wasn't teaching this man the way of salvation. He was teaching the man that he needed salvation because he was a law-breaker; he had fallen short of God's standard. The law was intended to bring this man to see his guilt and helplessness, and to cast him upon the grace of the Lord Jesus Christ.

The man went away sad, proving he neither loved God with all his heart, nor did he love his neighbour as himself – he went away

238

condemned by the law, but, sadly, he went away from the one who could have, and would have, saved him from the condemnation of the law if he had only turned to Him in repentance and faith.

When we come to Acts chapter 16 the attitude of the questioner is completely different:

> 'And he brought them out and said, "Sirs, what must I do to be saved?" So they said, "Believe on the Lord Jesus Christ, and you will be saved, you and your household"', Acts 16. 30-31, NKJV.

There is an increased urgency here – it's not merely, 'What . . . *shall* I do?' It's 'What *must* I do?' There is also a recognition of his danger – he's not just asking how to get eternal life, he wants to know how to be *saved*. There is no mention of 'What good thing shall I do?' He knows he isn't going to be saved by doing good things. That's why the answer was different – this was a man who knew his need and was ready for the gospel. It's the same principle as Romans chapter 2 verse 13 and chapter 3 verse 20; the self-righteous need to be humbled by the law to see their need of grace. These surface contradictions harmonize perfectly.[248]

Does God repent?

In one chapter, 1 Samuel chapter 15, we read that God tells Samuel He has repented, v. 11, and then Samuel says that God will not repent, v. 29, so which is it?

> 'Then came the word of the Lord unto Samuel, saying, It repenteth me that I have set up Saul to be king: for he is turned back from following me, and hath not performed my commandments. And it grieved Samuel; and he cried unto the LORD all night', vv. 10-11.

---

[248] I have written elsewhere about the harmony between Paul and James on the subject of justification. See PAUL McCAULEY, *He that Believeth, Establishing the Truth of Eternal Security*, John Ritchie Ltd, 2015, pp. 39-44.

239

'And Samuel said unto him, The Lord hath rent the kingdom of Israel from thee this day, and hath given it to a neighbour of thine, that is better than thou. And also the Strength of Israel will not lie nor repent: for He is not a man, that He should repent', vv. 28-29.

Before answering the problem directly, let's repeat what was said in relation to Paul supposedly contradicting himself. Any fair-minded person will acknowledge that the writer of 1 Samuel was not an idiot, and it is evident that he saw no contradiction, and so, if we see a contradiction, it is probably because we are not getting the intent of the author and we are misunderstanding his meaning.

Fair enough, so how do we square this? The answer is found in seeing the meaning of repentance, the contexts in which God repents, and the reasons for the repentance. Repentance means a change of mind or a change of attitude. Scripture shows that God repents when there is a change in the attitude or actions of men, so God says He is going to do something, e.g. bless or judge, but the people to whom or about whom He speaks change their behaviour or attitude to Him, for good or evil, that then leads to God changing the manner in which He acts towards them. Consider this, the Bible says the person who sins will perish, Rom. 2. 12, but it also says that the person who believes in Christ won't perish, John 3. 16, so we can state it like this, if we repent then God will repent. Our repentance changes our status before God so He acts towards us differently than He would have had we not repented. This isn't because of a change in God's character, it's because of the consistency of His character. The change has occurred in us, necessitating a change in how we are treated by God.

When we read that God doesn't repent, what it means is that God doesn't just change His mind – He doesn't think about things and discover a better way of doing things, or reflect on His actions and decide He was wrong. We often do that, we realize the way we had been going about something was wrong, ineffective or inefficient, and so we adjust – the repentance is based on us seeing something wrong in ourselves. In that sense, God never repents. He never has to change His mind and actions based on His behaviour, but He will change His actions towards us based on our behaviour. If there's no change in our attitude or behaviour there will be no change in His.

> 'What the first set of passages says [about God not repenting] is absolutely true, that God is absolutely unchangeable. He is "the same yesterday, and today, and for ever" (Heb. 13. 8). But the second class of passages is also true [about God repenting], for if God does remain the same in character, infinitely hating sin and absolutely unchangeable in His purpose to visit sin with judgement, then if any city or any person changes in attitude toward sin, God must necessarily change in His attitude toward that person or city. If God remains the same, if His attitude toward sin and righteousness is unchanging, then His dealings with men must change as they turn from sin to repentance'.[249]

Has anyone seen God?
David brought up the words of John chapter 1 verse 18:

> 'No man hath seen God at any time; the only begotten Son, which is in the bosom of the Father, he hath declared him'.

But then he cited references in the Old Testament where people saw God, such as:

> 'Then went up Moses, and Aaron, Nadab, and Abihu, and seventy of the elders of Israel: and they saw the God of Israel: and there was under His feet as it were a paved work of a sapphire stone, and as it were the body of heaven in His clearness', Exod. 24. 9-10.

---

[249] R. A. TORREY, *Difficulties in the Bible: Alleged Errors and Contradictions*, loc 894-902.

241

But John chapter 1 verse 18 doesn't contradict these Old Testament passages, *it explains them*. In John chapter 1 verse 18, God clearly refers to God the Father, and no one has seen Him at any time, so those Old Testament appearances of God were appearances of the Son. Because the Son shares the nature of God, the Old Testament passages are true, they saw God, and John chapter 1 verse 18 is also true, no one has ever seen God the Father.[250]

The attempts to catch the Bible out in a contradiction all fail. The supposed conflicts are only supposed.[251] The perfection is real.

Its perfection in regard to the person of Christ
We all make mistakes and it is especially easy when you are dealing with complex subjects. What subject could be more complex than the incarnation of the Son of God? The union of two natures in one person is something that we will never fully grasp, Matt. 11. 27, but the amazing thing is that when the writers of the Bible address the subject they never make a mistake. Every time they deal with it they capture the truth perfectly. I'll give you some examples.

I heard a man state in a presentation that Paul denied that Jesus was truly human. His proof text for this was Philippians chapter 2 verse 7, which he misquoted in this way, Christ 'was made in the likeness of man', meaning He wasn't really man. Now, if that had been what the verse said, then he would be right, it would be a denial of Christ's humanity, but that's not what Paul wrote. What Philippians chapter 2 verse 7 actually says is that Christ 'was made in the likeness of men'.

---

[250] The NET, following the oldest manuscripts, translates John chapter 1 verse 18 this way: 'No one has ever seen God. The only one, Himself God, who is in closest fellowship with the Father, has made God known'.

[251] For more information on supposed contradictions, see, for example, TORREY, *Difficulties in the Bible*; GLEASON L. ARCHER, *New International Encyclopedia of Bible Difficulties*; JAMES MONTGOMERY BOICE, *Dealing with Bible Problems, Alleged Errors and Contradictions in the Bible*; SIDNEY COLLETT, *The Scriptures of Truth*; KEN HAM, (ed.), *Demolishing Supposed Bible Contradictions*, vol. 1; TIM CHAFFEY, BODIE HODGE & KEN HAM, (ed.), *Demolishing Supposed Bible Contradictions*, vol. 2.

He was not like a man, He was like other men – there was a difference between the Lord and other men, but the difference was not physical because the next verse tells us he was 'found in fashion as a man'. He had all the physical attributes of a man. The difference was moral – He was not a sinner. So, a careful look at what is written shows the perfection of God's word because it guards not only the true humanity of Christ, but His sinless humanity too.

A similar statement is found in Romans chapter 8 verse 3. Paul writes about how God sent 'His Son, in the likeness of sinful flesh'. Notice he didn't write, 'in the likeness of flesh'. That would have denied the true humanity of Christ. Nor did he write, 'in sinful flesh'. That would have denied the sinless humanity of Christ. Just like Philippians chapter 2 verse 7, the expression used is perfect.

In these two passages in which the humanity of Christ is affirmed, we find His deity is asserted as well. The one who was made in the likeness of men was the one who was 'in the form of God', Phil. 2. 6. The one who was in the likeness of sinful flesh was the Son who was sent. The Bible not only teaches the real humanity of Christ, it always does so in connection with an affirmation of His deity. Consider the following examples:

Isaiah chapter 7 verse 14
> 'Therefore the Lord himself shall give you a sign; Behold, a virgin shall conceive, and bear a son, and shall call his name Immanuel'.

The humanity of Christ is clearly taught, the virgin bears a son, but His deity is just as clear, because He is to be called Immanuel, meaning *God with us.*

Isaiah chapter 9 verse 6
> 'For unto us a child is born, unto us a Son is given: and the government shall be upon his shoulder: and his name shall be called Wonderful, Counsellor, The mighty God, The everlasting Father, The Prince of Peace'.

This Messianic prophecy tells us that the child born, His humanity, would be the Son given, His deity. He would be the mighty God, the same title given to *Yahweh* in the next chapter, 10. 21.

Micah chapter 5 verse 2
> 'But thou, Bethlehem Ephratah, though thou be little among the thousands of Judah, yet out of thee shall he come forth unto me that is to be ruler in Israel; whose goings forth have been from of old, from everlasting'.

This famous prophecy of the birth of the Messiah shows that He is the eternally pre-existent one.

John chapter 1 verse 30
> 'This is he of whom I said, After me cometh a man which is preferred before me: for he was before me'.

As regards the Lord's human nature, He was after John the Baptist, but as regards His divine nature He was before him.

John chapter 18 verse 37
> 'Pilate therefore said unto him, Art thou a king then? Jesus answered, Thou sayest that I am a king. To this end was I born, and for this cause came I into the world, that I should bear witness unto the truth. Every one that is of the truth heareth my voice'.

This is the only time in the Gospels where the Lord Jesus Christ refers to His own birth, but notice what He adds; not only does He say He was born, but He says He *came into the world*, implying His pre-existence.

Romans chapter 9 verse 5
> 'Whose are the fathers, and of whom as concerning the flesh Christ came, who is over all, God blessed for ever. Amen'.

There is a statement about the human ancestry of the Messiah, but then a statement that, in another sense, He has no human ancestry – He is over all, God blessed forever.[252]

Hebrews chapter 2 verse 14
> 'Forasmuch then as the children are partakers of flesh and blood, he also himself likewise took part of the same; that through death he might destroy him that had the power of death, that is, the devil'.

Mere mortals are spoken of here as partaking of flesh and blood, but it doesn't say of the Lord Jesus that He was partaker; it says He took part of the same. It expresses the fact that He willingly entered into human experience and obviously, therefore, pre-existed.

Revelation chapter 22 verse 16
> 'I Jesus have sent mine angel to testify unto you these things in the churches. I am the root and the offspring of David, and the bright and morning star'.

The Lord describes Himself as David's offspring, but also as David's root. He came from David, yet David came from Him. How can this be? The answer is easy when we see that the Lord is both God and man. He is the root of David as regards His deity – He gave David life and brought him into existence. He is the offspring of David as regards His humanity – He came from David's family.

These are just a few examples of how the scriptures present the person of Christ so perfectly and consistently. There isn't one discordant note from all the different writers. If the Bible were just a human book, surely somewhere along the way there would be a

---

[252] Some (liberal) translations obscure the force of the verse by inserting a full stop before 'God blessed forever'. For proof that the verse is calling Christ God, see ROBERT M. BOWMAN JR & J. ED KOMOSZEWSKI, *Putting Jesus in His Place: The Case for the Deity of Christ*, Kregel Publications, 2007, pp. 147-148.

statement that would creep in that would jar with the others, but it never happens – it's all perfect.

Its perfection in relation to the Trinity
The early Christians took a lot of time and effort to craft their language and refine their understanding of the nature of God, but the remarkable thing is that the writers of scripture, who weren't thinking in formal creeds about the nature of God, present the truth of the plurality of persons within the nature of the one true God perfectly. Let's look at a few passages where the doctrine of the Trinity is implied and see the perfect accuracy of scripture.

Genesis chapter 1 verses 26-27
> 'And God said, Let us make man in our image, after our likeness: and let them have dominion over the fish of the sea, and over the fowl of the air, and over the cattle, and over all the earth, and over every creeping thing that creepeth upon the earth. So God created man in His own image, in the image of God created he him; male and female created he them'.

The use of the plural pronouns, 'Let *us* make' and 'in *our* image', imply a plurality of persons, but it is clear that God alone did the making and man is made in the image of God alone. The table shows the perfect correspondence of plurality and singularity.

	Plurality	**Singular**
Creation	'Let *us* make man'	'So *God* created man . . . created *he* him, male and female created *he* them'.
Image	'in *our* image'	'in *his* own image, in the image of *God*'

How do we account for the plurality of persons alongside the truth that creation was an act of God alone? The question is answered perfectly by the doctrine of the Trinity.

Isaiah chapter 6 verse 8

> 'Also I heard the voice of the Lord, saying, Whom shall I send, and who will go for us? Then said I, Here am I; send me'.

Isaiah's commission was from the Lord – 'Whom shall *I* send', and yet there was a plurality – 'and who will go for *us?*' The triune God is the one doing the sending.

Zechariah chapter 2 verses 8-11

> 'For thus says the LORD of hosts: "He sent Me after glory, to the nations which plunder you; for he who touches you touches the apple of His eye. For surely I will shake My hand against them, and they shall become spoil for their servants. Then you will know that the LORD of hosts has sent Me. Sing and rejoice, O daughter of Zion! For behold, I am coming and I will dwell in your midst," says the LORD. "Many nations shall be joined to the LORD in that day, and they shall become My people. And I will dwell in your midst. Then you will know that the LORD of hosts has sent Me to you', NKJV.

This passage throws up a paradox: the Lord of hosts, *Yahweh*, speaks about being sent by the Lord of hosts. He speaks about the nation of Israel as 'the apple of His eye', then says, 'I will shake My hand against them'. He says the nations shall be joined to *Yahweh*, and 'they shall become My people. And I will dwell in your midst'. There seems to be two *Yahwehs*, but that can't be; the confession of the Israelites was, 'Hear, O Israel: The Lord our God, the Lord is one!' Deut. 6. 4, NKJV.[253]

> 'Mystery of mysteries – here is Jehovah, yet sent by Jehovah! But it is the mystery of light and not of darkness to those who

---

[253] Despite the variety of ways different versions render this passage, C. F. KEIL shows that *Yahweh*'s words commence immediately after the introduction, 'For thus says the Lord of hosts', C. F. KEIL in *Keil & Delitzsch, Commentary on the Old Testament*, vol. 10, Hendrickson Publishers, 2006, p. 522.

have learned to know the blessed Triune God as He is revealed in the Scriptures'.[254]

There is no contradiction. Within the unique nature of the one true God there are three persons.

> 'Once again notice that Jehovah here says, "I will dwell", and then that Jehovah of Hosts sent Him. So the truth leaps again out of the page to us that Jehovah the Sender and Jehovah the Sent must be one'.[255]

The glory of the nature of God cannot be concealed. It received its full revelation with the incarnation of the Son and the descent of the Spirit, but the Old Testament provides a template for the being of God that only the Trinity can fill.

Matthew chapter 28 verse 19
> 'Go therefore and make disciples of all the nations, baptizing them in the name of the Father and of the Son and of the Holy Spirit', NKJV.

The Lord didn't say, 'baptizing them in the names of the Father, Son and Holy Spirit'. That would imply there are three distinct beings. Nor did He say, 'baptizing them in the name of Father, Son and Holy Spirit'. That could be taken to indicate that there are not three distinct persons, but merely three manifestations. The way He stated it shows that there is one divine name and nature, but three persons who share that name and nature. It is simply perfect.

Luke 15
The chapter commences with the complaint of the Pharisees and scribes, 'This man receives sinners and eats with them', Luke 15. 2,

---

[254] DAVID BARON, *Zechariah, A Commentary on His Visions and Prophecies*, Kregel, 2001, p. 74.
[255] JOHN J. STUBBS, *What the Bible Teaches, Zechariah*, John Ritchie Ltd, 2007, p. 338.

ESV. The Lord not only accepts the charge but gives a three-fold parable to show God's delight in receiving sinners.

The three stories He tells beautifully capture the activity of the triune God. The first story is to do with a shepherd who goes out after the sheep until he finds it, and then brings it home on his shoulders. We saw in chapter three how this shepherd portrays the Son of God; He was the one who left heaven 'to seek and to save that which was lost', Luke 19. 10. He is the one who carries the sinner home, 'He is able also to save them to the uttermost', Heb. 7. 25.

The woman seeking the silver illustrates the work of the Holy Spirit of God. The Holy Spirit is the divine person who takes the least prominent role in scripture; thus, a woman is used in the story. The woman lights the lamp and sweeps the house. The Spirit is the one who shines the light of God's word into the darkness of the human heart; He is the one who brings about conviction and illumination.[256]

Then, there is the story we call the prodigal son. The father in the story doesn't go out after the boy, he waits to receive him. Of course, God the Father didn't leave heaven. He sent His Son to go for the lost, and He sent His Spirit to do a convicting and illuminating work, and He waits to receive the repentant. There is another lovely touch about the story that shows the perfection of scripture: the boy comes to his senses in the far country, and decides to come home; he prepares his speech, 'I will arise and go to my father, and will say to him, "Father, I have sinned against heaven and before you, and I am no longer worthy to be called your son. Make me like one of your hired servants"', vv. 18-19, NKJV. However, when his father runs to embrace him, he starts to give his little speech, but he never gets to the bit, 'Make me like one of your hired servants'. The reason is we are not received by God on the basis of our works, nor are we received as those who have to earn their keep. We are received by grace.

---

[256] See, for example, John 16. 8-11; 1 Cor. 2. 4; 1 Thess. 1. 5.

The activity of the Trinity in the salvation of sinners is perfectly illustrated in this chapter.

John chapter 1 verse 1
> 'In the beginning was the Word, and the Word was with God, and the Word was God'.

This is how John commences his Gospel, and there are such depths of truth in this verse that it is sometimes difficult for the Christian to move beyond it to the rest of the Gospel. The more the verse is studied the more its perfections shine.

There are three clauses in the verse:

1) In the beginning was the Word,
2) And the Word was with God,
3) And the Word was God.

The first clause tells us the Word is eternal – when all things began the Word already was.

The second clause indicates the Word was equal *with* God but not equal *to* Him, that is, He is equal in position but distinct in person. 'God' in this clause has the definite article, and it is indicating that 'God' is being used as the name of a person here, so the Word was with the person called God.

The third clause tells us about the nature of the Word – the Word was God. The significant thing here is that 'God' does not have the definite article. If it did then it would mean that the Word was the person called God in clause two, and thus there would be a contradiction, i.e., the Word was with Himself. By dropping the article it is indicating that the Word has the same nature as the person called God. 'The Word is not who God is, but He is what God is'.[257]

---

[257] ANDREAS J. KOSTENBERGER & SCOTT R. SWAIN, *Father, Son and Spirit, The Trinity and John's Gospel*, Apollos, 2008, p. 113.

'If the Word is "all of God", and God is "all" of the Word, and the two terms are interchangeable, then how could the Word be "with" Himself. Such would make no sense. But John beautifully walks the fine line, balancing God's truth as he is "carried along" by the Holy Spirit', 2 Peter 1. 21, NIV.[258]

The way John puts his language is the only way he could have communicated that the Word is distinct in person but one in nature with God the Father.

Before we leave John chapter 1 verse 1, I want you to see how the three clauses of verse 1 weave themselves throughout the prologue, vv. 1-18, and the rest of the Gospel. Note the contrasts with John the Baptist:

'There was a man sent from God, whose name was John', 1. 6.

The word 'was' (*en* – imperfect tense) in the first clause of verse 1 indicates a timeless state of affairs, but in relation to John the word 'was' (*egeneto* – aorist tense) is different and indicates he came into existence. John was 'sent from God', but 'the Word was with God'. John was 'a man', but 'the Word was God'.

Look at the connections with verse 14:

'And the Word became flesh and dwelt among us', NKJV.

He who eternally *was*, *became*. He was *with God* came and *dwelt among us*. He who *was God* voluntarily *became flesh*.

John goes on to show us how the nation rejected this revelation of God in Christ. There are three occasions in John's Gospel prior to the cross when the Jewish leaders sought to kill Christ. In John chapter 8 verses 58-59 we read:

---

[258] JAMES R. WHITE, *The Forgotten Trinity, Recovering the Heart of Christian Belief*, Bethany House Publishers, 1998, loc 659.

'Jesus said unto them, Verily, verily, I say unto you, Before Abraham was, I am. Then took they up stones to cast at Him: but Jesus hid himself, and went out of the temple, going through the midst of them, and so passed by'.

The Lord wasn't merely claiming pre-existence; if He were, then He would have said, 'Before Abraham was, I was'.[259] He was claiming eternal existence, just as clause one of John chapter 1 verse 1 teaches.

John chapter 5 verses 17-18
'But Jesus answered them, My Father worketh hitherto, and I work. Therefore the Jews sought the more to kill Him, because He not only had broken the Sabbath, but said also that God was His Father, making Himself equal with God'.

The Jews rightly saw that the Lord Jesus was claiming equality with God, just as the second clause of John chapter 1 verse 1 teaches.

John chapter 10 verses 30-33
'I and my Father are one. Then the Jews took up stones again to stone him. Jesus answered them, Many good works have I showed you from my Father; for which of those works do ye stone me? The Jews answered him, saying, For a good work we stone thee not; but for blasphemy; and because that thou, being a man, makest thyself God'.

The Jews are rejecting the truth of the third clause of John chapter 1 verse 1 – the Word was God.

Now maybe John was just really careful and clever in placing all these things throughout his Gospel so that the three clauses link up in such a remarkable way with other passages, but as far as I'm concerned the perfection is clearly divine.

---

[259] And if that's all He was claiming He wouldn't have been guilty of blasphemy in their eyes or deserving of death.

1 Timothy chapter 5 verse 21
We have seen in Matthew chapter 28 verse 19 and John chapter 1 verse 1 how perfectly the definite article is employed to communicate the truth of the distinct divine persons sharing the same name and nature. Paul also shows how the definite article can be used to convey this fundamental truth.

> 'I charge thee before God, and the Lord Jesus Christ, and the elect angels, that thou observe these things without preferring one before another, doing nothing by partiality'.

In the Greek, Paul puts the definite article before *God*, but not before *Lord Jesus Christ* (or *Christ Jesus*, as the oldest manuscripts have it), but then he uses the definite article before *elect angels*. In doing so he creates two distinct groups, in one group there are God and Christ, in the other group there are the elect angels.

> 'The use of the one article with both 'God and Christ Jesus' unites them, both being Deity, while another article with 'the elect angels' sets them in contrast as creatures'.[260]

Had there been just one article it would have grouped angels with God. Had there been three articles it would have put Christ in a group between God and angels, but by the using the definite article twice, as Paul did, he puts Christ on the Creator side of the Creator/creature divide. It is a tiny detail, but it shows that the word of God is perfect right down to the tiny details.

Its perfection in relation to divine attributes
The *omni* attributes
The Bible is not a book of systematic theology. It doesn't have a chapter on the attributes of God. Our view of God's attributes is gleaned from looking at how the entirety of scripture reveals Him. There are three great incommunicable attributes that emerge from the Bible that are often linked – the three *omni* attributes: God is

---

[260] D. EDMOND HIEBERT, *First Timothy*, Moody Press, 1957, pp. 103-104.

omnipotent (all-powerful), omniscient (all-knowing) and omnipresent (active at every point in creation). I want to draw your attention to a few passages in which we see these three attributes portrayed perfectly.

Psalm 2 verses 1-4
> 'Why do the heathen rage, and the people imagine a vain thing? The kings of the earth set themselves, and the rulers take counsel together, against the Lord, and against his anointed, saying, Let us break their bands asunder, and cast away their cords from us. He that sitteth in the heavens shall laugh: the Lord shall have them in derision'.

The nations are raging and plotting. The kings of the earth set themselves, that is, they are setting themselves for a fight, a fight against an omnipotent God. The rulers are in their council chambers conspiring against an omniscient God. They want to break the cords of deity asunder and get away from an omnipresent God. Fighting against omnipotence, plotting against omniscience, and trying to get away from omnipresence; little wonder 'He that sitteth in the heavens shall laugh'.

Psalm 139
This psalm is built on these three attributes. In the first six verses the psalmist extols the truth of God's omniscience:

> 'O Lord, thou hast searched me, and known me. Thou knowest my downsitting and mine uprising, thou understandest my thought afar off. Thou compassest my path and my lying down, and art acquainted with all my ways. For there is not a word in my tongue, but, lo, O Lord, thou knowest it altogether. Thou hast beset me behind and before, and laid thine hand upon me. Such knowledge is too wonderful for me; it is high, I cannot attain unto it'.

In verses 7 to 12 he contemplates the omnipresence of God:

'Whither shall I go from thy Spirit? Or whither shall I flee from thy presence? If I ascend up into heaven, thou art there: if I make my bed in hell, behold, thou art there. If I take the wings of the morning, and dwell in the uttermost parts of the sea; even there shall thy hand lead me, and thy right hand shall hold me. If I say, Surely the darkness shall cover me; even the night shall be light about me. Yea, the darkness hideth not from thee; But the night shineth as the day: the darkness and the light are both alike to thee'.

Then in verses 13 and 14 he considers God's omnipotence:

'For thou hast possessed my reins: thou hast covered me in my mother's womb. I will praise thee; for I am fearfully and wonderfully made: marvellous are thy works; and that my soul knoweth right well'.

Philosophers speak about God having *maximal greatness*. Before such a phrase ever came into the mind of a philosopher, David in this psalm presented God as the maximally great being. He captured his greatness perfectly in Psalm 139.

1 Kings chapter 18 verse 27
The glory of the true God can be set in contrast with the emptiness of false gods. This is seen in Elijah's contest with the prophets of Baal. He is calling the nation of Israel away from idolatry and back to the living God, *Yahweh*, with whom they were in covenant relationship.

He challenges the prophets of Baal to call on their god to send fire to accept their sacrifice. All morning they jump around, crying and pleading. Then Elijah starts to poke fun at them:

'And so it was, at noon, that Elijah mocked them and said, "Cry aloud, for he is a god; either he is meditating, or he is busy, or he is on a journey, or perhaps he is sleeping and must be awakened"', NKJV.

255

Elijah is showing that their god isn't omniscient – *If he's meditating or busy he can't listen to your prayers at the same time*; he's not omnipresent – *Baal sometimes goes on journeys so perhaps he's absent at the moment*; and he's not omnipotent – *Your god gets tired and needs a rest.*[261]

What a contrast with the true God. Isaiah tells us, Isa. 40. 28, that He is 'the Creator of the ends of the earth', thus He is omnipresent – there's nowhere in creation where He is not present. He 'fainteth not, neither is weary', showing He is omnipotent. 'There is no searching of His understanding' because He is an omniscient God.

Daniel chapters 1-3
Daniel was whisked away from his home and dropped into the midst of a cesspit of idolatry in Babylon, but the glory of the God of Israel had captured his heart and wouldn't let him go.

In the first three chapters of his book we get a sight of these three attributes. In chapter one, although Daniel is far from Judah, God was still with him and working for him, e.g., 1. 9, 17, proving that God is omnipresent. He isn't confined to the borders of the Promised Land.

In chapter 2, Nebuchadnezzar wanted his wise men to tell him his dream and the interpretation. Daniel and his friends took this problem to the Lord in prayer, and when Daniel got the answer he praised God as the one who 'knoweth what is in the darkness', 2. 22. When he told the king the dream and its meaning, Nebuchadnezzar exclaimed, 'Of a truth it is, that your God is a God of gods, and a Lord of kings, and a revealer of secrets', 2. 47. God is omniscient.

Then, in chapter 3, Daniel's three friends were threatened with the fiery furnace if they wouldn't bow to Nebuchadnezzar's image. Nebuchadnezzar concluded his rant to them with these words, 'and who is that God that shall deliver you out of my hands?' 3. 15.

---

[261] I'm indebted to Mr Brian Currie for this insight.

Shadrach, Meshach and Abed-nego answered, 'our God whom we serve is able to deliver us from the burning fiery furnace', 3. 17, and that's exactly what He did, causing Nebuchadnezzar to confess that 'there is no other god that can deliver after this sort', 3. 29. Nebuchadnezzar learnt that God is omnipotent.

Luke chapter 7
When we come into the New Testament we see that the Lord Jesus has these three attributes, and there are several places where all three of them are evident. In Luke chapter 7 there are three people who are blessed by the Lord. The first one is the centurion's servant, 7. 1-10. The Lord healed this man from a distance, proving that He is omnipresent. Distance is nothing to Him.

The second person blessed is the widow of Nain, 7. 11-17. Her son, a young man, was dead and was being carried to the grave when the funeral cortege encountered Christ and His company. The Lord raised him from the dead, proving that He is omnipotent. Others had raised people from the dead in scripture, but they did it by crying to the Lord, 1 Kgs. 17. 20-22, praying to the Lord, 2 Kgs. 4. 33, kneeling down and praying, Acts 9. 40. The Lord Jesus didn't cry to God or kneel and pray, He said, 'Young man, *I say unto thee*, Arise', 7. 14, (emphasis added) – it was a display of His own power.[262]

The third person who receives blessing from the Lord in the chapter is the woman of the city who was notorious for her sin. The Lord Jesus was in the home of Simon the Pharisee, and this woman crept in and came to the feet of Christ. When Simon saw this he was disgusted, and figured that Jesus obviously didn't know what this woman was like, 7. 39, but the Lord showed Simon that He not only knew this woman's history, He knew Simon's heart – He truly is omniscient. He was able to pronounce that the woman's many sins were all forgiven.

---

[262] Significantly it is in this section that Luke for the first time in his narration of events calls Jesus 'Lord', v. 13. Luke, as a physician, could help the sick, but he could do nothing for the dead. He sees someone here who can do what no physician can do – raise the dead.

Three people blessed, each one by coming into contact with one of these three divine attributes.

Colossians chapter 1 verse 17; Hebrews chapter 1 verse 3
These two texts are found in very rich sections extolling the deity of Christ.

> 'He is before all things, and by him all things consist', Col. 1. 17.
> 'upholding all things by the word of his power', Heb. 1. 3.

If all things consist or hold together in Christ as Colossians chapter 1 verse 17 says, and if He upholds all things as Hebrews chapter 1 verse 3 says, then He must know about all things, that's omniscience, He must be active at all places, that's omnipresence, and He must have unlimited power, that's omnipotence, all expressed in the span of a few words.

Revelation chapter 5 verse 6
> 'And I looked, and behold, in the midst of the throne and of the four living creatures, and in the midst of the elders, stood a Lamb as though it had been slain, having seven horns and seven eyes, which are the seven Spirits of God sent out into all the earth', NKJV.

In John's vision the Lamb, the Lord Jesus, has seven horns. Horns in scripture denote power, see, for example, Daniel chapter 8, and the number seven speaks of completeness. Seven horns can mean nothing other than complete power, He is omnipotent. He also is seen as having seven eyes, telling us of complete insight, He is omniscient. And these seven eyes are sent forth into all the earth, telling us He is omnipresent.

These writers were not writing textbooks on the attributes of God, and I don't know if they had a definitive list of God's incommunicable attributes in their mind, yet these three *omni*'s come up again and again, and are presented so perfectly.

God's righteousness and grace

The Bible proclaims over and over that God is a God of absolute righteousness, and yet, at the same time, a God of abounding grace, for example:

> 'And the Lord passed by before him, and proclaimed, The Lord, The Lord God, merciful and gracious, longsuffering, and abundant in goodness and truth, keeping mercy for thousands, forgiving iniquity and transgression and sin, and that will by no means clear the guilty; visiting the iniquity of the fathers upon the children, and upon the children's children, unto the third and to the fourth generation', Exod. 34. 6-7.

God proclaims Himself to be merciful and gracious, forgiving iniquity and transgression and sin, and yet He will by no means clear the guilty. But it is the guilty who need forgiveness, so how can God be forgiving and yet not let sin go unpunished?

> 'Tell ye, and bring them near; yea, let them take counsel together: who hath declared this from ancient time? who hath told it from that time? have not I the Lord? and there is no God else beside me; a just God and a Saviour; there is none beside me', Isa. 45. 21.

We could understand scripture saying, 'He is a just God *or* a Saviour', but how can He be a just God *and* a Saviour? Justice demands sin be answered for; salvation means the sinner goes free. How can these two titles both belong to God at the same time? The answer is found at the cross:

> 'But now the righteousness of God apart from the law is revealed, being witnessed by the Law and the Prophets, even the righteousness of God, through faith in Jesus Christ, to all and on all who believe. For there is no difference; for all have sinned and fall short of the glory of God, being justified freely by His grace through the redemption that is in Christ Jesus,

whom God set forth as a propitiation by His blood, through faith, to demonstrate His righteousness, because in His forbearance God had passed over the sins that were previously committed, to demonstrate at the present time His righteousness, that He might be just and the justifier of the one who has faith in Jesus', Rom. 3. 21-26, NKJV.

God's righteousness has been displayed in that sin has been punished, but His grace has been shown in that He stepped in Himself in Christ to be the sin-bearer so that the guilty could go free. Christ became man's representative and answered to God for human guilt, so God can righteously justify all who avail themselves of the provision.

> 'Because the sinless Saviour died,
> My sinful soul is counted free,
> For God the just is satisfied
> To look on Him and pardon me',
> [CHARATIE DE CHENEY LEES SMITH BANCROFT]

God's righteousness wasn't softened by His grace, nor was His grace hardened by His righteousness. They are both fully and perfectly displayed at Calvary.

Its perfection regarding the provision of salvation
'It's too good to be true' is a wise attitude to take with the vast majority of special offers we hear about, but when it comes to the offer of salvation in the Bible it is too good not to be true. The salvation the Bible presents is light years above anything found in other faiths. The biblical gospel doesn't merely offer forgiveness and rescue, but it says we can become God's children and share His life, John 1. 12-13; we can be united with Christ so that God accepts us as He accepts His Son, Eph. 1. 6; and we can become heirs of God so that all the glory of God is going to be shared with us, and it is all through faith in Christ, Rom. 8. 16-17; 1 Peter 1. 3-5. Little wonder the Bible calls it *so great salvation*, Heb. 2. 3.

Why does humanity need salvation anyway? It is because of the entrance of sin into the world. We call this event *the Fall*, because mankind fell into sin, and when man fell, the whole of his personality (mind, emotions and will) was affected. The mind became darkened, Eph. 4. 18, the emotions were robbed of the joy and peace of fellowship with God and, instead, experienced guilt, shame and fear, Gen. 3. 9-10, and the will became rebellious, Rom. 8. 7-8. The perfection of salvation is seen in the fact that the Saviour is called *the Christ*. The title *Christ* means anointed. In Israel, there were three anointed offices: the prophet, 1 Kgs. 19. 16; the priest, Lev. 8. 12; and the king, 1 Sam. 10. 1; 16. 13. The Christ is the fulfilment of each of these three offices, and as such He meets the need of fallen humanity:

> 'As *Prophet* He brings knowledge, i.e. light, delivers the understanding from sin's darkness, and establishes the kingdom of truth.
> As *Priest* He brings the sacrifice, cancels the guilt and thereby the consciousness of guilt, thus delivering the feelings from the crippling pressure of misery and an accusing conscience, and establishes the kingdom of peace and joy.
> As *King* He rules the will, guides it in paths of holiness, and establishes the kingdom of love and righteousness . . .
> His threefold office sets man free in the three powers of his soul the understanding, the feelings and the will. A full, free, and complete salvation is introduced, so that *the redemption could not be more perfect than it is'*.[263]

The systems of salvation in man-made religions have man's fingerprints all over them. The provision of a perfect Saviour in Christ, to meet the complete need of the whole man, is manifestly divine.

Its perfection regarding its function
> 'But evil men and imposters will grow worse and worse, deceiving, and being deceived. But you must continue in the

---

[263] ERICH SAUER, *The Triumph of the Crucified*, The Paternoster Press, 1964, pp. 18-19, emphasis added.

things which you have learned and been assured of, knowing from whom you have learned them, and that from childhood you have known the Holy Scriptures, which are able to make you wise for salvation through faith which is in Christ Jesus. All Scripture is given by inspiration of God, and is profitable for doctrine, for reproof, for correction, for instruction in righteousness: that the man of God may be complete, thoroughly equipped for every good work', 2 Tim. 3. 13-17, NKJV.

When Paul wrote to Timothy, many were defecting and deserting, ground was being given up and people giving in, but Paul tells Timothy to continue in the things he has learned from him and the other witnesses, 2. 2. He is talking about New Testament revelation. Then, in verse 15, he introduces something additional, 'and that from childhood you have known'. He is talking there about Old Testament revelation. Then, in verse 16, he puts the two together and says, 'All scripture is given by inspiration of God'. This is a clear indication that the apostles knew that their teaching was on the same level of authority as the Old Testament scriptures.

Paul says that all scripture is profitable that the man of God may be complete. There are two things to notice here: first, it's all profitable so we should not take from it, and it is given that the man of God may be complete, that means it's sufficient, so we should not add to it. It has been the error of liberal Protestantism to take from the word of God and it has been the error of Roman Catholicism to add to the word of God. There are serious warnings against both courses of action, Rev. 22. 18-19. The truth that Paul expressed in these words so succinctly answers these errors. It's almost as if he saw down the line and pre-empted them, but of course, he couldn't have done that. But God could.

This is a miniscule sampling of the ways in which scripture presents truth so perfectly. I have often told younger Christians that if they want to be sure that the Bible is the word of God then the thing to do is study it. The more closely and carefully you look, the more the perfection is apparent and the more convinced you will become that you are looking at a work of God.

You can experience God's presence in His word

This is perhaps the greatest joy possible for a human being to know on earth, the experience of God's presence. There is a mix of excitement and subdued awe that floods the soul when God is encountered in a personal way through scripture.

Anyone who has been on the Christian pathway for any length of time knows what this is like. Let me give you a few examples, and almost every Christian will say, *I've been there.*

A Christian has a dreadful worry, and in her daily reading she reads a promise of God that exactly answers to her circumstances. It lifts the burden and lets her know God is with her and in control.

Another Christian is tolerating a particular sin in his life, justifying it and sanitizing it, trying to convince himself it doesn't matter; he goes along to a Bible teaching meeting and the preacher nails that particular sin from scripture and the sinning Christian recognizes that God is speaking to him.

A believer is struggling with regrets from sins of the past. He thinks there is no way God could use him, then he happens to come across a passage that looks as if it was written just for him, reminding him that God is the God of restoration – it was just *what* he needed, just *when* he needed it.

Another Christian is perplexed about the answer to a particular Bible problem, she doesn't feel free to voice it and it is robbing her of her joy and shaking her confidence. She goes along to a meeting or switches on the radio and there is a preacher addressing that very subject from the Bible.

These are examples of what Psalm 46 verse 1 teaches: 'God is our refuge and strength, a very present help in trouble'. So many of us can testify to the truth of this. We have erected our little monuments along life's pathway where God drew very near to us in our need through His word.

But there need not be a crisis in order for God's presence to be known in the word. Paul prayed for the Ephesians that God would grant them 'the Spirit of wisdom and revelation in the knowledge of him', Eph. 1. 17, and what he meant by that is that God would grant that the Spirit of God would minister to them in giving them wisdom to understand what had been revealed, see 1 Cor. 2. 9-14, all with a view to knowing God more and more. Many a time, just through the study and contemplation of the Bible, Christians have known the indescribable sensation of the reality of God – the Spirit of God has caused the truth to hit home with freshness, the glory of God shines with a particular splendour, the beauties of the Saviour are so clear, and the experience causes the heart to bow in wonder and the spirit to rise in worship. It is the reality of the presence of God.

For those who have never been there, all I can do is tell you it is real and it is wonderful, and probably the closest thing to heaven on earth. And I can call on multitudes of others to testify to the truth of what I'm telling you.

This experience isn't brought on by mood music, emotional manipulation and collective euphoria. It is something known by the individual believer studying the text of scripture in the fear of God and in dependence on the Holy Spirit.

As 1 Samuel chapter 3 verse 21 puts it, 'the Lord revealed himself . . . by the word of the Lord'. This is why the Christian who doesn't have access to apologetics materials or answers to objections is still justified in saying he knows the Bible is a revelation *from* God, because in it he has encountered a revelation *of* God. When God confronted any individual *in scripture,* they did not need something else to verify that experience – it was self-authenticating, and when God confronts an individual *through scripture* it is exactly the same.

Conclusion

There are lots of things we are entirely justified to say we know, and yet if we were put on the spot and asked – *How do you know?* – we might struggle to articulate our reasons. We just know from our experience. For the vast majority of Bible-believers that is where they stand in regard to the Bible – it is their meat and drink, their strength and comfort, their treasure and delight. They love it with all their hearts. Its message has changed their lives, its perfections thrill them, and God has met with them through it.

That doesn't mean that evidence and arguments are superfluous or redundant. John the Baptist had a real experience of seeing the Spirit of God descend on Christ, and hearing God say, 'This is my beloved Son, in whom I am well pleased', Matt. 3. 16-17. John didn't need any additional validation for him to know that was real, but, during a dark period in his life, that moment seemed distant, doubt crept into his mind, and he sent two of his disciples to ask the Lord, 'Art thou he that should come, or do we look for another?' Matt. 11. 3. The Lord didn't direct him to that experience in the past, but rather gave him objective evidence that would hold his faith during that difficult time. Every Christian has experienced the power of the word in regeneration; the majority of Christians can look back to transcendent, self-authenticating, undeniable experiences of the presence of God in the word, but during dark times those times, though still real, seem remote, and it is then that having access to evidences and arguments can be very helpful.

Furthermore, the use of evidences and arguments can be the means of unbelievers coming to accept, or at least be open to the possibility, that the Bible is God's word. The Christian's personal experience might not be terribly compelling to the unbeliever, and can be ignored with a wave of the hand, but the stubborn facts of prophecy, reality, oneness and verification can't be so easily dismissed.

The point of this chapter is to show that the Christian is not on the outside, looking at evidence before him and weighing it up. He has come to *know* that the Bible is God's word. The claims of scripture can be put to the test.

God's power
The Bible says that those who trust Christ for salvation will receive new life.

God's perfections
This life provides an appetite for scripture and causes the eyes of the heart to be opened to see beauties in God's revelation that were hidden to them before.

God's presence
They have undeniable experience of God meeting with them and meeting their spiritual and emotional needs through His word.

Those who have believed the gospel and trusted the Lord Jesus as Saviour have proved by experience that the Bible is God's word.

Conclusion

We have looked at five areas that provide proof that the Bible is God's word. I hope that it has been encouraging to my fellow Christians, and will strengthen your faith in the Bible and your commitment to it. Our society would like us to take a chisel to the scriptures and chip away at certain bits that wound our pride and condemn our lifestyle. If the Bible is divinely inspired then we don't have that liberty. In Paul's last letter, his appeal to Timothy was to hold fast, 2 Tim. 1. 13, and herald forth, 4. 4, the word of God. That is your commission. You can take your stand on and for God's word without embarrassment, and continue to sing from your heart,

Jesus loves me, this I know,
For the Bible tells me so.

To those of you who are not Bible-believers, I am so grateful you have allowed me to present this evidence to you. What is your response?

Prophecy

The Bible has proved itself to get it right when it talks about the future. Are you going to take seriously what it says about your future?

Reality

The Bible says it as it is, and has the only adequate explanation for the reality we know and encounter every day. Are you going to accept that what it says about you is also true?

Oneness

The Bible has many writers, but they all act as the fingers of a master pianist who uses the different notes to produce a wonderful symphony. They are like the different colours an artist uses to paint a masterpiece. All these writers join together to play one song and paint one picture. They point to the same person and tell the same story, we need a Saviour, and that Saviour is Jesus of Nazareth, the Son of God.

Verification

The Bible encourages you to do some fact-checking. It makes claims that can be verified. The scientific data shows that the writers of scripture weren't merely writing from the limited resources of their own experience. The archaeological findings reveal footprints that can only be filled by God. Then God Himself, in the person of the Son, gave His own seal of divine approval to the Bible. The Bible is trustworthy, God Himself has said it. You can safely and sensibly put your confidence in what it says.

Experience

You can come to know the author. God doesn't just want you to believe the Bible is His word; He wants you to respond to its message and enter a relationship with Him. Let me summarise the Bible's message of salvation:

You have sinned against God, Rom. 3. 23, and your sin carries a penalty that you can never pay, Rev. 20. 11-15.

God loved you so much that He gave His Son to pay the penalty of sin at Calvary, John 3. 16; 1 Cor. 15. 3; Isa. 53. 5.

The Lord Jesus paid the penalty in full, and as proof of that God raised Him from the dead, Rom. 4. 25; 1 Cor. 15. 4-8.

If you acknowledge your guilt, admit your helplessness and trust Christ for salvation, then He will save you and bring you into God's family, Acts 16. 30-31; Eph. 2. 8-9; John 1. 12.

You may have questions about certain things in the Bible; you're not the only one. There are things that I wonder about and puzzle over. I'm not saying there are no difficulties, I'm saying there are no *defeaters*. While there may be some difficulties, my point is that to deny that the Bible is God's word causes *far more* difficulties. There is ample evidence that the Bible is what it claims to be, and you can know it in your own experience. Having received salvation, you can embark on the journey of finding answers to the questions you have. And you will do so in the enjoyment of fellowship with God and with the help of the indwelling Holy Spirit.

Remember what Frank Turek's friend said? *'I don't believe the Bible. But if it is true, then I'll be in big trouble'.* If you are going to reject the gospel you will need to be 100% sure that all of the evidence presented here (or anywhere else) is false, and that the experience of every Christian is a delusion. Your eternal destiny hinges on your response to the Saviour offered in scripture.

Don't ignore the evidence. Paul thanked God for the Thessalonians, 'because when you received the word of God which you heard from us, you welcomed it not as the word of men, but as it is in truth, the word of God, which also effectively works in you who believe', 1 Thess. 2. 13, NKJV. They welcomed the gospel as God's word; it made a powerful difference in their lives, and it will in yours too.

Recommended Reading

For those wishing to explore the subjects of this book in more detail I recommend the following. Their inclusion here is not an unqualified endorsement.

Books marked with * are at a more advanced or scholarly level rather than a popular level.

On the authority of the Bible

BRIAN H. EDWARDS, *The Bible – an authentic book,* Day One Publications, 2015.

NORMAN L. GEISLER & WILLIAM E. NIX, *A General Introduction to the Bible,* Moody Press, 1986.

JOHN F. MACARTHUR, *Why Believe the Bible?* Regal, 2007.

On the Canon of Scripture

*ANDREAS J. KOSTENBERGER & MICHAEL J. KRUGER, *The Heresy of Orthodoxy, How Contemporary Culture's Fascination with Diversity Has Reshaped Our Understanding of Early Christianity,* Apollos, 2010.

*MICHAEL J. KRUGER, *Canon Revisited: Establishing the Origins and Authority of the New Testament Books,* Crossway, 2012.

*MICHAEL J. KRUGER, *The Question of Canon, Challenging the status quo in the New Testament debate,* Apollos, 2013.

General Apologetics

JOHN ANKERBERG & JOHN WELDON, *Fast Facts on Defending your Faith,* ATRI Publishing, 2013.

JOHN BLANCHARD, *Does God Believe in Atheists?* Evangelical Press, 2000.

KENNETH BOA & ROBERT M. BOWMAN, *20 Compelling Evidences that God Exists*, David C. Cook, 2002.

WILLIAM LANE CRAIG, *On Guard, Defending your Faith with Reason and Precision*, David C. Cook, 2010.

*WILLIAM LANE CRAIG, *Reasonable Faith, Christian Truth and Apologetics*, Third Edition, Crossway, 2008.

NORMAN L. GEISLER & FRANK TUREK, *I Don't Have Enough Faith to Be an Atheist*, Crossway, 2004.

JOHN C. LENNOX, *Gunning for God, Why the New Atheists are Missing the Target*, Lion Hudson, 2011.

C. S. LEWIS, *Mere Christianity*, HarperCollins, 2002.

Dealing with Bible difficulties

GLEASON L. ARCHER, *New International Encyclopedia of Bible Difficulties*, Zondervan, 2011.

JAMES MONTGOMERY BOICE, *Dealing with Bible Problems, Alleged Errors and Contradictions in the Bible*, CLC Publications, 2013.

R. A. TORREY, *Difficulties in the Bible: Alleged Errors and Contradictions*, Moody Press, 1972.

Prophecy

J. ALLEN, *Daniel Reconsidered*, Scripture Teaching Library, 2013.

*DARRELL L. BOCK AND MITCH GLASER (Ed.) *The Gospel According to Isaiah 53*, Kregel, 2012.

MICHAEL L. BROWN, *Answering Jewish Objections to Jesus*, vol. 3, Baker Books, 2003.

R. C. NEWMAN (Ed.), *The Evidence of Prophecy*, Interdisciplinary Biblical Research Institute, 2012.

R. E. SHOWERS, *The Most High God*, FOI, 1994.

JOHN F. WALVOORD, *Every Prophecy of the Bible*, David C. Cook, 1999.

Reality

J. P. MORELAND, *The Soul: How we know it's real, and why it matters*, Moody, 2014.

NANCY PEARCEY, *Finding Truth, 5 Principles for Unmasking Atheism, Secularism, and Other God Substitutes*, David C. Cook, 2015.

FRANK TUREK, *Stealing from God, Why atheists need God to make their case*, NavPress, 2014.

J. WARNER WALLACE, *God's Crime Scene, A Cold-Case Detective Examines the Evidence for a Divinely Created Universe*, David C. Cook, 2015.

Oneness

J. M. FLANIGAN, *Christ in the Levitical Offerings*, John Ritchie Ltd. 2011.

DAVID GOODING, *The Riches of Divine Wisdom, The New Testament's Use of the Old Testament*, Myrtlefield House, 2013.

F. W. GRANT, *The Numerical Bible,* Loizeaux Brothers, 1932.

F. W. GRANT, *Genesis in the Light of the New Testament*, Loizeaux Brothers, 1887.

ADA R. HABERSHON, *Study of the Types*, Kregel, 1997.

ALBERT LECKIE, *The Tabernacle and the Offerings*, Precious Seed Publications, 2012.

C. H. MACKINTOSH, *Notes on the Pentateuch, Genesis to Deuteronomy*, Loizeaux Brothers, 1980.

THOMAS NEWBERRY, *Types of Levitical Offerings*, John Ritchie Ltd., n.d.

HENRY W. SOLTAU, *The Holy Vessels and Furniture of the Tabernacle*, Kregel, 1982.

HENRY W. SOLTAU, *The Tabernacle, the Priesthood and the Offerings*, Kregel, 1972.

Verification

Scientific evidence
*JOHN C. LENNOX, *God's Undertaker, Has Science Buried God?*, Lion, 2007.

LEE STROBEL, *The Case for a Creator, A Journalist Investigates Scientific Evidence That Points Toward God*, Zondervan, 2004.

Archaeology
CLIVE ANDERSON & BRIAN EDWARDS, *Evidence for the Bible*, Day One Publications, 2015.

DOUG POWELL, *iWitness Biblical Archaeology*, available as an app or paperback (Apologia Educational Ministries, 2014).

The ultimate verification
*MICHAEL F. BIRD (ed.), *How God Became Jesus: The Real Origins of Belief in Jesus' Divine Nature – A Response to Bart D. Ehrman*, Zondervan, 2014.

ROBERT M. BOWMAN JR & J. ED KOMOSZEWSKI, *Putting Jesus in His Place: The Case for the Deity of Christ*, Kregel, 2007.

LEE STROBEL, *The Case for Christ, A Journalist's Personal Investigation of the Evidence for Jesus*, Zondervan, 2016.

LEE STROBEL, *The Case for the Real Jesus, A Journalist Investigates Current Attacks on the Identity of Christ*, Zondervan, 2014.

Experience

ALVIN J. SCHMIDT, *How Christianity Changed the World*, Zondervan, 2004.

LEE STROBEL, *The Case for Grace, A Journalist Explores the Evidence for Transformed Lives*, Zondervan, 2015.